DATE DUE			

A Cognitive Theory of Metaphor

⊐Ɫ Bradford Books

A Cognitive Theory of Metaphor

Earl R. Mac Cormac

A Bradford Book
The MIT Press
Cambridge, Massachusetts
London, England

This book was set in Palatino by The MIT Press Computergraphics Department and
printed and bound by Halliday Lithograph in the United States of America.

Library of Congress Cataloging in Publication Data
Mac Cormac, Earl R.
  A cognitive theory of metaphor.
  "A Bradford book"
  Bibliography: p.
  Includes index.
  1. Metaphor. 2. Cognition. 3 Semantics.
4. Languages—Philosophy. I. Title.
P301.5.M48M33 1985   401'.9   85-7904
ISBN 0-262-13212-5

To my wife Nancy and my daughters Ann and Susan; without their emotional support, love, and encouragement I would never have completed this odyssey.

Contents

Preface

An undergraduate student at Davidson College first interested me in the question of metaphor in 1966. At that time I was interested in the propositions used in science and religion to make knowledge claims. Since both disciplines employ figurative language, a comparative study of their uses of metaphor seemed desirable. My investigation culminated in my first book, *Metaphor and Myth in Science and Religion* (Duke University Press, 1976). In that work I suggested that metaphor was not only a linguistic category but also a cognitive process. A conference on metaphor at the University of Illinois in 1977 stimulated me to think of the possibility of developing metaphor as a cognitive process by applying philosophical arguments to evidence and theories produced by linguists and psychologists. This work results from years of reading, thinking, and writing about this problem. A different version of chapter 1 was presented to a meeting of the Society for the Philosophy of Technology in New York in 1983 and will appear as "Men and Machines: The Computational Metaphor," in *Philosophy and Technology II: Information Technology and Computers in Theory and Practice*, edited by Carl Mitcham and Alois Huning, Reidel, 1985. Chapter 1 appears here with permission. Parts of chapter 4 appeared in my article, "Metaphors and Fuzzy Sets" (*Fuzzy Sets and Systems*, vol. 7 (1982)) and are reprinted with permission. Except for these two previous publications, the rest of this work is original and attempts to develop the first unified cognitive theory of metaphor. As the reader will see in both the introduction and the afterword, this book does not complete the task; rather it offers a beginning for further analysis.

Professor Donald T. Campbell, University Professor at Lehigh University, has been a colleague, mentor and friend for almost twenty years. Many of the ideas in chapter 5 were stimulated by him. Professor Campbell, like others whom I cite, should not be held accountable for the ideas expressed here, for he does not necessarily agree with all of them even though he served as a catalyst for many. I do wish, however, to express my profound gratitude to him and others. Similarly,

Mary Hesse, Professor of the History and Philosophy of Science at the University of Cambridge, has been a constant source of encouragement and constructive criticism. She read earlier versions of several chapters, offering suggestions for improvements. Paul Durbin, Professor of Philosophy at the University of Delaware, Professor Robert Hoffman, Department of Psychology at Adelphi University, and Dr. Eric Wanner of the Alfred P. Sloan Foundation have all read versions of the manuscript and offered criticism and advice. Not only have I adopted ideas developed by Thomas Saaty, University Professor at the University of Pittsburgh, in his decision theory, but we have become warm friends—perhaps a manifestation of the humanizing function of mathematics.

In writing this book and the earlier one, I have become convinced that effective writing requires strong intellectual and emotional support. At Davidson College I have been fortunate in having excellent philosophical colleagues who have challenged my ideas and offered constructive criticism. George Abernethy, Irwin Goldstein, Robert Maydole, Alfred Mele, Michael Smith, and Lance Stell have all helped in this work. Frank Bliss, Professor of English and Chair at Davidson College, read many of the earlier chapters and offered suggestions for improvements in style. Ann Callahan, an exceptional secretary, typed the manuscript. Institutional support and encouragement were provided by T. C. Price Zimmermann, Professor of History and Dean of Faculty at Davidson College. Funds for faculty development from the Andrew Mellon Foundation were used to support this work.

Introduction

Philosophers and psychologists face the challenge of presenting an explanatory account of metaphor that describes how one can understand the juxtaposition of referents not normally associated. Although only a decade ago the legitimacy of metaphors was vigorously debated, today metaphors are so widely accepted as proper cognitive devices that the issue has shifted to the question of how they can be described in an adequate explanatory account. We want to understand how John Donne combined the concepts of sonnets and funeral urns in his famous poem, the *Canonization*.

> We'll build in sonnets pretty roomes;
> As well a well wrought urne becomes
> The greatest ashes, as halfe-acre tombes,
> And by these hymnes, all shall approve
> Us *Canoniz'd* for Love.[1]

What enabled Donne to put together the ideas of "sonnets" and "burial rooms"? The normal semantical associations that we have with sonnets are "writing" and "poetry," not funeral urns. Through a cognitive process Donne searched various locations in his long-term semantic memory, found these two referents, comprehended a meaningful relationship between them, and finally generated the metaphor. Scientists, like poets, also generate new metaphors through a cognitive process when they want to suggest a new hypothesis. Kenneth Johnson introduced the highly speculative metaphor of colored quarks (red, blue, and yellow) as follows: "Quark color has nothing whatsoever to do with visual color. The word color is used because the way different colored quarks combine in quantum mechanics is reminiscent of the way visual colors combine."[2] Physicists seeking to explain the attributes of theoretical particles comprehended an analogy between the properties of colors and the possible properties of quarks.

To explain metaphor as a cognitive process, I presume the existence of deep structures of the human mind as a language generating device.

When I speak of the "existence" of deep structures, I mean "existence" in the sense of rational reconstructions and not in the sense of specific actual biologically based mechanisms. Through brain processes the human mind operates hierarchically to juxtapose widely disparate semantic concepts which produce metaphors that can be comprehended. The semantic referents of a metaphor depend on some analogy between their attributes to be understood and some disanalogy between their referents to be suggestive. I have arranged this hierarchy of rational reconstructions into two levels of deep structures: a semantic level and a cognitive level. These levels are not mutually exclusive but are posited to indicate my belief that the cognitive process underlies the semantic process. I do not identify the two processes because I assume the existence of nonverbal cognitive functions, like those allowing painters to express their feeling and insights without resorting to words.

Surface language in the form of the actual metaphors, "Sonnets are pretty rooms" and "Quarks are colored," exists at the top of the hierarchy of rational reconstructions. Nor does surface language escape from interaction with the deeper structures of semantics and cognition. The surface language plays an important role in providing a context for interpretation, especially in determining the meaning of the semantic components of the referents of a metaphor. One might not be able to understand "colored quarks" as anything more than nonsense if one did not know enough of the theory of quarks to comprehend the analogy between the combination of colors and the interaction of quarks. I postulate the following three levels of explanation as nonexclusive rational reconstructions of the cognitive process by which metaphors are generated:

Level 1: Surface Language

Level 2: Semantics and Syntax

Level 3: Cognition

These hierarchical levels can also be viewed as heuristic devices to aid in understanding the cognitive process by which metaphors are produced. The same conceptual process represented in rational reconstructions by these three levels also interrelates the levels in the production of metaphors through a more comprehensive process, which I describe as a "knowledge process." Viewed internally, metaphors operate as cognitive processes that produce new insights and new hypotheses. Viewed externally, metaphors operate as mediators between the human mind and culture. New metaphors change both the ordinary language we use and the ways in which we perceive and understand the world. As metaphors enter common usage, dictionary entries grow. Metaphors often fade or die as they become commonplace. Since metaphors change language, they play a part in cultural evolution. As language affects our behavior, metaphors may also play a part in biological evolution. By participating in these parallel but different types of evolution, metaphor can be included as an integral ingredient in what some like Donald T. Campbell have described as "evolutionary epistemology."

The problem of circularity immediately confronts this explanatory account of metaphor based on a hierarchy of deep structures. How can one presume to have explained anything when the very account given to provide understanding of metaphor as a cognitive process assumes that very same cognitive process as providing the organization of the three levels? This circularity cannot be fully avoided but it can be assuaged. This kind of circularity parallels the circularity found in attempting to describe the nature of "meaning" without presuming "meaning" in the description. I attempt to assuage circularity by maintaining a division between two kinds of language found at level 1: ordinary language, which is literal, and metaphorical language, which I claim is figurative or nonliteral. The existence of literal language as distinct from metaphors offers a common objective standpoint from which to judge the meaning and the partial truth of metaphors. This independence of literal language from the cognitive process of metaphor allows judgments about metaphor that are free from the vicious circularity of employing only the process that the investigator seeks to explain as the very nature of the explanation itself. But one does not escape the circularity completely, for as I have already noted, the meaning of the referents of metaphors must often be decided by reference to the context of the metaphor found in surface language (level 1).

A kindred circularity is uncovered by the discovery that any explanatory theory of metaphor must inevitably presume an underlying "basic metaphor" on which the explanatory account is constructed. Basic metaphors are those fundamental theoretical assumptions about the nature of metaphor posited by theorists, such as "metaphor produces a contradiction when read literally" (controversion theory) or "metaphor is an analogy" (comparison theory). Again we cannot fully avoid circularity since, if we are to construct a nontrivial explanatory account of metaphor, we must assume that the metaphor partially identify with what it is literally not. The recognition that theories of metaphor presume underlying basic metaphors does not necessarily generate the assertion that all language, therefore, must itself be metaphorical. This claim does not follow from the acknowledgment that theories about metaphor are themselves metaphorical. I argue extensively in chapter 3 that one can successfully maintain a distinction between the two and that failure to mark the differences between metaphors and literal language not only impairs the intelligibility of the descriptions of the nature of metaphor but also commits the theory to an undesirable relativistic theory of truth. My defense of the existence of a literal language has important ramifications for my entire theory of metaphor, including the nature of the meaning of metaphor, its truth value, and its role as mediator between mind and culture.

Perhaps one of the most controversial assumptions about a theory of metaphor in this study is my contention that the deep structures at levels 2 and 3 can be best represented by abstractions. Advantages of this assumption include the universality of mathematical structures and a greater precision of expression than that found in natural languages. In striving to be as precise as possible about a phenomenon that possesses an inherent ambiguity, I have resorted to formal structures, like fuzzy sets and many-valued logics, that offer both precision and flexibility. By adopting abstractions to describe deep structures, I do not intend to claim any more objectivity than one might establish using ordinary words set off in a metalanguage to explain metaphor. Formal language employed in formal structures offers an alternative method of expressing an explanation. The origins of chapter 4 lie in a partial visual image of the nature of the organization of natural language. Imagine a hierarchical network in n-dimensional space with each of the nodes of the network a fuzzy set (a set in which membership may be partial rather than either/or). Each fuzzy set defines a word. Some of the words defined by fuzzy sets are categories that describe objects or events in the physical world. The image of this formal structure appears much like some of the models used by chemists to represent molecules. This image of intuition about language remains only partial because of the difficulty of seeing in more than three dimensions, and I have posited an n-dimensional space.

My assumption of formal abstractions organized in a quasi-mathematical hierarchy reflects the dominant, current metaphorical assumption of computation as the basis of cognition. In this spirit I begin chapter 1 with an analysis of the computational metaphor. This treatment of the computational metaphor serves both to illustrate the problems of metaphor and to introduce the reader to the major assumption of this study, namely, the presumption that metaphor itself can best be explained by viewing the human mind as a computational device. Under this assumption, metaphors result from the operation of a cognitive process on formal semantic structures. Much of the cognitive process, especially its creative aspects, remains hidden, but I specify some of the parameters of that process, including the organization of memory, necessary to allow the unusual juxtaposition of referents found in metaphors. After considering various possibilities, I conclude that for now finding an algorithmic description of the creative cognitive process by which metaphors are generated seems unlikely. That one cannot fully explain metaphor with formal abstractions alone does not invalidate the applicability of abstract structures to the aspects of metaphoric production that can be properly explained. Hence my explanation of metaphor can be better described as quasi-formal rather than as entirely formal. If I had succeeded in producing algorithms for the universal production of metaphors, I might have reduced metaphor to a recursive function, but the creativity and often unexpected variability of metaphor seems to defy recursion. I would also have asserted that properties of the unknown could be not only predicted but also deduced. My confidence in the Kantian notion of the limits of conceptualization makes me content with a quasi-formal account of metaphor. Employing a quasi-formal, hierarchical structure to explain metaphor is much like deciding to use a mathematical model to represent an event or experience. One must decide first to use a mathematical model, and then one must decide which one to use. I decided that a formal structure would be desirable to explain deep aspects of a cognitive process that generates metaphors. I also selected a particular quasi-formal structure based on networks, hierarchy, and fuzzy sets. I might just as easily have chosen a different formal structure with different advantages and disadvantages. My model seeks to solve the problems of semantical change necessary for the generation of metaphors, and I hope that I have been successful in that endeavor.

Among the standard theories of metaphor, my theory can best be described as a formal version of the interaction theory of metaphor usually identified with the work of Max Black. I argue that metaphor results from a cognitive process that juxtaposes two or more not normally associated referents, producing semantic conceptual anomaly, the symptom of which is usually emotional tension. The conceptual process that generates metaphor identifies similar attributes of the referents to form an analogy and identifies dissimilar attributes of the referents to produce semantic anomaly. The degrees of similarity and dissimilarity determine the truth value of the metaphor. I employ a four-valued logic to express a range of truth values so that a metaphor need not be classified solely as either true or false in the standard form of two-valued logic. I deny the contention of the controversion theory of metaphor that metaphors necessarily express falsity when interpreted literally. I argue that metaphors can be understood as insightful and as conveying partial truth without first understanding the metaphor as an intentional expression of falsity.

Metaphor can be described as a process in two senses: (1) as a cognitive process by which new concepts are expressed and suggested, and (2) as a cultural process by which language itself changes. To illuminate both processes, I adopt Philip Wheelwright's distinction between epiphors and diaphors. Wheelwright characterized epiphors as those metaphors that express more than they suggest. Diaphors suggest more than they express. Since metaphors depend on both analogies and disanalogies among the attributes of their referents, all metaphors possess both epiphoric and diaphoric elements. Those metaphors possessing more analogy among the attributes of their referents, however, can be said to be epiphors, whereas those possessing more disanalogy can be said to be diaphors. This distinction is especially useful in describing the second cultural process. Metaphors can begin life as either diaphors or epiphors and then change their status through usage or testing. Diaphors can become epiphors as their hypothetical suggestions find confirmation in experience or experiment. Epiphors can become ordinary language when they are used so often that they express what the speakers now consider to be commonplace. When this occurs, a new lexical account of the word or words (referents) usually enters the dictionary. Some metaphors remain as diaphors, others remain as epiphors, whereas others change with diaphors becoming epiphors and epiphors becoming ordinary language. Rather than serving as a static grammatical category, metaphor exists both as a dynamic cognitive process proposing new hypotheses and as a dynamic cultural process changing the language we speak and write.

Not only have I proposed a cognitive interaction theory of metaphor but I have also presumed an interdisciplinary interaction between philosophy and psychology. I have written this work from the point of view of a philosopher interested in establishing an explanatory theory of metaphor based on evidence and theories provided not only by previous philosophers but even more importantly by contemporary linguists and psychologists. I believe that in paying serious attention especially to the evidence of psychological experiments and theories supported by experiments, I have moved in the direction of returning philosophy to a proper empirical stance. Positivists in the past thought that by advocating "testability" they retained an empirical orientation. In developing a theory of metaphor, they sought an explanation that rendered metaphor capable of empirical testability. Instead, I look at the evidence of tests applied to metaphor by psychologists, believing that evidence produced by testability is more important than a rule or analysis that guarantees the testability of metaphor. This move allows me to generalize the work of others and to formulate arguments on the basis of empirical evidence accordingly. A philosopher hostile to this method might object that a psychologist could easily perform the function of generalization and that I have methodologically put myself out of business. I readily and happily concede that psychologists (and even others) and not just philosophers can generalize the data about metaphor and formulate arguments. Many psycholinguists have already done just that. But by adopting this methodology, I claim not only a legitimate empirical basis for philosophy but a better modeling procedure as an approximation to actuality. In studying the cognitive process of metaphor generation and comprehension, why should one confine the investigation only to what previous philosophers have said and the appearance of metaphor in ordinary language or in logic? Why not examine the various ways in which other disciplines have approached metaphor? In this work I could have easily spent more time examining the work of literary scholars on metaphor, but I have not done that because my focus has intentionally been on metaphor as a cognitive device. And if one wants to examine theories about cognition, psychology offers the most. With my commitment to formal structures (employing the computational metaphor), computer science and mathematics also offer argument and evidence. The new discipline often called "cognitive science," combining philosophy, psychology, linguistics, and computer science, best represents my approach.

The interdisciplinary nature of this work necessarily means that often and intentionally my approach is eclectic. At its worst an eclectic approach juxtaposes ideas and evidence that clash or lead to outright contradictions. I hope that I have avoided that disaster, but if reviewers of this work find them, then I will gladly retreat and reformulate the theory. Moving from the worst scenario to that which is less bad but still nevertheless not good, I find the possibility of juxtaposing ideas and evidence that find no relationship with each other. In the range of good eclecticism I find combinations of ideas and evidence that can be justified by good theoretical arguments, especially in this work, quasi-mathematical structures. I have strived, perhaps unsuccessfully at times, to use psychological and linguistic evidence without distortion (but sometimes with reinterpretation) as a basis to support philosophical arguments about metaphor as a cognitive process. This approach has been suggested by others in articles, chapters, and in the organization of conferences.[3] Not to my knowledge, however, has anyone tried this cognitive science approach to metaphor at such length. That such an effort will be controversial seems inevitable, but I look forward to engaging in further debates over the nature of metaphor with those who are serious about this problem but may have different ways of explaining metaphor.

To provide this work with as much focus as possible, the numerous examples of metaphor introduced to make concrete many of the abstractions have been drawn from two major areas: (1) literature, especially poetry, and (2) science. When I have been unable to find just the right example from either of these areas to illustrate a point, I have invented my own.

Finally, before letting the reader plunge into the theory, let me suggest one or two other caveats, including several suggestions of what this book intentionally does not attempt. I include the latter for reviewers because of my experience with an earlier book on metaphor.[4] First on the positive side, in an effort to maintain consistency in my empirical approach in the treatment of both semantics and truth, I combine a many-valued logic of truth with a combination theory of truth that includes coherence and correspondence theory aspects. This may seem to the reader to be something like one of Houdini's feats; let me assure the reader that I have not found the task easy and that I am still worried about what I have done to the traditional notion of contradiction in chapter 8. While in a mood of admissions, let me candidly state that I have introduced chapter 6 because I believe that metaphor does function as a speech act and because I would feel guilty in omitting it. To present a semantic analysis of metaphor and ignore the performative functions of metaphor is to render the semantic analysis incomplete. The treatment of metaphor as a speech act, however, is not essential for the theory of metaphor as a cognitive process. The work on speech acts primarily extends my theory. But if I have extended the theory in this direction, why have I not extended it in other directions, like those of literary criticism, the role of metaphor in myth, and the relation between metaphor and symbolism? My only reply to these and other omissions comes from my desire to focus this work in the cognitive aspects of metaphor, leaving the other topics to the future. In the afterword I suggest future topics for research drawn from issues discussed in this book. Now I wish the reader bon voyage on a journey through the computational and cognitive world of metaphor.

1

The Computational Metaphor

The Computational Metaphor in Cognition

Explanations without metaphor would be difficult if not impossible, for in order to describe the unknown, we must resort to concepts that we know and understand, and that is the essence of a metaphor—an unusual juxtaposition of the familiar and the unfamiliar. On the frontiers of contemporary research exploration of the relationship between the mind and the brain depends on using basic metaphors as foundations on which to construct theories. Among the various metaphors presumed to underlie the interconnection between brain and mind, the computational metaphor occupies center stage. Under the computational metaphor the brain can be viewed as a computational device similar to a computer, and the mind emerges as a series of programs by means of which the brain functions. Human thinking does not necessarily reduce to brain functions; rather, human thinking and brain functions combine to produce a computational process. The "hardware" of the brain operates under the control of the "software" of the mind to produce computation, which traditionally is called cognition.

Zenon Pylyshyn describes the core of the computational metaphor:

> The view that cognition can be understood as computation is ubiquitous in modern cognitive theorizing, even among those who do not use computer programs to express models of cognitive processes. One of the basic assumptions behind this approach, sometimes referred to as "information processing," is that cognitive processes can be understood in terms of formal operations carried out on symbol structures. It thus represents a formalist approach to theoretical explanation. In practice, tokens of symbol structures may be depicted as expressions written in some lexicographic notation (as is usual in linguistics or mathematics), or they may be physically instantiated in a computer as a data structure or an executable program.[1]

The computational metaphor for cognition is tangible evidence of a success of an interactionist view of metaphor. The advent of the modern computer brought with it the metaphorical suggestion that these machines think; the discipline of artificial intelligence was developed by those computer scientists, philosophers, and psychologists who accepted the metaphorical suggestion that computers engage in mental activities similar to those of humans. In an interaction metaphor both parts of the metaphor are altered. When we claim metaphorically that "computers think," not only do machines take on the attributes of human beings who think—we ask whether computers have intentions and feelings as well as the ability to make rational deductions—but "thinkers" (human beings) take on the attributes of computers. And that is exactly what has happened in the case of the computational metaphor: the mind of a human being is described in terms of the attributes of a computer. We talk about the neuronal states of the brain as if they were like the internal states of a computer; we talk of the mental processes of thinking as if they were algorithmic. Computers are like minds in many respects; they can store data, recall it, manipulate it, learn to recognize new patterns, and even create new cognitive patterns. Human cognition is like machine computation; humans can manipulate strings of symbols according to rules in language and mathematics. Although computers are faster and more efficient than humans in many of their computations, most of the differences between the two remain on the side of humans who have emotions, possess more creativity, and are intentional in many of their actions. Those who deny intelligence to computers emphasize the uniqueness of these human functions, whereas those who affirm artificial intelligence in computers downplay the differences by dismissing the significance of human emotions for computers and by claiming that computers have intentionality. Before discussing the computational metaphor further, let me note the first major problem for a theory of metaphor—examination of the interaction metaphor raised by "Man is a computer."

What makes the identification of human beings with computers a metaphor and not just an analogy? We could not understand the computational metaphor if we could not recognize the similarities between humans and computers. These differences do not preclude the formation of an analogy because most fruitful analogies are not isomorphic, expressing a one-to-one correspondence among all their parts. Although metaphors presume analogies of features and parts of their referents, they possess a strangeness arising from the juxtaposition of their referents. If we claim that metaphors differ from analogies, then we have to explore more carefully the basis of this "strangeness." A necessary condition for a metaphor is the existence of some similarity between the parts of a metaphor, but I argue later that analogy is by no means a sufficient condition.

Historical Versions of the Computational Metaphor

The illumination of human nature through the formation of mechanical metaphor did not arise as a new phenomenon in the twentieth century, for La Mettrie published his famous *Man a Machine* in 1748. Many who have not read this work imagine that La Mettrie only compared man to a mechanical device like a watch. Indeed he did, as one can see in the following quotation, but he also recognized that "man is so complicated a machine that it is impossible to get a clear idea of the machine beforehand and hence impossible to define it" and so resorted to a variety of metaphors.[2] First the strictly mechanical metaphor:

> The human body is a watch, a large watch constructed with such skill and ingenuity, that if the wheel which marks the seconds happens to stop, the minute wheel turns and keeps on going its round, and in the same way the quarter-hour wheel, and all the others go on running when the first wheels have stopped because rusty or, for any reason, out of order. Is it not for a similar reason that the stoppage of a few blood vessels is not enough to destroy or suspend the strength of movement which is in the heart as in the mainspring of the machine; since, on the contrary, the fluids whose volume is diminished, having a shorter road to travel, cover the ground more quickly, borne on as by a fresh current which the energy of the heart increases in proportion to the resistance it encounters at the ends of the blood vessels?[3]

La Mettrie likens the recall of ideas to a gardener who in knowing plants "recalls all stages of growth at the sight of them."[4] He compares the images produced in the brain to a "magic lantern."[5] Even the "soul" is described as an "enlightened machine."[6] But in comparing the human body to machine, La Mettrie becomes fascinated with the biological part of the metaphor and speaks of the brain as having muscles for thinking and declares that to know man better we must not only look to machine but to animals as well.

> Thus, the diverse states of the soul are always correlative with those of the body. But the better to show this dependence, in its completeness and its causes, let us here make use of comparative anatomy; let us lay bare the organs of man and of animals. How can human nature be known, if we may not derive any light from an exact comparison of the structure of man and of animals?[7]

This is the message hidden from those who know of La Mettrie's metaphor of man as a machine only by reputation. La Mettrie's "machine" is a blood and guts machine that can be illuminated not only by the mechanical parts of artifices but also by comparison with animals. Thus along with the computational metaphor stands the twin metaphor "Man is an animal." Perhaps the most fascinating proposal that La Mettrie made was his suggestion that it should be possible to teach human language to apes, thus furthering our knowledge of human nature. La Mettrie's suggestion was based on the successful teaching of language to deaf-mutes, and it is an interesting note that his suggestion presaged Washoe and Lana by almost 250 years.

> But, because of the great analogy between ape and man and because there is no known animal whose external and internal organs so strikingly resemble man's, it would surprise me if speech were absolutely impossible to the ape.[8]

A contemporary version of *Man a Machine, The Metaphorical Brain* by Michael Arbib, explicitly invokes these twin metaphors (man as machine and as an animal) as the basis for understanding people.

> We want to understand how people think and behave, and in particular we wish to understand the role of the brain in thought and behavior. In some ways the brain of a man is like the computer of a robot, in others it is more akin to the brain of a frog. Our aim here is to convey an understanding of the brain in terms of two main metaphors: The cybernetic metaphor, "Humans are machines," and the evolutionary metaphor, "Humans are animals." We shall not downgrade the differences, but we hope to learn much from the similarities.

> Thus, when we call this book *The Metaphorical Brain* we do not imply that the understanding of the brain that it affords will be any less "real" than that afforded by other books—rather we are simply making explicit the aid that metaphor provides us, as well as lessening the risk of misunderstanding that results when an implicit metaphor is mistaken for reality.[9]

As a product of evolution, the biological aspects of humans must be described by any metaphor or series of metaphors that attempts to explain human nature. Where Arbib used the twin metaphors of "Humans are machines" and "Humans are animals" to account for the biological nature of man, Pylyshyn employed only the computational metaphor of "Cognition is computational" and assigned the animal nature of humans to an instantiation of what he called the "functional architecture" of the mind. Pylyshyn speaks of computation and mind on two levels: (1) the theoretical requirements for computation (mind) and (2) the biological structures and processes of the brain that carry out these computations. These correspond to the software and hardware of a computer. But even with this distinction, Pylyshyn has difficulty accounting for intentionality and consciousness that humans exhibit in forming self-conscious goals that alter their mentality.

A Literal Version of the Computational Metaphor

More startling than Pylyshyn's attempt to include the biological component in the functional architecture of a computational device is his insistence that the computational metaphor be taken *literally*.

> Given that computation and cognition can be viewed in these common abstract terms, there is no reason why computation ought to be treated as merely a metaphor for cognition, as opposed to a hypothesis about the literal nature of cognition. In spite of the widespread use of computational terminology (e.g., terms like "storage," "process," "operation"), much of this usage has had at least some metaphorical content. There has been a reluctance to take computation as a *literal* description of mental activity, as opposed to being a mere heuristic metaphor. In my view this failure to take computation literally has licensed a wide range of activity under the rubric of "information processing theory," some of it representing a significant departure from what I see as the core ideas of a computational theory of mind.[10]

Pylyshyn wants us not just to conceive of mental activity *as if* it were computational like the algorithms of a computer but to identify cognition *as* computation. This does not mean that human beings are identical with computers (for Pylyshyn has carefully formed a hierarchy of levels of theory with computation as a theoretical level that can be instantiated in either machines or humans) but rather that the computational algorithms for both computers and minds are the same. This identity follows if we change the way in which we theorize about humans and the world. He invokes the analogy in the seventeenth century of the acceptance of Euclidean geometry as the nature of space. Only in the time of Newton were the axioms of Euclid taken as a literal description of the physical world. This acceptance "profoundly affected the course of science"; acceptance of the computational metaphor will similarly affect theories about cognition—positively, of course.

> Accepting a system as a literal account of reality enables scientists to see that certain further observations are possible and others are

not. It goes beyond merely asserting that certain things happen "as if" some unseen events were taking place. In addition, however, it imposes severe restrictions on a theory-builder, because he is no longer free to appeal to the existence of unspecified similarities between his theoretical account and the phenomena he is addressing—as he is when speaking metaphorically. It is this latter degree of freedom that weakens the explanatory power of computation when it is used metaphorically to describe certain mental functions. If we view computation more abstractly as a symbolic process that transforms formal expressions that are in turn interpreted in terms of some domain of representation (such as the numbers), we see that the view that mental processes are computational can be just as literal as the view that what IBM computers do is properly viewed as computation.[11]

Pylyshyn ignores, however, the consequences of taking Euclidean geometry literally; the Euclidean beliefs about the absoluteness of length were shattered by the advent of relativity theory in the twentieth century. What guarantee does Pylyshyn offer that conversion of the computational metaphor into a literal description by an act of belief will not impede cognitive science by constraining how we think about the problem into narrow channels of thought? Metaphors can be most dangerous when we forget that they are metaphors; we often become beguiled by familiarity rather than by corroborating evidence into accepting a metaphor as literal. Pylyshyn asks theorists to accept the computational metaphor as literal, not because of corroborating evidence but because he believes acceptance will produce better theories that are more constrained and thereby more focused.

Whether to take the computational metaphor as literal illustrates one of the major problems facing any theory of metaphor—drawing the line between the "literal" and the "metaphorical." Until recently, many linguistics, philosophers, and scientists viewed metaphor with disdain, as an ungrammatical device characteristic of sloppy thinking rather than as a legitimate theoretical tool. In the eyes of these critics, mystics seeking to express the rapture of the moment of union or poets yearning to express their anguish could resort to metaphor because intuitions and feelings could not be presented in precise terms; but when scientists resort to metaphor, they are accused of substituting mushy, imprecise figurative uses of language when they should be improving the theory to the point where it can be presented in more precise terms. Yet the growing recognition that theories require metaphors to be both hypothetical and intelligible brings with it the need to differentiate between the metaphorical and the nonmetaphorical or literal.

Some theorists of metaphor claim that all language is metaphorical and that no such thing as literal language exists. They do admit that many metaphors lose their strangeness and become "dead metaphors," but even these, they claim, retain their metaphorical status of combining two different referents. In the sense of representation all symbols are metaphors, for they present the meaning of an object, event, or idea not necessarily present at the moment of utterance. If we admit that all language is metaphorical, then when faced with choosing among metaphors in any particular case (such as that of the nature of recognition), why do we choose the computational metaphor over other possible metaphors? And contrary to Pylyshyn, the computational metaphor cannot be converted to a literal statement because no difference exists between the two. Pylyshyn might choose a metaphor that is less metaphorical than others but he can never seek the literal. This view possesses some harsh consequences not only for making sense of a metaphor (one has no standard of literal language by which to make a distinction) but also for a theory of truth. Since corroboration of metaphors never converts them into the literal, we are faced with a relativistic linguistic realm with no anchor points in that which could be experienced as literal.

On the other hand, if we claim a distinction between literal and metaphorical, then we must make good on this assertion by producing a plausible criterion for demarcation. Such a criterion must be linguistic as well as cognitive; we have to show how the literal can be experienced or perceived as literal and the metaphorical as metaphorical. The cognitive notions of resemblance, similarity, and difference are all involved as parts of a knowledge process that makes distinctions possible. The presentation of such a knowledge process inevitably entails the invocation of metaphors, or at least an intuitive distinction between literal and metaphorical, so that the development of the criterion is rooted in circularity. The only partial escape from this possible paradox is to differentiate levels of discourse; when we speak about distinctions between literal and metaphor in the context of cognitive processes we necessarily have to speak on a metalevel of language. The fact that my theory of metaphor on the metalinguistic level is itself metaphorical does not necessarily entail that distinctions between literal and metaphorical on the object-language level do not exist.

The Computational Metaphor and Conceptual Changes

Any theory of metaphor that claims a distinction between the literal and the metaphorical also has to explain how metaphors differ from everyday language and how metaphors die and become part of ordinary discourse. Metaphors serve as catalysts for linguistic change; the metaphors of one generation become banal expressions of another generation. Metaphor exists as a quite normal creative human cognitive process that combines normally unrelated concepts to produce new insights. John McCarthy, reputedly the originator of the appellation "artificial intelligence," argues that the ascription of mental qualities to machines is perfectly legitimate and should not be prohibited.[12]

> To ascribe certain 'beliefs', 'knowledge', 'freewill', 'intentions', 'consciousness', 'abilities' or 'wants' to a machine or computer program is legitimate when such an ascription expresses the same information about the machine that it expresses about a person. It is useful when the ascription helps us understand the structure of the machine, its past or future behaviour, or how to repair or improve it. It is perhaps never logically required even for humans, but expressing reasonably briefly what is actually known about the state of a machine in a particular situation may require mental qualities or qualities isomorphic to them. Theories of belief, knowledge and wanting can be constructed for machines in a simpler setting than for humans and later applied to humans. Ascription of mental qualities is most straightforward for machines of known structure such as thermostats and computer operating systems, but is most useful when applied to entities whose structure is very incompletely known.[13]

McCarthy's argument hinges on the word "same"; when does an ascription express the *same* information about a person as a machine? To a thermostat McCarthy ascribes the simple belief statements of "The room is too cold," "The room is too hot," and "The room is OK." Yet this does not entail that the thermostat understands the concept of "too cold," which humans certainly do understand. If belief means only specific actions or dispositions to act, then the thermostat certainly does possess the three beliefs ascribed to it by McCarthy. If belief includes understanding and assent to a proposition, then it remains doubtful that the thermostat possesses beliefs in the *same* way that humans do. The metaphorical ascription of human traits to computers or attributes of computers to humans raises the question of just what parts of the metaphor are the same for both. Pylyshyn rightly recognized that to take literally the computational metaphor meant that only certain features of human computation and computer computation are the same. If the brain and the computer are hardware instantiations of the functional architecture of the computational metaphor, then few physical processes of computations are similar. When metaphorical ascriptions are made, we must be careful to decide just how far the similarities between the two referents of the metaphor can be extended. Some critics of artificial intelligence claim that, because human beings who manifest intelligence can feel pain and presumably computers cannot feel pain, computers, therefore, cannot be intelligent beings. But such an argument assumes that if something possesses intelligence, then it must necessarily possess all the other attributes that humans possess. Daniel Dennett showed that asking if computers feel pain when it is claimed that computers simulate human intelligence is like asking whether computers experience hurricanes since they also simulate them.[14] If a machine possesses a belief in the sense of a disposition to act, then it need not necessarily possess other attributes that human beings, who also have dispositions to act (beliefs), possess.

In 1950, A. M. Turing proposed a conceptual game called the imitation game that presumed the identification of computers and minds.[15] An interrogator faces the challenge of deciding which of two people separated from him is a woman and which is a man. He questions them and receives answers by means of a telecommunicator. When a computer is substituted for one of the participants in the other room, the interrogator cannot tell the difference. The machine can appear just as intelligent and just as plausibly human as the actual human participant. In artificial intelligence circles this conceptual procedure, the imitation game, has come to be known as the Turing test. In any question involving the qualities of a computer, if one cannot tell the difference between the output of the machine and that of a human, then one is justified in ascribing the human attribute to the computer.

Metaphors can be dangerous not only in bewitching us into thinking that what they suggest really does exist but also in leading us to believe that the attributes normally possessed by any of the referents in the metaphor are possessed by the others. If humans and computers possess memories or beliefs, then we may be seduced by the metaphorical usage to assume that the properties of human memory can be found in the computer or that the notion of belief in humans should be limited to dispositions to act since they are so limited in computers. Metaphorical personification, which has probably existed since the advent of human speech, has become extensive in computer science. Primitive cultures often personify natural objects by giving them a divine status; perhaps we have shifted the deification from nature to technology. The naming of computers began in laboratories and later appeared in science fiction novels and movies. A recent introductory work on computers heads a section on Winograd's computer program "SHRDLU."[16]

Metaphors allow us to extend our knowledge by juxtaposing normally unrelated referents and by suggesting that some of the attributes of each referent are similar. Other attributes of each referent remain dissimilar. Drawing the line between those attributes that are similar and those that are dissimilar strains the imagination and perception of those confronting new metaphors. In the computational metaphor, many of the similarities between humans and computers are obvious—both entities can add, subtract, and multiply; both can make decisions; both can store information and retrieve it; both can learn to recognize new patterns; both can process language. But can both *think*? If thinking is defined in terms of the preceding incomplete list of functions performed by both, then certainly computers think. But if one argues that thinking depends on embodiment of the computational device in a biological organism, then computers clearly do not think.[17]

One could also view this analysis from the point of the computer and claim that thinking only occurs when an entity follows formal rules. Because much of what passes for thought among humans rests on haphazard associations rather than on the instantiation of formal rules, a critic might argue that computers think much more often than humans do, and only occasionally when people emulate computers by strictly following formal rules can they be said to be thinking rationally.

When one affirms that machines possess beliefs or intentions, as McCarthy did in arguing that a thermostat has three types of belief, we can wonder whether belief includes among its proper attributes understanding and self-awareness. The notion of a belief must be limited in its attributes if it is to apply to a thermostat.

Both the production and the recognition of a metaphor demand the ability to link attributes of normally unrelated referents. The more difficult the comprehension of the linkage, the more suggestive the metaphor. The computational metaphor that demands association of a full range of human attributes, like feelings, consciousness, and intentionality, with computers is a much more suggestive metaphor than a more constrained computational metaphor that allows analogies only among certain deductive functions.

In later chapters I will develop a semantic theory that allows semantic change to take place in the formation of metaphors. Underlying this semantic theory is a cognitive process. The production of metaphors is not just a linguistic phenomenon occurring on the surface of language; it arises from a deeper cognitive process that creatively envisages new possibilities for meanings. The coiner of vibrant metaphors somehow combines seemingly unrelated concepts to produce a new fluid concept that expresses analogies among some of its features and reveals disparities among others. The metaphor may be so suggestive that it finds little confirmation in experience or it may be so expressive of analogies that had been little noticed before the advent of the metaphor that it comes to be widely used and finally fades into ordinary language. For the computational metaphor to become accepted as a literal expression, the evidence confirming the association between formal programs and minds should become so overwhelming that the computational metaphor loses its tension. Pylyshyn, however, wanted to transform the computational metaphor into a literal statement as a means of producing a better theory.

The Computational Metaphor as a Basic Metaphor

The example of the computational metaphor illustrates another aspect of metaphor—its use as a basic presuppositional insight or intuition that undergirds an entire theory. I call this type of metaphor a basic metaphor. Metaphors can also be employed to express a particular feeling or to suggest an individual possibility. I call this second type of metaphor a conveyance metaphor. I have much more to say about both of these later; here, let me draw out some of the issues posed by the use of the computational metaphor as a basic metaphor for the investigation of mind and brain.

The first form of the computational metaphor was presented in the "artificial intelligence" metaphor, which was suggested by the algorithmic functions that computers execute so efficiently and that before the advent of the computer only humans were known to perform. Another expression of this basic metaphor is "computers think." This basic metaphor, which rested on a startling suggestion when it was first proposed in the 1950s, combines the referent intelligence, which before this time had been confined to humans and animals, with the referent computing machine. From the earliest forms mentioned in the *Oxford English Dictionary* to the present, intelligence has been associated with the mental faculties and understanding so that one of the usual attributes of intelligence is "biological," i.e., pertains to humans and animals. Machines are normally interpreted as having nonbiological attributes. Positing the computational metaphor suggests the examination of both computing machines, to see just how much in fact they are like humans, and human beings, to see just how much in fact they correspond to computing machines in cognitive functions. As a basic metaphor, the computational metaphor proposes to treat human cognition *as if* it were computation and computation *as if* it were human cognition. When the metaphor was first proposed, it was widely recognized as a metaphor and not as a literal assertion because too many differences were recognized between human thinking and the functioning of computers. Gradually, more similarities were found, and the strangeness of the metaphor, its tension or suggestiveness, diminished.

Often the process of investigation, which began with the recognition of a basic metaphor as the presupposition of the entire enterprise, follows the line of positing conveyance metaphors that grow out of the basic metaphor. McCarthy moved in this direction through the attribution of numerous human traits to machines. He extended the attributes beyond those of cognition to attitudes, feelings, and consciousness. He also extended the notion of machine beyond that of the computer to those like the thermostat. The extension of the basic metaphor through other metaphors to a wider range of possible experience tests the comprehension of the identification of the referents.

This procedure of extending knowledge through the postulation of basic metaphors arising from intuitions about ourselves and the world has been occurring for centuries. From Plato's presumption of an unchanging realm of forms to Einstein's presuppositions that the world is orderly and mathematical, philosophers and scientists have invoked implicitly or explicitly basic metaphors as foundations on which to construct their explanations. The invocation of the computational metaphor as a basic metaphor was done explicitly and with awareness that this presuppositional act brought with it tentativeness and speculation—characteristics that Pylyshyn thought led to theory construction that was too unfocused. At other times in the history of thought, basic metaphors have been covertly assumed, as in the case of the early twentieth-century logical positivists who believed that they had no first principles and had thereby avoided a dreaded metaphysical stance and yet *assumed* that language mirrored the world (a basic metaphor).

I have noted that in examining the computational metaphor we face a possible paradox; the theory of metaphor that is described in this book is itself grounded in a theory of cognition that presumably can be expressed only metaphorically. I have hinted that by differentiating between a theory and a metatheory paradoxes of self-reference may be avoided. But I have to do more than that, for I also want to avoid the commitment to a view that all language is metaphorical and that one can easily identify literal language, even though grounded in a cognitive process. I am faced with the problem that my account of literal language is guaranteed by a theory of cognition that can be formed only with a basic metaphor (it need not be the computational metaphor that I have cited here only as an example at this point). My theory of metaphor presumes a cognitive theory that presumes the use of at least a basic metaphor (and probably conveyance metaphors as well). This circularity seems like a process of mirroring: the image of metaphor is reflected back to cognition and that of cognition is reflected back to metaphor. But are there one or two images? At this point we cannot tell, but I can offer a possible escape from this reflected circularity.

The metaphorical process not only involves the mind and the brain but it also presumes the external world with its wealth of symbols and culture.

An adequate theory of metaphor presents not only semantic, syntactic, and cognitive theories that explain how unusual combinations of words can produce new concepts but also contextual theories about the external world that provide depositories of associations of words and interactions between individuals and their environment that produce knowledge. The cognitive process that produces metaphors is embedded in a wider knowledge process that involves the individual in a contextual evolutionary process: evolution of both the brain that provides the hardware for cognition and the culture that provides the context in which through interaction with the linguistic environment metaphors emerge. But biological evolution and cultural evolution proceed according to different mechanisms. The mind that produces metaphors may well mediate between its own neural processes and the cultural processes.

In the development of a knowledge process that includes interaction between individuals and their environment, I hope to develop a theory of metaphor that accounts for literal expression, allows for individual creativity, and yet acknowledges that the meaning of metaphors depends largely on context. The circularity of self-reference between metaphor and cognition can be overcome only by appeal to the objectivity of the external world. My preliminary intuition finds metaphor as a mediating device among mind, brain, and the external world; a metatheory of metaphor that seeks to explain the nature and meaning of metaphor inevitably will presume elements from all three. In one schema we might view the levels of metaphor as follows:

1. Surface level: culture

2. Deeper level: semantics and syntax

3. Deepest level: cognition

The problem with this attempt to set out metalevels in accord with the computational metaphor is that levels 2 and 3 are not independent of level 1 and that both levels 2 and 3 are embodied in a biological organism whose evolution is partially affected by culture. As a knowledge process, metaphor seems much more complicated because of its linguistic expression in a cultural context by an embodied cognition (mind).

I describe metaphor as an evolutionary knowledge process that combines brain, mind, and culture in the creative formation of language. Before proceeding to this account, however, I need to describe carefully the nature of metaphor—what makes a metaphor a metaphor, how one can distinguish a metaphor from an analogy, and how one can distinguish a metaphor from literal language. I am concerned with developing a linguistic theory that is sufficient to produce metaphors and that can be embedded in this larger knowledge process. I also look at the status of metaphors as truth functions and at the issue of how metaphors achieve meaning.

2
The Nature of Metaphor

Metaphor and Analogy

When confronted by a metaphor, ordinary people can usually understand the unusual combination of words. When they read "His mind bred vermin. His thoughts were lice born of the sweat of sloth," from James Joyce's *A Portrait of the Artist as a Young Man*, the average person knows that Stephen Dedalus's mind has been corrupted by laziness.[1] Readers do not have to consult grammatical rules to comprehend its meaning; they are told that a "metaphor" combines referents in an unusual way and because they intuitively know that "thoughts" are not literally "lice," they can comprehend Joyce's vivid juxtaposition of words as a metaphor. The philosopher, however, desires to go beyond this native ability to understand metaphors and wishes to produce a theory of metaphor that explains how it is possible for someone to generate meaning out of a linguistic construction that seems on the surface to be an anomaly, if not a contradiction in terms. Although "thoughts" are embodied, unless one is an identity theorist who reduces all thinking to brain processes, the usual intuition about thoughts places them apart from biological entities. How can these nonanimal things, thoughts, be identified with insects that infest animal bodies? And even if one did identify the mind solely with the brain, how could one find vermin running through the head when we know that the brain meshes with the nervous system, an electrochemical network? Only in death could lice perhaps literally run through the physical meat of the brain, and we know from the context of the story that Stephen remains alive.

Our ability to identify "thoughts" with "lice" rests on our knowledge that thoughts can be corrupted and that lice are a sign of bodily corruption. Perhaps Joyce does mean to suggest that Stephen is dying spiritually through the corruption of his mind by sloth. If there was not some similarity between "thoughts" and "lice," we could not recognize the combination as meaningful. An analogy serves as a necessary but not a sufficient condition for the existence of a metaphor. In the computational metaphor, described in chapter 1, the analogous functions of mathematical calculation, learning of patterns, and storage and retrieval of information provided some of the similar features that allowed the identification of the human mind with a computer. But why isn't the locution "The mind is a computational device" an *analogy* between the human mind and a computer? What makes this combination a metaphor and not just an analogy? Many analogies occur that few would call metaphors. The toy model of the USS *Missouri* possesses numerous analogous parts to the actual ship. When built to scale, the model exhibits a similar shape, similar superstructure, the same number of guns in the same locations, etc. Unless built as a working model, the toy also exhibits some differences: no machinery operates below deck nor do the guns fire. A photograph also presents an analogy with the subject photographed with the obvious difference that the tactile features of the photograph are lost as compared with the real subject. How can one draw the line between an analogy and a metaphor? One might argue that although the line of demarcation is not a sharp one, the difference between an analogy and a metaphor depends on the degree of difference between the two referents. Referents that differ substantially can be called metaphors, whereas those that possess more similarities are analogies. This move places metaphor in the category of a subset of analogy. Although I have acknowledged that analogy is a necessary condition for metaphor, I claim that metaphors possess additional necessary conditions beyond those of simple analogies, especially models. For example, when we see the toy *Missouri*, we are not emotionally shocked by the model and wonder how it could possibly represent that mighty dreadnaught on whose decks the Second World War ended. Yet the identification of "thoughts" and "lice" produces an emotional tension within us. Although understanding the association of the two, we worry that mental corruption differs from physical corruption sufficiently to produce a possible contradiction.

Difficulties with the Tension, Controversion, and Deviance Theories

Theorists of metaphor have located the difference between metaphor and analogy in (1) the emotional tension generated by the juxtaposition of anomalous referents (the tension theory), (2) the falsity or contradiction produced by a literal reading of the identification of the two referents (the controversion theory), and (3) the ungrammaticality of the juxtaposition of the two referents (the deviance theory).[2] In talking about the two referents in the context of differentiating between metaphor and analogy, theorists have described the metaphorical referents as tenor/vehicle, focus/frame, and topic/vehicle.[3] Much confusion exists about the identification of the metaphorical referents. I. A. Richards described the underlying idea (principle subject) of a metaphor as the tenor and the less well known as the vehicle of imagined nature. This seems to imply that the two referents of a metaphor arise from cognition beneath the surface language words appearing in the metaphor. There remains the possibility, however, of having the tenor refer to the first surface language term of a metaphor as the familiar term and to the second surface language term as the less familiar. Yet both of the surface language terms may well be familiar—we are acquainted with "minds" and with "computers," and we are acquainted with "thoughts" and "lice." Although suggesting identification of the familiar with the tenor and the unfamiliar with the vehicle (and leaving ambiguous whether this identification is with the actual surface language terms of the metaphor), Richards was careful to acknowledge that this association may not be correct and that the terms tenor and vehicle may be inverted in their reference to the parts of a metaphor. What seems to be the tenor may actually be the vehicle, and vice versa. Black's interaction theory of metaphor accounted for this possible inversion and employed focus and frame to talk about the two referents. He also left ambiguous the level, cognitive or surface, at which focus and frame operate. Through interaction, focus and frame combine in a relationship called the ground. Black's interaction theory allows for a reversal of his own terms—the focus may become the frame and the frame the focus.

I agree with these theorists that another necessary condition for metaphor must be the presence of at least two referents, but I resist suggesting that one referent be identified with the familar and the other with the unfamiliar. Later, I will attempt to clarify the relationship between the surface language of a metaphor and the deeper cognitive structure. I identify the referents with the latter rather than with the former.

Consider the metaphor, "The wind thinks outrageous thoughts aloud." One might identify the two referents as "the sounds of the wind" and "thoughts." Or one might identify the "wind" with "a person who thinks." One might also propose three referents, "wind," "thoughts," and "person." Among these three referents one may find an interaction, the wind is a person who thinks outrageous thoughts, or a person who thinks outrageous thoughts is like the wind howling in the wilderness. There may be many other possible interpretations but the point remains that metaphors may possess more than two referents. Finding metaphors with more than two referents is easy and confirms my contention that to be a metaphor, a linguistic combination must have *at least* two referents but may possess more. Tom Robbins in *Another Roadside Attraction* wrote, "Stars are merely projections of the human psyche—they are pimples of consciousness—but they are at the same time quite real."[4] Here again there are at least three referents: "stars," "consciousness," and "pimples." One might object that this mixed metaphor confuses the mental and physical in application to stars. A defender might reply that consciousness in this metaphor becomes like the skin of the body when projected to the universe and by no means mixes the metaphor—rather, consciousness is first transformed to a skin, and then the stars become pimples on that surface when projected to the celestial realm.

Most commentators on metaphor have followed Max Black's advice to begin their analysis with banal metaphors, simple identifications of the form "A is B," and then to see if they could make sense of these constructions before going on to tackle more complicated metaphors such as "stars are the pimples of consciousness." A wise strategy, but one that leads to the preoccupation with two referents, one familiar (the tenor) and the other unfamiliar (the vehicle). Metaphors may be much more complicated than that and may involve at least two but often more than two referents, and these referents cannot be divided simply into the familiar and the unfamiliar.

Let us now return to the question of how to differentiate between metaphor and analogy and consider the possibilities of tension, controversion, and grammatical deviance. Each of these contains a partial truth, but none of them satisfactorily offers an adequate demarcation. I propose a fourth alternative, a conceptual theory of semantic anomaly, which offers a better method of demarcation. A fuller justification of my conceptual theory of semantic anomaly is offered in a later chapter.

Metaphors usually produce tension among their hearers. The tension theory by no means exists as necessarily exclusive from either the controversion or the deviance theories. Confronted by the identification of the human mind with a computer or with stars as the pimples of consciousness, the hearer may *feel* tension in the metaphor. The seeming misuse of language produces this tension, but the hearer also finds meaning in the metaphor. How can this be? If the metaphor is literally false and/or ungrammatical, then how can we account for its apparent meaning? A tension theorist may propose that the meaning arises out of the metaphor's emotive import. Convinced that literature could not be tested in the same way as scientific language, I. A. Richards proposed that poetry expresses its meaning through its emotive nature, the feelings that it stirs in its audience.[5] Like poetry, then, metaphors can express emotive meaning; the tension that they produce is the very expression of meaning. But how do they do this? Can a metaphor be false and yet meaningful? Certainly, many nonmetaphorical false statements are meaningful. But if a metaphor is ungrammatical, how can it be meaningful? Ungrammatical metaphors seem to be conceptually confused rather than meaningful false statements. Yet metaphors that were false seem to become true, and metaphors that were ungrammatical seem to become grammatical, both through usage. The numerous dead metaphors in ordinary conversation were once tension-filled seemingly false statements such as "time flies"—how can "time," an inanimate entity, "fly" like a bird? The metaphor also may be ungrammatical in the sense that it combines words inappropriately. Now, however, "flies" has taken on the connotation of "passes rapidly," so that it produces no tension when we hear the metaphor. Through continued misuse of language, a false metaphor became true, lost its ungrammaticality, and lost its tension. Why would a poet or even a scientist choose to misuse language intentionally, producing false statements in order to produce an emotively meaningful statement? Human beings, unless they wish to lie or deceive, usually do not intentionally set out to produce false but meaningful statements. The poet wants to express an insight or suggest a possible new and creative meaning and resorts to an unusual juxtaposition of words that he or she hopes will convey a glimmer of truth, not express an obvious falsehood. We may *feel* some meaning in a metaphor, but that meaning cannot rest solely on emotion; it must have some cognitive support. Few words depend solely on their emotive import for their meaning; most depend on recognition of their cognitive content.

Under the tension theory, ungrammaticality, falsehood, or unfamiliarity, or any combination of these produces emotional "tension" in the hearer of a metaphor. But the hearer's unfamiliarity may diminish when encountering the same metaphor over and over. For the cognitive scientist, encountering the computational metaphor frequently, even as a critic of it, may diminish the tension associated with that metaphor. To criticize a position, one must adopt at least the vocabulary and some of the basic assumptions of that position in order to present arguments against it. Ironically, the opponent of the computational metaphor in offering arguments and evidence against it may gradually assume many of the implications of the metaphor as part of her own critical position. The metaphor may become less ungrammatical, and its falsehood diminishes through modification of the metaphor. Familiarity reduces tension and thereby may eliminate falsehood and ungrammaticality. This indeed brings about a most peculiar state of affairs—a hypothetical theory or speculative poetical insight can become true not through the confirmation of experience but through continued expression of a metaphor. Through continued misuse, tension lowers, truth increases, and the utterance becomes grammatical.[6] Truth and grammatical deviance become functions of emotional tension. When tension disappears, truth and proper grammar appear. But a metaphor may become extremely familiar and still remain hypothetical. In the history of science, so familiar did Newton's description of the world become that scientists forgot the speculative nature of his metaphoric assumptions about the world—that the world was mathematical and operated according to the Newtonian mechanical laws. A tension theory does explain psychologically how people succumb to metaphors through familiarity, but it does not suffice to differentiate between metaphors and analogies. Many metaphors are characterized by tension, but other metaphors remain metaphors even though they have lost their psychological shock. These often entice people into believing that they are literal rather than metaphorical, presenting a clear and present danger to the poet and scientist.

Before leaving the tension theory, let me note that there remains an ambiguity about emotional feelings associated with metaphors. Not only may the unusual juxtaposition of referents produce an emotional shock in the hearer, but the cognitive meaning of the metaphor may also convey the feelings of the author and/or produce similar or different feelings in the hearer. On hearing our previous example of "The wind thinks outrageous thoughts aloud" the average person may comprehend the emotional feeling of the author that the "wind" is ominous and howling as well as experience the hearer's own shivering feeling of foreboding and mild terror. I deal with this distinction further in chapter 7.

The controversion theory differentiates between metaphor and ordinary language by observing that a literal reading of a metaphor produces statements that are false.[7] To avoid this falsehood, the metaphor must be read speculatively *as if* it were true or false. In Sir Charles Sherrington's vivid metaphor "The brain is an enchanted loom where millions of flashing shuttles weave a dissolving pattern," the identification of the "brain" with an "enchanted loom" is literally impossible—brains are flesh and blood parts of an organism and, therefore, according to the controversion theory, can be identified only with any kind of loom, even an enchanted loom in a *false* assertion.[8] Neither poets nor scientists, however, want to be trapped into making false assertions when they propose speculative metaphors. Sherrington probably wanted to suggest an insightful way of looking at the brain rather than intentionally propose a false assertion about it. To eliminate the intentional perpetration of falsehood by otherwise honest people, metaphors must be either paraphrased or converted into statements of similarity—analogy. The metaphor cannot be taken as it is; it must be transformed into an analogy—the "brain" becomes *like* an "enchanted loom" in certain respects and different from it in others. This conversion to a simile (as if) with further restriction of the features to those that are similar prevents falsehood but robs the metaphor of its suggestive meaning. Paraphrase to ordinary language and reduction to explicit analogy makes *true* metaphors a subset of analogies. Metaphors that have not been paraphrased or reduced to analogy remain falsehoods. For metaphors to assert true propositions, their creativity has to be sacrificed. The image of flashing shuttles weaving dissolving patterns promotes a way of thinking about the neuronal activity of the brain. Is it necessarily false? If one answers yes, then many well-accepted theories that rely on models for their interpretation may also fall from grace.

The controversion theory poses a dilemma for the philosopher seeking an explanatory account of metaphor: either metaphors assert falsehoods or the only legitimate metaphors are the least interesting ones, the ones that collapse into ordinary language or into explicit analogy. The emotive theory of metaphor, a subset of the tension theory, argues that metaphors may be false but that they are meaningful through their expression of emotive import. Metaphors present the emotive feelings of the author as well as stimulate similar and other emotional feelings in the hearer. Emotive theorists thought that they had resolved the dilemma uncovered by the controversion theory. Metaphors did not have to be paraphrased or reduced to analogies; they could remain metaphors even though false and yet could be meaningful and insightful. The emotive theory responded to demands by positivists that for a statement to be meaningful it must be capable of test. Under the controversion theory, metaphors are meaningful but false; yet their falsity arises not from empirical test but usually from semantic contradiction. When juxtaposed, the referents produce incongruity and therefore falsity. By admitting falsity, the emotive theorists claimed meaning, but the meaning that they claimed for metaphors, and even for ethics when a similar objection was made by positivists to moral statements, was that the metaphor produced not only an intelligible *sense* of meaning but also an *insightful* meaning. They could produce the latter by conveying the emotions of the author of the metaphor and by stimulating the emotions of the hearer of the metaphor.

The dilemma posed by the controversion theory and the solution offered by the emotive theory assume that the truth or falsity of a metaphor is an *either/or* matter. Either the metaphor is true or it is false. Because of its semantic anomaly it must be false, and if false it can either become true by reduction to analogy and therefore cease to be a metaphor or it can remain false and find useful meaning only through emotive expression and stimulation.

Suppose, however, that metaphors can be partially true and partially false, that the truth or falsity of a metaphor is not an either/or matter but rather a matter of degrees. In the respect that the attributes of the two referents are similar, the metaphor can be said to be true, whereas with respect to the difference of certain attributes it can be said to be false. The more suggestive the metaphor, the greater the degree of falsity; the more expressive of analogy, the greater the degree of truth. As a corollary, the more suggestive, the more tensive a metaphor.

Do these notions of partial truth and partial falsehood wreak havoc on our usual notions of truth to the extent that making any such move creates a separate category of truth reserved for metaphor, called "metaphorical truth"? The application of a two-valued logic and the law of excluded middle (either a statement is true or it is false) to metaphor seems to produce an inadequate theory of metaphor. Is this enough to warrant a revision of our normal intuitions of truth? Perhaps not, but there remain many areas in human experience, including science, in which a two-valued logic constrains our explanatory account unduly. Not only does complementarity as an explanation of light come to mind but also the various forms of decision theory, which are better explained by Bayesian probability than by either/or logic.

The development of fuzzy-set theory and fuzzy logic allows for the development of the associations of terms with degrees of truth and falsity. In fact, a many-valued logic can be constructed and applied to a fuzzy semantics, allowing for functions relating terms that change.[9] I develop these notions extensively as they apply to metaphor in a later chapter. For now I agree with the controversion theory that metaphors do produce falsehoods among some of the attributes of the two referents, but I deny that this leads to the conclusion that the entire metaphor is false and must be paraphrased or reduced to analogy in order to convey any truth. Instead, I propose that metaphors possess a fluidity with respect to truth and falsehood and that a many-valued logic rather than a two-valued logic can better explain metaphors. I add that this many-valued logic can best express the truth functions of metaphors in the context of a fuzzy-set theory that ranges over semantics.

The deviance theory holds that metaphors differ from analogies by their misuse of language, claiming that literally read metaphors are ungrammatical. Metaphors sin grammatically most often when they attempt to combine semantically words that have opposite semantic selection markers. Consider the metaphor, "The telephone is my umbilical cord to the world." "Telephones" are inanimate objects, whereas "umbilical cords" are animate. The semantic selection markers of Animate and Inanimate clash.

Transformational generative grammarians early held that metaphors violated grammatical rules and therefore were deviant linguistic structures.[10] The construction of semantic trees for the surface language referents of a metaphor reveals anomalies if not contradictions. Having moved down the tree for "telephone" and passing the node of the semantic marker Inanimate, one cannot then move back up the tree to the alternative node Animate to connect "telephone" with "umbilical cord." But language changes; the word "fly" once referred only to animate objects since no inanimate objects were known to fly. Perhaps when rocks were thrown, they were described as "flying" through the air because they were like birds in that respect. Since the advent of the balloon and airplane, the word "fly" can easily be associated with the semantic marker Inanimate, and we have already seen in the dead metaphor "time flies" that this verb extends beyond observed physical motion to the rapid passage of time. Recognizing that metaphors can involve words as referents that change their semantic markers led grammarians to admit that metaphors are semigrammatical devices.[11] Metaphors cannot be presented as fully grammatical because they violate semantic rules. Yet, neither can they be viewed as *absolutely* deviant in grammar because so many of them die and become part of ordinary language through the change in meaning of their referents.

Some theorists, however, have attempted to maintain the distinction between grammatical and ungrammatical as the basis of difference between metaphorical and nonmetaphorical. Robert J. Matthews contended that "the performance distinction between metaphor and non-metaphor is correctly characterized on the competence level in terms of a distinction between semantically deviant and non-deviant sentences."[12] Recognizing that not all semantically deviant combinations of words are necessarily metaphors, Matthews further differentiated between these two groups by noting that metaphors involved the *intentional* misuse of language.[13] Confronted by the problem of how to handle the opposed semantic markers (selection restrictions), he suggested that features of these markers be de-emphasized. But to do that would emaciate the metaphor. If we de-emphasize the Inanimate of "telephone" and the Animate of "umbilical cord," then we move in the direction of converting the metaphor into an analogy, and the difference between metaphorical and nonmetaporical is lost.

Defining metaphor as the intentional misuse of language to present a new insight or to propose a new hypothesis finds support in the recognized difficulty of developing grammatical rules for the production and interpretation of metaphors. Metaphors do seem to violate the normal associations of words; in metaphoric constructions referents that normally remain separate are juxtaposed. And the context in which a metaphor finds interpretation varies so greatly as to defy interpretations that follow a set of rules. Thus the deviance theory seems to offer a viable way of distinguishing between metaphor and non-metaphor.[14] The consequences of this theory, however, separate the linguistic world into ordinary language that operates according to semantic rules and the metaphoric world of intentionally ungrammatical but insightful constructions. But the two worlds are not unrelated, as metaphors die and become part of the corpus of ordinary discourse. Under this theory no explanation exists for this. The deviance theory does not provide an explanation of semantic change. Furthermore, the deviance theory might be acceptable if metaphors were exceptions to normal grammatical use, if they occurred only on rare occasions. Metaphors, however, occur in great profusion; so riddled is ordinary language with dead metaphors and so often do we resort to the construction of metaphors to express and suggest new insights that a theory such as the deviance theory, which claims metaphors to be unusual, seems inherently wrong. Metaphor appears so usually and so regularly a part of ordinary language that instead of contending that metaphor deviates from a normative grammar, one might better consider that any grammar which cannot account for metaphor is too limited in comprehension to be useful. Grammars that view metaphor as deviant may themselves be deviant in their failure to account adequately for metaphor.

The tension theory, the controversion theory, and the deviance theory all fail to present a theory of metaphor that can differentiate successfully between metaphor and nonmetaphor. The tension theory fails because many metaphors remain hypothetical metaphors even though they become familiar and lose their tension. It is not an unusual occurrence in science for a speculative theory to become so familiar that its surprise is lost, and yet the basic metaphor underlying the theory does not become a literal expression. In the tension theory the grammaticality and the truth of metaphor often depend on a loss of tension—grammar and truth become functions of emotional effect rather than subject to independent rules and independent tests.

The controversion theory places the formulator of metaphor in the position of intentionally constructing falsehoods to promote new insights. Even in the most hypothetical metaphors, poets and scientists want to propose possibilities based on some insight, no matter how tiny or budding, that they consider to be at least partially true. Yet they must resort to a false statement to do so. And metaphor can be rescued from falsity only by paraphrase or by reduction to analogy. If a metaphor finds expression in a true statement, it can only do so under the controversion theory by ceasing to be a metaphor, and that is hardly the way to distinguish metaphors from nonmetaphors.

The deviance theory defines metaphor as an intentional misuse of language and assumes that a semantical theory should not encompass metaphor. But metaphor pervades language so extensively that any semantic theory that excludes metaphor fails as a linguistic theory by being far too narrow.

Although each of these theories fails, insights into the nature of metaphor can be gleaned from them. From the tension theory we learn that metaphors can convey emotional feelings and stimulate emotions through both the unusual juxtaposition of referents and the cognitive content of the metaphor. From the controversion theory we learn that an either/or theory of truth does not apply easily to metaphor, and I suggest that metaphors might better find interpretation under a theory of degrees of truth and falsity. From the deviance theory we learn that metaphors do produce semantic deviance; the semantic markers of the referents of a metaphor do indeed clash and seem to contradict one another. From this observation, to conclude that metaphors are therefore deviant need not follow. Rather I conclude that a semantic theory that cannot account for metaphor and semantic change is itself insufficient. On the ruins of these failures, I propose to construct a theory of semantic conceptual anomaly.

The Theory of Semantic Anomaly

My use of the word anomaly recognizes that many metaphoric juxtapositions of referents seem both contradictory and ungrammatical. I also recognize that this anomaly may produce an emotional tension in the hearer. But the anomaly is by no means strictly a contradiction (falsehood) nor is it ungrammatical. In the metaphor, "My lawnmower is a wild animal," the semantic markers Inanimate and Animate clash, for lawnmowers are not literally animals.[15] But that is just the point of a good metaphor, to consider a lawnmower *as if* it were an animal lunging in different directions despite attempts to restrain it. If we have vivid imaginations, we may actually imagine the mechanical beast in the form of a lion or tiger viciously biting hunks of grass. The lawnmower remains a lawnmower and the wild beast a wild beast; in metaphoric conceptual comprehension the one is seen as the other. We might even think of tigers as lawnmowers rather than lawnmowers as tigers. That lawnmowers are wild beasts is partly true and partly false. The grammatical combination is unusual but not necessarily deviant, as the association of the two referents may be the beginning of a process of linguistic change leading finally to such widespread usage that the entry for "beast" in the dictionary includes the lexical meaning "mechanical monster." We do not have to reduce this metaphor either to ordinary language by paraphrase or to analogy in order to understand the truth of the metaphor. Nor do we have to extend the word beast to mechanical devices to prevent grammatical deviance. Rather, we can understand the metaphor "My lawnmower is a wild beast" as both partially true and grammatical and as the beginning of the process of semantic change. The comprehension of the metaphor follows from the conceptual ability to hold two disparate things in mind at the same time; Douglas Berggren called this ability stereoscopic vision.[16] In part, this conceptual ability and the ability to transform one referent into another results from our imaginative powers. Later, I will show that metaphor not only performs semantic changes in meaning but also serves as the engine for conceptual change in images and ideas.

The theory of semantic conceptual anomaly asserts that the difference between metaphor and nonmetaphor, especially analogy, rests on the conceptual recognition of the semantic anomaly of metaphor and its interpretation as meaningful. Emotional tension exists as a symptom of this recognition rather than as the origin of it. Not all semantically anomalous constructions are metaphors; only those semantic anomalies that we can interpret as suggesting new insights and new possible meanings are metaphors. Strange juxtapositions of referents that produce semantic anomaly are not necessarily ungrammatical, for if they bring about metaphoric conceptual understanding, then they are quite normal; they are the initiation of a process of semantic change that may terminate when semantic markers change and new lexical entries enter the dictionary.

My advocacy of the theory of semantic conceptual change remains incomplete, for I have only shown the faults of the tension theory, the controversion theory, and the deviance theory and given the reader promissory notes for further development of theories of truth and semantics that will undergird my theory. I hope the reader will cash these notes in chapters 4 and 8. Before then I must sketch further my account of the nature of metaphor by giving attention to traditional grammatical forms and their relation to metaphor.

Metaphor and Other Figurative Language

I have already noted that reducing a metaphor to an analogy emphasizes the similarities among the referents and diminishes the dissimilarities. A simile also makes explicit the similarities among the referents. Discussions over the relation between metaphor and simile began with Aristotle, who thought of metaphor as the genus and simile as one of the species.[17] Cicero and Quintilian reversed the relationship with simile as the genus and metaphor as the species. Recently, John Middleton Murry described the two as "essentially the same," with metaphor as "compressed simile."[18] W. Bedell Stanford argued the opposite, namely, that metaphor and simile possess an essential difference.

> The essence of metaphor is that a word undergoes a change or extension of meaning. In simile nothing of this kind occurs; every word has its normal meaning and no semantic transference is incurred. This is a fundamental difference in the verbal sphere. It means that metaphor is primarily a treatment of *language*, simile is primarily a treatment of *thought*; metaphor, then, logically (but not psychologically as has been shown) belongs to the order of tropes, simile to the order of figures; and this being so, on linguistic grounds they can never be classed together.[19]

Metaphor seems hardly to be a "compressed simile" because when confronted with a metaphor, hearers must not only consider the similarities between the referents, as they do in the presence of a simile, but also ponder the differences. In this respect, it is better to talk about simile as "compressed metaphor," compressed in the sense that the incongruities of the semantic markers associated with the referent may be ignored. Viewing simile as compressed metaphor agrees with Aristotle in making metaphor the genus and simile the species. But what about Stanford's claim of an essential difference between the two, that metaphor treats language, whereas simile attends to thought? Stanford correctly notes that metaphors involve semantic transference, and I agree that changes of semantic meaning are less likely, though not prohibited, in similes. Compare Joyce's metaphor quoted earlier, "His mind bred vermin. His thoughts were lice born of the sweat of sloth," with Wallace Stevens's simile that thoughts are like insects in the lines, "Or is the multitude of thoughts,/Like insects in the depth of the mind."[20] Joyce's metaphor makes us know and feel the evil of sloth; in our heated languor (sweat), our minds become infested with lice. Through his metaphor we may begin to think of lazy thoughts as if they were insects (vermin). This semantic possibility may begin a process of semantic transformation modifying our semantic conception of both "thoughts" and "lice." In Stevens's simile, thoughts and insects are deemed similar—many thoughts can kill a single thought (next line, not quoted) just as many insects can destroy another insect. Although in a simile we may be less likely to consider the differences between "thoughts" and "insects," the presence of the "like," an admonition to look for analogies, does not prohibit such a consideration. When reading Stevens's lines, we may wonder just how thoughts can act like insects when they are *so different*. Similes evoke less tension in the hearer and propose an explicit comparison of similarities, but they do not prohibit a consideration of differences. Both metaphors and similes involve conceptual activity; the creator of the metaphor or simile must imagine a combination of referents, and the hearer must search out the connections among the referents as well as take cognizance of the differences (less so in the simile). Stanford wrongly relegated metaphor to language and simile to thought; both are linguistic devices that find their origin and understanding in cognition.

As an expression of language (with a conceptual origin), metaphor exists along with metonymy, synecdoche, personification, irony, and catachresis as a figure of speech, a trope—a nonliteral use of words. Given our description of metaphor as a combination of referents that produces semantic conceptual anomaly, few metonymies or synecdoches are likely to be metaphors; metonymy employs an attribute as an expression of the entity, and synecdoche takes a part and lets it stand for the whole or takes the whole and lets it stand for a part. These two figures of speech do not often juxtapose referents with contradictory semantic markers. When giving the name "speedy" to a fast runner, this metonymy does not cross categories and does not produce semantic anomaly. But if we call him "flash," we may have a metonymy that is also a metaphor because we are taking a category of light (the "flash" of lightning or the "flash" of a "flashgun" on a camera) and applying it to a human being, a category with the semantic marker Animate.

Synecdoches may also be metaphoric when they take an attribute of an individual or of the whole that normally would not apply to the other. Referring to workers as "hands" generates no semantic anomaly, but referring to the "altruism" of an individual ant may be metaphoric in that, although the entire anthill possesses a division of labor in which certain groups of ants function altruistically, as do soldier ants when they fight to the death, each individual ant, even the soldiers, may be operating in a completely determined manner. By some human standards, if behavior is completely determined, then it cannot be altruistic. The synecdoche of calling an ant "altruistic" may be founded in semantic anomaly, that of applying a category to individual human beings, which is perhaps applicable through personification to an ant colony but not to the individual ant in the same way.

We have already seen personification as synonymous with many metaphors; the computational metaphor began with the application of the human attribute of intelligence and applied it to computers. Through interaction, the process became inverted when the computational properties of the machine were then applied to human cognition. Perhaps a new figure of speech should be invented, "mechanicification," the transformation of the living into the mechanical, a process that has been with us since at least the seventeenth century. Numerous metaphors exist that are not personifications, as in Carl Hempel's identification of scientific concepts with knots—"Thus the concepts of science are the knots in a network of systematic interrelationships in which the laws and theoretical principles form the threads."[21] And we know that some of the most interesting, significant, and fruitful metaphors are personifications. For centuries mankind has taken what is known about humans and applied these insights to the physical world, thereby creating speculative hypotheses that can be tested physically. Aristotle's observation that humans experience forces as pushes or pulls was applied to physical objects, forming a theory of motion that demanded contact of impressed force to cause motion and that prohibited action at a distance without contact.

Are all personifications necessarily metaphoric in that they almost necessarily generate semantic anomaly by taking human attributes and juxtaposing them with nonhuman referents? Although not all metaphors are personifications, it certainly seems that all personifications are metaphors. One might object that primitive peoples who believe that rocks and trees are inhabited literally by animistic spirits presume personifications that are not metaphors. In applying human attributes to these nonhuman objects, primitive peoples do not think that they are crossing semantic categories. Or do they when these rocks and trees take on an aura of mystery? It remains almost impossible to reconstruct the semantic comprehension of primitive peoples let alone their animistic belief structure. Let us rest with the observation that most, if not all, personifications are metaphoric in their anomalous juxtaposition of semantic referents.

Irony rarely conveys a metaphoric comprehension because irony almost automatically forces the hearer to switch one of the referents to the opposite. When we say to a sullen and sour breakfast companion, "You certainly are brimming with cheer this morning," the hearer understands "cheer" to mean "unhappy" or "depressed." Saying the opposite does produce shock, tension, but one does not consider how this woeful person could be cheerful but rather sarcastically realizes that he or she presents anything but a cheerful countenance. If tension and the literal falseness of a statement were the measures of a metaphor, then many ironical constructions would qualify as metaphors. Irony forces us to see the incongruity of the juxtaposition of the referents and when we become aware of the irony, we do not transform one referent in terms of the other but replace it completely.

The *Oxford English Dictionary* defines catechresis as "improper use of words; application of a term to a thing which it does not properly denote; abuse or perversion of a trope or metaphor." The first part of this lexical entry fits metaphor well, but without the semantic anomaly there could be no metaphor. One might modify the definition to add the possibility of connotation as well as denotation to cover all cases of metaphor. The last part of the *OED* description fits the case of mixed metaphors. But can a metaphor be misused by mixing it? One can be beguiled by familiarity with a metaphor into thinking that it describes literally rather than metaphorically, forgetting that the metaphor is a metaphor. Since I allow metaphors with more than two referents, mixed metaphors are not only possible but legitimate. Mixed metaphors often betray confused and even inconsistent thinking. We laugh when a politician exclaims, "The President is plowing this ship of state through an interstate highway." Here we have Plato's metaphor identifying the state with a ship and then this "ship" plowing like an agricultural implement not through the water, but through concrete! Our unfavorable response arises from our discernment of confusion and not just from the existence of absurdity. Ordinary metaphors, especially highly suggestive ones, seem absurd on first contact. But nothing prevents us from constructing a highly speculative and hypothetical mixed metaphor that takes three or more referents and juxtaposes them in a series of insightful semantic anomalies. Max Black defined catachresis as "the putting of new senses into old words."[22] And sometimes metaphors can be extended into mixed metaphors that suggest further possibilities rather than confusing the ones already proposed by the metaphor.

Epiphor and Diaphor

Although distinguishing between metaphor and other figures of speech, such as simile, assists in clarifying the nature of metaphor, more important to that task is the recognition of two types of metaphor arising from its expressive and suggestive functions. Philip Wheelwright distinguished between metaphors whose primary function is to express (epiphors) and metaphors whose primary function is to suggest (diaphors).[23] He elaborates on epiphor as follows:

> Since the essential mark of epiphor—which is to say, metaphor in the conventional Aristotelian sense—is to express a similarity between something relatively well known or concretely known (the semantic vehicle) and something which, although of greater worth or importance, is less well known or more obscurely known (the semantic tenor), and since it must make its point by means of words, it follows that an epiphor presupposes a vehicular image or notion that can readily be understood when indicated by a suitable word or phrase. In short, there must be a literal base of operations to start from.[24]

Epiphors express insights of which we were previously unaware or only dimly aware until we confronted the metaphor. Their success depends on our ability to recognize features of similarity between the referents. When we first hear the metaphor "Billboards are warts on the landscape," we immediately comprehend the similarity between ugly billboards on the verdant landscape and ugly warts on the skin of smooth bodies.[25] So strongly does the similarity of ugliness between a "billboard" and a "wart" strike us, that the semantic anomaly between the semantic marker Inanimate of the former and the semantic marker Animate of the latter does not disturb us greatly. This metaphor can be classified as an epiphor; for it expresses so strong an analogy that the semantic anomaly between the referents recedes to the background. No pure epiphors exist, for if they did, then metaphors would possess no semantic anomaly and would be analogies rather than metaphors. In "Billboards are warts on the landscape," the clash between the animate and inanimate attributes of the referents provides the suggestive element—the diaphoric aspect of the metaphor. And because emotional tension usually appears as a symptom of semantic anomaly, epiphors are less tensive than diaphors.

So successful do some epiphors become that they lose their semantic anomaly and fade into ordinary language. Through usage, the similarities between the referents of an epiphor are so well accepted that one or both of the words has an additional meaning added to its lexical entry in the dictionary. "Wart" now means an ugly protuberance on either the skin of an animal or the skin of a plant. If the billboard metaphor becomes well enough accepted, then the dictionary entry for "wart" may include the more general meaning "an ugly protuberance on a surface."

Diaphors suggest new possible meanings by emphasizing the dissimilarities between the referents rather than expressing the similarities. No pure diaphors exist, for if there were no analogy between the parts of the metaphor, we could not understand it as intelligible. Wheelwright says of diaphor:

> The purest diaphor is doubtless to be found in nonimitative music and in the most abstract painting; for wherever any imitative or mimetic factor is present, whether an imitation of nature or of previous art or a mimesis of some recognizable idea, there is an element of epiphor. The late Gertrude Stein was evidently striving as far as she could toward the purely diaphoric in such word-combinations as "Toasted Susie is my ice-cream" and "A silence a whole waste of a desert spoon, a whole waste of any little shaving. . . ."[26]

Perhaps the purest musical diaphor would be John Cage's "Symphony of Four Minutes and Thirty-Three Seconds of Silence." But in Stein's "toasted Susie is my ice-cream," whether Susie is thought of as crisp, fresh, and firm, as suntanned or as warm, as associated with bread, breakfast, or a party, the sentence clearly says "I like Susie," and it would be impossible to read it as saying the opposite.[27] Moreover, it says "I really like Susie." The attractiveness of the sweetness and the appearance of ice cream and the color and the fragrance and the warmth of toast are not all that implied, of course, for the juxtaposition of "toasted" and "ice cream" suggests rich paradoxes—the diaphoric aspect of this metaphor. These paradoxes range all the way from Susie's being at once warm and dry and cold and moist, to her being likeable despite—or because of—the contradictions she embodies. She seems associated with the beginning of the day and the end of the party; she is relatively stable and relatively unstable; special and ordinary; firm and changeable; not vulnerable and vulnerable. She is warm and living, cold and dying. Susie is an experience of the movement which is time, of the moment. We would not have her any other way than the way she is; we could not. Even the purest diaphor must have some similarities, even paradoxes between the two referents. We can identify the juxtaposition of any two words on the basis of searching for common elements in those words and a context in which those common elements would be present.

All genuine metaphors possess epiphoric and diaphoric elements arising from the similarities and disparities among the attributes of the referents. Some metaphors tend to be more epiphoric in expression, whereas others tend to be more suggestive in proposing new possibilities, and still others may be equally epiphoric and diaphoric and hard to classify into one or the other category. One may question whether this typology is really necessary at all; in describing the nature of metaphor I have already noted the presence of analogy and semantic anomaly. Identifying these types of metaphor based on similarities and dissimilarities of the referents' features may be helpful in preventing the construction of a theory of metaphor that draws on only one type of metaphor. I have already pointed out that the controversion theory tends to measure the truth of metaphors in terms of their capacity for reduction to simile or their paraphrase into ordinary language. Epiphors fit this theory much more readily than do diaphors, for the latter cannot be reduced or paraphrased easily without destroying them. Northrop Frye tended to use the diaphor as the paradigm for all metaphors in his theory of literature as a self-contained world of meaning developed in *Anatomy of Criticism*.[28] Northrop Frye in his emphasis on the autonomy of literature and Monroe Beardsley in his advocacy of the controversion theory offer polar approaches to metaphor that can be avoided by cognizance of epiphors and diaphors. Frye tended to look at all metaphors as confined to literature; Beardsley wanted them to be available to the empirical world through paraphrase. Both seized on those aspects of metaphor that would support their literary theory, Frye emphasizing the suggestiveness of diaphor in a self-contained world of literature and Beardsley emphasizing the expressiveness of epiphor readily accessible to the empirical world. Every theory of metaphor must take into account both types of metaphor, epiphor and diaphor. To consider mainly one type in an explanatory account of metaphor chooses the facts to fit the theory.

Consideration of metaphors as epiphors and diaphors also suggests a dynamic theory of metaphor. Metaphors are formed as either diaphors or epiphors by juxtaposing the referents of ordinary language. This may be done by taking two words and putting them together or by taking an old, familiar word and infusing a new meaning into it by setting it into a different context or by coining a new word that combines normally unrelated referents. Changes in the meaning of the word "force" presented by Newtonian mechanics offered a metaphoric use by juxtaposing the referents of the meaning of force in Aristotelian and Cartesian mechanics with the new hypothesis proposed by Newton. Similarly, "force" to Einstein juxtaposes the meaning of "force" in relativity theory with the traditional meaning of "force" in Newtonian mechanics. The recent neologism of the "tachyon," a particle that travels faster than the speed of light, illustrates the invention of a diaphor in which the two anomalous referents are the contemporary-physics notion of a "particle," which cannot travel faster than light, and the "particle" that can violate Einstein's basic and fundamental assumption of the constancy of light's velocity.

Let us trace the possible history of a diaphor. After initial formation, a diaphor may spend the rest of its life as a diaphor, the "tachyon" remains a diaphor since no experimental evidence has been found to confirm it. But if some slight evidence was found that hinted at the actual and not just the hypothetical existence of tachyons, the diaphor could become an epiphor—more expressive of analogy than it is suggestive of only possibility.

An epiphor can remain an epiphor, expressive of analogies of the features of two, normally unrelated referents. This often takes place in literature: poetic epiphors remain metaphors since they are only used when reading poetry. Other epiphors, however, become so widely used that the semantic anomaly among the referents becomes eliminated when the meaning of the attributes changes their meaning. Dictionaries add lexical meanings to words as lexicographers observe the widespread changes in usage in ordinary language.

In the process that I have been describing, a diaphor can become an epiphor and an epiphor ordinary language. Not every metaphor traverses this path. Some metaphors remain diaphors, some diaphors become epiphors and never are reduced to ordinary language, and some epiphors begin linguistic life as epiphors never to become ordinary language. This process of metaphor takes place through time and exists as a possible path rather than as a necessary route that all metaphors must follow.

Metaphor as a Process

Since I have introduced the notion of metaphor as a process, I should elaborate on that idea, as I speak of metaphor throughout this book as a process in a variety of interrelated ways. Throughout most of this chapter I have been describing metaphor at the level of surface language, the language that we speak. In discussing the tension theory, the controversion theory, and the deviance theory, I characterized metaphor at deeper levels, the semantic and cognitive levels. My description of metaphor as the juxtaposition of referents that produces semantic conceptual anomaly moved the operation of metaphor into semantic theory and into cognition. This move was made with promissory notes to the reader to be cashed in later chapters. My return, however, to considerations of simile, metonymy, synecdoche, and catachresis brought us back largely to considerations of surface language. Epiphor and diaphor measure the likeness and dissimilarity of attributes of the referents and require cognitive intuitions to make these judgments, but the description of epiphor and diaphor is neither a linguistic explanation nor the explanation of metaphor as a knowledge process.

Throughout this book I speak of metaphor as a process that exists at three interrelated levels: (1) metaphor as a language process—the possible movement from ordinary language to diaphor to epiphor and back to ordinary language, (2) metaphor as a semantic and syntactic process—the explanation of metaphor in terms of linguistic theory, and (3) metaphor as a cognitive process set in the context of a larger evolutionary knowledge process—metaphor explained not only as a semantic process but as an underlying cognitive process without which new knowledge might not be possible. One might be tempted to conceive of these three levels as blocks set on one another but such an image would be misleading since these three processes depend on one another and interpenetrate one another. In describing metaphor as a semantic process, one must resort to comprehension of the surface language context in which the metaphor occurs; as a cognitive process, the perceptual environmental context in which knowledge occurs must be considered. Why not talk about one metaphoric process with three aspects: surface language, semantics, and cognition? Metaphor *is* a single process with these three aspects but to explain metaphor in terms of all three aspects at once confuses the explanation. My strategy is to separate the aspects into three processes, always remembering that when a poet or a scientist coins a new metaphor, a single process takes place with three aspects. The artificial separation into three processes at three levels, with cognition the deepest, acknowledges that value of deep-structure abstract explanations. Chomsky's construction of abstract deep structures for language has proven fruitful not only for linguistics but for cognition as well. Descriptions of metaphor that remain at the first level, that of treating metaphor as a surface language phenomenon, lack explanatory power and leave us unsatisified. These theories tell us how to form metaphors and how to use them rather than explain the fundamental nature of a metaphor as part of human cognition.

Grammatical Forms of Metaphor

Christine Brooke-Rose produced an excellent study of metaphor in terms of traditional surface language grammar.[29] Analyzing the texts of fifteen poets, she classified the metaphoric inventions of these writers into verb metaphor and five types of noun metaphor. Before investigating grammatical relations, she noted that two different methods were previously used to study metaphor:

> . . . the philosophical approach, which concerns itself with idea— content, and the linguistic approach (or rather, abortive attempts at a linguistic approach) which concerns itself, as one might suppose, with language. Most exponents of the latter, however, fall back continually on the former.

There are four main types of analysis by idea-content:

(1) *The species/genus classification* (Aristotle)

(2) *The animate/inanimate classification* (Aristotle's successors)

(3) *The classification by domain of thought* (implicit in Cicero and some Renaissance rhetoricians, taken up by 19th and 20th century critics for detailed linguistic and literary analysis)

(4) *The Analysis by dominant trait* (Modern German School).[30]

Brooke-Rose divided the study of metaphor into two levels but found the deeper mental level overemphasized, leading to an ignorance of the style of metaphor. She tended to assume no relationship between the two levels; my construction of three interrelated levels assumes that semantics mediates between surface language and cognitive processes.

The most constructive of the four main classifications by mental process is, from my point of view, that which concentrates on the animate/inanimate relationship, though it is barely developed. The verb metaphor animates, by transferring to an object an action not normally associated with it; and many nonmetaphors, as I hope to show, have a strong element of activity and "bring the thing before the eyes in action," as Aristotle would say.

The other three approaches all seem to me to over-emphasize the mental process through which one thing is called another, the "why" of metaphor, not the "how," the idea and not the ways in which it can be expressed with words or the different effects of these different ways. And since only a few of these different means of expression have been indiscriminately selected to exemplify the transfer of ideas, logician-critics have frequently got into difficulties, language being less complex than thought. These approaches have all contributed a great deal to the criticism of thought and ideas, and if the classifiers are seldom good critics, at least they have provided the material for the more imaginative minds to work on (for instance Cleanth Brooks makes brilliant use of Caroline Spurgeon's discoveries). As such, however, they contribute little to the study of style. They offer no criteria, except by encroaching on the poet's prerogative, his imagination.

Whatever the mental process involved in calling one thing by another name, the poet must use nouns, verbs, adverbs, adjectives and prepositions.[31]

In separating thought processes from style, Brooke-Rose forgot that one must have some means by which to recognize a metaphor as a metaphor. She might argue that her typology offers paradigms by which one can compare combinations of referents to see if they are in fact metaphors, but the very construction of those paradigms requires some initial intuition that they are metaphors. And the justification of these intuitions (which Brooke-Rose assumes and does not present) would require at least some semantic analysis. It would seem impossible to decide when a word juxtaposed with another word is being used in an unusual fashion unless one knew not only the standard meanings of the two referents but also that some of the attributes of the two referents were similar and others dissimilar. It takes an act of cognition to make this discernment of likeness and difference.

In Brooke-Rose's defense, let us remember that she wanted to correct an oversight, the inattention to style and grammar in metaphor, and that she has produced the best study of metaphoric style thus far. I chide her only for bypassing the need to recognize the cognitive function in any theory of metaphor, even a theory that proposes to describe "how" rather than "why" metaphors are formed.

Brooke-Rose classifies five types of noun metaphor:

(1) *Simple Replacement*: the proper term is replaced altogether by the metaphor, without being mentioned at all.

(2) *The Pointing Formulae*: the proper term A is mentioned, then replaced by the metaphor B with some demonstrative expression pointing back to the proper term (A . . . that B).

(3) *The Copula*: a direct statement that A is B, which is authoritative in tone and even didactic.

(4) *The link with "To Make"*: a direct statement involving a third part: C makes A into B.

(5) *The Genitive* (in the very wide sense of provenance from): this is the most complex type of all, for the noun metaphor is linked sometimes to its proper term, and sometimes to a third term which gives the provenance of the metaphoric term: B *is part of*, or *derives from*, or *belongs to* or *is attributed to* or *is found in* C, from which relationship we can guess A, the proper term (e.g., the *Hostel* of my heart = body).[32]

This classification with its numerous supporting examples serves well to remind the student of metaphor that relatively few poetic metaphors occur in the form "*A is B*" (Brooke-Rose's copula metaphor). She rightly criticized other studies of metaphor for ignoring this complexity; most start with simple banal metaphors of the form "*A is B.*" Brooke-Rose rediscovered the complexity of metaphor. As supporting examples for the "make-link" metaphor, she cited the following passage from John Donne's "Twicknam Garden":[33]

> Love, let mee
> Some senseless peece of this place bee;
> Make me a *mandrake*, so I may groane here,
> Or a stone *fountaine* weeping out my yeare.

(Italics added by Brooke-Rose). As a link between *A* and *B*, the verb *to make* can convey paradox as well as ambiguity bordering on the literal. Whatever the form of linkage, the copula, the verb "make," or the genitive, Brooke-Rose interpreted the grammatical metaphorical process as one that juxtaposes nouns. She did not explain a process of semantic change of meaning, but did indicate the richness of meaning possible through the complexity of various grammatical forms. Even when she considered the verb metaphor, she interpreted it as performing the same function as the noun metaphor, only the verb metaphor does it implicitly.[34] Verb metaphors implicitly change one noun into another, often by implication. "The verb metaphor, then, changes a noun implicitly instead of explicitly, and this means that the change can be much less decisive: the noun can become one of many things."[35] Brooke-Rose observed the preponderance of intransitive verb metaphors used in English and how often they animate personifications, but even this evidence did not dissuade her from viewing the metaphoric process as the juxtaposition of nouns with the transformation of one noun into another. In metaphors joined by the copula, referents are juxtaposed, and the reader must search out just how *A* is like *B* and how *A* is unlike *B*. In a diaphor the reader considers how *A* might be like *B*. But in a verb metaphor the reader may be told how *A* is like *B*; the verb conveys the process of semantic transference. When we are told "the ship ploughs the waves," the likeness of a ship to a plough seems much more *explicit* than in the metaphor "a ship is a plough." It does not seem clear that the verb metaphor is weaker than or subservient to the noun metaphor.

Conveyance Metaphors and Basic Metaphors

The ways in which metaphors are used also seems to be a description that occurs at the first level of explanation—metaphors as parts of surface language. Poets consciously or unconsciously grasping a feature of life or the world seek to convey their insights in the most meaningful, vibrant, and fresh manner. They select words and juxtapose them to form metaphors that both express their intuition and suggest new possible meanings. Wallace Stevens identifies "death" as the "mother of beauty" in his poem "Sunday Morning."[35] Another example is the scientist grappling with a hypothetical possibility for a new explanation. He does not know quite how to formulate his glimmer of what physical reality might be, and so he takes some old concepts and infuses them with new meaning by juxtaposing them with other less familiar terms or with familiar but not ordinarily associated terms, by inventing a neologism, or by changing the theory in which the terms normally find their contextual meaning. To explain the regulation of genes, the "operon" was invented, a diaphoric metaphor that suggests a possible explanation.

The detailed mechanisms that regulate the activity of genes are far from fully understood. For bacteria the generally accepted model of gene regulation is the "operon" proposed by Jacob and Monod (1961). An operon consists of an operator and several structural genes, all adjacent or in close proximity to each other. The operator, interacting with the cell environment through the products of regulatory genes, determines when the structural genes of the operon will be transcribed.[36]

Are there such *real* entities as "operons"? Perhaps, but the term was invented as a hypothetical explanation of how genes operate. Experimental confirmation of the existence of "operons" may transform the "operon" from a diaphor to an epiphor and perhaps even to ordinary language.

A third example is a politician who wants to create a new image and so invents a metaphor like "the war on poverty," which at first seems exciting and idealistic. The weapons in this war become federally funded social programs and as the "war" finds practical elaboration and embodiment, the metaphor fades.

All these uses of metaphor and a host of others occur regularly in our language; metaphor is employed as a linguistic device to *convey* semantic changes of conceptualization for a variety of purposes. As I noted in chapter 1, this common and ordinary use of metaphor can be given the name of *conveyance* metaphor. I also noted in dealing with the computational metaphor that a second use of metaphor exists— the postulation of *basic* metaphors serving as fundamental presuppositions underlying a theory or even an entire discipline. Stephen Pepper called these metaphors root metaphors. I changed the name, however, to basic metaphors to avoid the limited association with metaphysical theories that Pepper described.[37] A basic metaphor can serve as the hypothetical presupposition for a single theory, a discipline, or a theology, and not just as the basis of a metaphysical theory. Since my basic metaphor is an extension of Pepper's notion, let me return to his definition of the root metaphor and extend it from there. Pepper describes the root metaphor method as follows:

A man desiring to understand the world looks about for a clue to its comprehension. He pitches upon some area of commonsense fact and tries [to see] if he cannot understand other areas in terms of this one. This original area becomes then his basic analogy or root metaphor. He describes as best he can the characteristics of this area, or if you will, discriminates its structure. A list of its structural characteristics becomes his basic concepts of explanation and description. We call them a set of categories. In terms of these categories he proceeds to study all other areas of fact whether uncriticized or previously criticized. He undertakes to interpret all facts in terms of these categories. As a result of the impact of these facts upon his categories, he may qualify and readjust the categories, so that a set of categories commonly changes and develops.[38]

The inventor of a basic metaphor wants to comprehend an entire area of human experience or of the physical world; the scientist may adopt consciously or unconsciously the basic metaphor, "The world is mathematical," as a hypothetical assumption that motivates her theory construction. She knows that the world is not literally mathematical, for if it was, science would collapse into mathematics and scientists would have no need for experiments. But she accepts the basic metaphor as a diaphor that suggests a particular way of looking at the world; she strives to confirm the intuition by creating mathematical theories that do find empirical confirmation. And in the case of particle physics, the mathematical postulation of particles such as the positron and the neutrino (subsequently confirmed experimentally) led some to assert the dictum, "What mathematics demands, nature provides." But even in particle physics, so many experimental anomalies remain that the basic metaphor, "The world is mathematical," remains a diaphor.

Theologians also wittingly or unwittingly postulate basic metaphors about humanity and the world. The religious belief that God acts in history forms the basic metaphor, "The world is the arena of God's actions." This also serves as a diaphor since direct empirical confirmation of an invisible God performing overt acts in this world seems difficult if not impossible. As a basic metaphor, however, God's acting in history forms the basis for the construction of a series of theological categories that find indirect confirmation and interpretation in the lives of the faithful.

The difference between conveyance and basic metaphors follows from their scope and function. Conveyance metaphors usually propose a metaphoric insight limited in scope, whereas basic metaphors underlie an entire theory or discipline devoted to description of widespread phenomena. The computational metaphor seeks to serve as the basis for an explanation of all human thinking. Individual conveyance metaphors can be used as basic metaphors. The many metaphors employed to personify organisms and objects in the world have also been used as a single basic metaphor: "The world is a human being," forming the basis of primitive theories like animism. Pepper rejects animism as imprecise and rejects mysticism—"The world is a spirit" or "The world is divine"—as abstract. He allows only the world hypotheses of formism, mechanism, contextualism, and organicism, founded on the root metaphors of similarity, a machine, a historical event perceived from the present, and a process, respectively. These hypotheses are precise enough, not too eclectic to be ruled out as overly general; they are also independent and autonomous. I resist the temptation to deal with the requirements of each of these hypotheses; suffice it to expand the notion of a "root metaphor" beyond Pepper's four hypotheses and rename the expanded concept a basic metaphor, allowing it to range over all kinds of imprecise and eclectic theories.

The basic metaphoric method seems so natural and fundamental to human beings in their quest for knowledge that to deny it would make the acquisition of new knowledge almost impossible. Pepper's motive in developing the idea of four world hypotheses constructed on the basis of root metaphors was to offer a knowledge process, structural corroboration, that produced cognitive insights called "danda" that could parallel and incorporate the "data" that strict empiricists, especially the positivists, thought of as the basis of knowledge. Pepper argued that a strictly empirical position degenerates into either an impossible skepticism or a heinous dogmatism, hence the need for a nondogmatic and nonskeptical alternative form of epistemology, that of corroboration within a structural framework, a series of categories constructed in accord with an underlying root metaphor. In making this argument, Pepper observed the same problem of self-reference that I found with respect to the computational metaphor in chapter 1. The root metaphor theory proposes a theory of truth based on the success or failure of root metaphors. What guarantee do we have that the root metaphor theory itself is true and/or should be accepted?

> Strangely enough, if this root metaphor theory is correct, its truth could only be established by the adequacy of the theories which constitute its evidence. For this theory is itself a structural hypothesis—at least, it would be such in its ultimate corrobora- tion—and, as we have seen, a structural hypothesis only attains full confirmation in a world theory. Hence, if this theory is true, an adequate world theory will support it. This theory would then, so to speak, become absorbed in its own evidence, that is, become an item in the very theory which it is a theory about.[39]

I noted the same phenomenon in the computational metaphor; if the computational metaphor serves as a presupposition for a theory of mind, then the evidence for accepting the computational metaphor will be part of the theory in which it is embedded. Why? Because the theory that I present to account for mental activity is a product of mental activity—that of metaphoric thinking. If we were faced with justifying a theory about a physical phenomenon, we would not be faced with the same problem of self-reference, since the theory would refer to a series of entities and actions other than itself. But a theory about theory construction or a theory of metaphor that invokes metaphor to support it or a theory of mind that presupposes mental entities like metaphors all face the potential circularities and paradoxes of self-reference.

No longer do we speak at level 1 of explanation—surface language; to deal with basic metaphors we have plunged to level 3—the cognitive level—almost without regard to level 2, that of semantic theory. Dealing with this problem of self-reference requires consideration of semantic theory as it relates both to surface language and cognition. The problem of an explanation of a theory of metaphor can be viewed as a mirror reflected by another mirror; an entity—semantic theory—must be interposed between the two mirrors to break the endless series of reflections.

Metaphor and Creative Possibility

Metaphors perform the cognitive function of creating new meanings through the juxtaposition of referents in language. Without them, humanity would find it difficult to extend its knowledge into the unknown, and language would be largely static. The diaphor offers the possibility of taking a familiar referent and transforming it by juxtaposing it with a referent or referents not normally associated with the familiar referent. The combination of referents that produces semantic anomaly forces the hearer or reader of a metaphor to locate the similarities among the attributes of the referents as well as the dissimilarities. Not only does the recognition of similarities not seen before produce new insights or new meanings, but especially the identification of dissimilarities allows for the possibility of transformation of these dissimilarities into previously unthought of similarities, thereby ensuring the creation of a new meaning. This process of transforming the attributes of referents fuels semantic change. Comprehension of the meaningfulness of semantic anomalies may produce widespread usage of a metaphor as it traverses the route (or partial route) from diaphor to epiphor to ordinary language. When a metaphor reaches this final position as a dead metaphor in ordinary language, commemoration of the return of the metaphor to ordinary language takes place as dictionaries add new lexical meanings to traditional words. Take the word "birth," which in the *Oxford English Dictionary* finds its first lexical entries for the biological event of bringing life into the world with the first references in the 1300s. By the sixteenth century, however, "birth" had come to have a figurative sense as in the "birth of an idea" or the "birth of the Roman Empire." In contemporary dictionaries, "birth" in the sense of the origin of an idea or event no longer is considered a figurative use of language. The meaning of "birth" has been metaphorically extended (through generalization) from biological origins to nonbiological origins.

The conceptual semantic anomaly of metaphors frightened past philosophers because they demanded precision in language and a decision procedure for ascertaining the truth or falsity of statements. Many metaphors defy determination into strictly true or false statements; with respect to the similarities of the attributes of the referents, a metaphor may be partially true and, with respect to the differences of the attributes of the referents, a metaphor may be partially false. And as a metaphor, especially a diaphor, becomes more widely confirmed in its suggested meaning and, perhaps, becomes an epiphor, the truth value of the metaphor may increase. If a metaphor dies and enters the promised land of ordinary language, then it becomes a literal statement, and it also becomes a true statement.

Suppose, however, that those philosophers and linguists who viewed metaphors as false and ungrammatical statements could have cleansed our language by eliminating these deviant uses of language. Without metaphor, what kind of conceptual world would we face? I have just noted that without metaphor, the formation of hypotheses would be drastically limited and that semantic change might not occur. One could stipulate new meanings, but the manner in which one did so probably would involve a conceptual process identical with the metaphorical process. If one wants to describe a new insight, how can one do so except in terms of what is already familiar, extending the meaning of the known to the unknown. Suppose that the philosopher cares not a whit for new meanings but asserts his function as describing accurately *what is* rather than *what might be*. Could the philosopher do this without metaphor? Perhaps, yet some of the most fruitful and insightful descriptions of reality depend on abstractions that are only indirectly confirmed through empirical tests. The philosopher could resort to cataloging the obviously perceived items of the universe. When he got to entities such as "minds" and "persons" he might be hard pressed to describe these in a manner acceptable to all without some speculative hypotheses that could be considered before agreement was given. Even if the philosopher could abandon metaphor and produce a simple, literal description of *what is* and still have it recognized as legitimate philosophy, the scientist could hardly construct tentative, hypothetical theories about the physical nature of what is without some resort to metaphor, the intentional conceptual formation of semantic anomalies to speculate about the unknown in terms of the known. The scientist's very goal of producing an explanatory account of the nature of the physical world that penetrates deeper in conceptual understanding than a mere catalog of the objects and events that men and women perceive presumes some assumption, a basic metaphor, specifying the form that such an explanation takes—the world is a mechanism or the world is an organism or the world is mathematical. Philosophers tend to do the same when they assume that language mirrors the world or that the world is conceptual or that the world is composed of atoms of sense data or objects instantiated in logic.

My argument that metaphor can be recognized as metaphor on the basis of the conceptual semantic anomaly produced by the juxtaposition of referents awaits cashing the promissory notes of justificatory accounts of semantics and of metaphoric knowledge processes. But I have presumed an intuitive difference between metaphors and ordinary language. And not all theorists of metaphor make that assumption, for others presume that all language is metaphorical. In this chapter I have scrutinized those who assume a difference between ordinary language and metaphor and constructed criteria for the determination of that difference. I rejected the tension theory, the controversion theory, and the deviance theory and proposed the theory of semantic conceptual anomaly. Before proceeding to redeem the promissory notes, I must consider the possibility that all language is metaphoric, and so I devote the next chapter to a denial of that contention. Along the way I hope also to refine the notions of "the literal" and of "ordinary language."

3
The Literal and the Metaphorical

The Problem of Distinguishing between the Literal and the Metaphorical

If language is described as metaphorical, does such a classification rest on the presumption of the existence of literal language against which the metaphor finds contrast? Can one know a metaphor to be a "metaphor" without also knowing that *it is not literal*? Although I have assumed a recognizable difference between "literal" and "metaphorical" in the preceding two chapters, there are those who deny such a distinction by claiming that all language is metaphorical. This claim can be based on the belief either that a basic metaphor, such as "Language mirrors the world," underlies all language activity or that each and every sentence expresses metaphorical thinking—comprehending one thing in terms of another. Defenders of the first claim understand everyday language as a theory about the world, and because all theories rest on basic metaphors, ordinary language necessarily presumes a basic metaphor, usually some form of the metaphor that "the world (including the physical world) is composed of language." Proponents of the second claim base their assertion on the observation that ordinary language is filled with dead metaphors. When new metaphors fade and die, they are still metaphors, and when we forget the metaphorical nature of ordinary language, we beguile ourselves into thinking that the hidden figurative meaning of dead metaphors no longer exists. Those who claim that all language is metaphorical view the literal as disguised metaphors.

I examine the arguments that language is metaphorical, uncover their deficiencies, and then proceed to describe the contrast between the literal and the metaphorical. This last task, however, is not free from presumption of a basic metaphor nor from the use of certain conveyance metaphors. Here, I begin to fight the battle of circularity noted in chapter 1, namely, that any theory of metaphor probably employs a basic metaphor and perhaps even employs conveyance metaphors. This circularity becomes further entangled by the nature of the literal, for any explanatory account of the literal entails an investigation of perception and its relation to the conceptual aspects of language. Can there be "direct perception" or the "emergence" of concepts that are not themselves mediated by other concepts? Complete escape from this circularity is not possible, but mitigation by shifting to a naturalistic epistemology is possible. The claim that the distinction between metaphorical and literal is superior to a denial of the literal is justified by the avoidance of a problem like linguistic relativity and the greater facility thus offered for describing the inner cognitive and semantic operation of metaphors.

The Metaphorical Nature of Theories of Metaphor

In the *Myth of Metaphor*, Colin Turbayne presents the case for the first claim—that all language is metaphorical in the sense that ordinary language as a theory about the world presumes a basic metaphor.[1] Turbayne set out to examine the metaphorical assumptions of Newton and Descartes that the world is a machine. He found nothing wrong with their presumption of a basic metaphor on which to found their physical and metaphysical theories; when they assumed their theories to be "literal," however, they created myths by being victimized by their own metaphor. Forgetting the metaphoric basis of a theory eliminates the tentative, hypothetical nature of the explanation. Familiarity rather than evidence transforms a metaphoric hypothesis into a literal account. Only by uncovering the basic metaphor can one show how this beguiling process has taken place; Turbayne advocates the exposure of the metaphor and then its replacement by another metaphor, a sure indication that the hidden metaphor is not literal. Turbayne attempts to show that Newton's basic metaphor of mechanism can be replaced by the basic metaphor "The world is language."

> I shall therefore treat the events in nature *as if* they compose a language in the belief that the world may be illustrated just as well, if not better, by making believe that it is a universal language instead of a giant clockwork; specifically, by using the metalanguage of ordinary language consisting of "signs," "things signified," "rules of grammer," and so on, instead of the vocabulary of the machine consisting of "parts," "effects," "causes," "laws of operation," and so on, to describe it.[2]

How can we discover that we have been victimized by a metaphor if we have become so familiar with the metaphor that we believe it to be literally true? Often this can be accomplished by extending the metaphor and by finding that such an extension produces absurd results. Or one can attempt to "undress" the metaphor by presenting the literal truth. Many have attempted to show the inadequacy of preceding theories or metaphysics by giving a contemporary account of the world and claiming that this present description really does literally describe how things are. The earlier theories can be seen from the present *true* explanatory account to be nothing more than myths. But such an effort to unclothe earlier theories by assuming the present account to be literal forgets that what we describe now as reality may later be similarly unclothed and exposed as resting on the metaphorical.

The attempt to re-allocate the facts by restoring them to where they "actually belong" is vain. It is like trying to observe the rule "Let us get rid of the metaphors and replace them by the literal truth." But can this be done? We might just as well seek to provide what the poet "actually says." I have said that one condition of the use of metaphor is awareness. More accurately speaking, this means *more* awareness, for we can never become wholly aware. We cannot say what reality is, only what it seems like to us, imprisoned in Plato's cave, because we cannot get outside to look. The consequence is that we never know exactly what the facts are. We are always victims of adding some interpretation. We cannot help but allocate, sort, or bundle the facts in some way or another.[3]

Turbayne argues that whatever account we give of the world, scientific, poetic, or metaphysical, it is inevitably metaphorical in the sense that we can never present a "literal" account of what is literal or real. To describe what is really real, we must inevitably resort to mediating devices, such as words or paint strokes, and when organized into a coherent account, these presume a basic metaphor as the organizing feature of their structure. If we purport to offer an account of the literal as contrasted with the metaphorical, we face the dilemma that either (1) we present a literal account of the literal that is likely to be shown to be a myth by later theories when our presumed basic metaphor is exposed and shown to generate absurdities through extension, or (2) we explicitly presume a basic metaphor as underlying our differentiation between literal and metaphorical, which seems to imply that one cannot present such a distinction without the circularity of assuming a knowledge of the nature of a basic metaphor. In discussing the nature of the literal later in this chapter I will show that a "literal" description of the literal is impossible because description of *what is* always involves cognitive mediation. To avoid the consequences of the first horn of the dilemma, I must choose the second horn. But what are the consequences of this admission? Have I admitted defeat in my attempt to distinguish between the literal and the metaphorical by accepting the conclusion that all theories, even those about metaphor, rest on basic metaphors?

Does this mean that all language is metaphorical and that since circularity is inevitable in theories about metaphor, I must lie back and enjoy it?

By accepting the second horn, I admit that all theories are metaphorical in that they assume basic metaphors as their foundations. And a theory about metaphor must presume a basic metaphor. Score one for circularity. But this admission does not mean that all language is metaphorical, only that a theory about metaphor is metaphorical. What remains true of a theory of language does not necessarily apply to each and every sentence or combination of words. That a theory of metaphor inevitably presumes a basic metaphor does not entail that every form of language must be metaphorical. When Turbayne labels dead metaphors as possessing literal meanings, he seems implicitly aware of the difference between the claim that all theories, even those about metaphor or language, assume basic metaphors and the claim that each and every utterance is metaphorical.

> In dead metaphors, such as "perceive," "comprehend," and "metaphor," however, the questions of homogeneity and likeness do not arise because, although the etymon overlaps its metaphorical meaning, these are overlooked by all but scholars. In dormant metaphors also, such as "high note," "to see meanings," and "lay bare feelings," both meanings have become literal.[4]

One can admit that a theory of metaphor is itself metaphorical without the further admission that one cannot distinguish between what is literal in ordinary language and what is metaphorical. Some of those who assert that it is not possible to distinguish between the literal and the metaphorical because all language is metaphorical wrongly draw this conclusion from the discovery that theories of metaphor presume basic metaphors.

How can this circularity be treated so that it is similar to that of attempting a definition of meaning? Any definition of meaning inevitably presumes a knowledge of what the definition means. Must I resort to a Russellian theory of types or to the invocation of a metatheory to prevent my theory of metaphor from referring to itself? A basic metaphor can be a primitive term or a term like an axiom, accepted intuitively, assumed to provide the basis for a theory of metaphor, existing in the metalanguage, and not referring to itself. Such a move might be successful in preventing paradox and avoiding circularity, but it would also imply that there is at least one kind of metaphor, the basic metaphor, that relies on intuition and that does not require an explanatory account. Our cognitive capacities would have to include a primitive metaphorical intuition. If we possess such a primitive capacity, why not stretch this intuitive capacity to all forms of metaphor and eliminate the need for any explanatory account at all. Rather than following this line of argument, I prefer to accept the circularity. My acceptance rests on the belief that I am constructing a naturalistic cognitive account of metaphor instead of an axiomatic, logical, epistomological one. To construct a theory of metaphor, one must presume some knowledge of metaphor and a host of other assumptions (already learned) about language, culture, and the physical world. In dealing with natural kinds, Quine found himself in a similar circularity, and his answer with respect to induction could be mine with respect to metaphor.

At this point let me say that I shall not be impressed by protests that I am using inductive generalizations, Darwin's and others, to justify induction, and thus reasoning in a circle. The reason I shall not be impressed by this is that my position is a naturalistic one; I see philosophy not as an a priori propaedeutic or groundwork for science, but as continuous with science. I see philosophy and science as in the same boat—a boat which, to revert to Neurath's figure as I so often do, we can rebuild only at sea while staying afloat in it. There is no external vantage point, no first philosophy.[5]

One cannot talk about language de novo without some knowledge of language; similarly, one cannot talk about metaphor without certain presumptions about metaphor. Yet I resist going so far in this direction as to posit a full metaphoric intuition that preempts the need for a theory of metaphor. Such an explanatory account, especially one that distinguishes between the literal and the metaphorical, will enable us to understand better how metaphors are formed semantically, how they convey meaning, and how they convey truth. Now let us turn to that other assertion—that all language is metaphorical.

Rejection of Claims that All Language Is Metaphorical

George Lakoff and Mark Johnson recently claimed in *Metaphors We Live By* and in "Conceptual metaphor in everyday language" that "metaphors partially structure our everyday concepts and that this structure is reflected in our literal language."[6] Much of the language that many of us call "literal" they argue is really "metaphorical." They further contend that the metaphorical nature of natural language prevents the development of an explanatory account of meaning based solely on literal language. Nor can one present, they assert, an account of metaphor that derives its meaning from functions performed on literal discourse.

They devote much of their analysis to a demonstration of the systematic conceptual structures in which what they call literal or conventional metaphors of ordinary language exist. Metaphors such as "Argument is war," "Time flies," and "Theories are buildings" are exemplified, carefully examined, and shown to presuppose a conceptual structure that is partially expressed in natural language. These metaphors are "alive" because they find daily use. In contrast, isolated metaphors, such as "The *foot* of the mountain," "a *head* of cabbage," and "the *leg* of a table," which are not parts of an overall conceptual scheme, are described as dead metaphors.[7] Figurative or nonliteral metaphors arise through the extension of used parts of literal metaphors, the use of unused parts of literal metaphors, or the creation of a novel or new metaphor. Lakoff and Johnson present the metaphor "These facts are the bricks and mortar of my theory" as an example of the figurative type. This is an extension of the metaphor "Theories are buildings." "His theory has thousands of little rooms and long, winding corridors" is presented as an instance of the unused part of a metaphor, whereas "Classical theories are patriarchs who father many children, most of whom fight incessantly" offers an instance of a novel metaphor. Throughout this discussion of forming figurative or imaginative metaphors from conventional or literal metaphors, Lakoff and Johnson assume that the concept "building" includes only the outer shell and foundation as the proper parts of the metaphor "Theories are buildings."

> The parts of the concept BUILDING that are used to structure the concept THEORY are the foundation and the outer shell. The roof, internal rooms, staircases, and hallways are parts of a building not used as part of the concept THEORY. Thus the metaphor THEORIES ARE BUILDINGS has a "used" part (foundation and outer shell) and an "unused" part (rooms, staircases, etc.). Expressions such as *construct* and *foundation* are instances of the used part of such a metaphorical concept and are part of our ordinary literal language about theories.[8]

Presumably, if these figurative metaphors become widely used and common, they lose their tension and become conventional metaphors. Most theories of metaphor describe this process as one of dying or fading, where the metaphor becomes part of ordinary, literal language. Lakoff and Johnson, however, are adamant that even if figurative metaphors become conventional or literal metaphors, they retain their metaphorical status.

We note in passing that all of the linguistic expressions we have given to characterize general metaphorical concepts are figurative.

Examples are TIME IS MONEY, TIME IS A MOVING OBJECT, CONTROL IS UP, IDEAS ARE FOOD, THEORIES ARE BUILDINGS, etc. None of these is literal. This is a consequence of the fact that only *part* of them is used to structure our normal concepts. Since they necessarily contain parts that are not used in our normal concepts, they go beyond the realm of the literal.[9]

By considering hundreds of dead metaphors, Lakoff and Johnson succeeded in showing that natural language presumes and expresses many hidden conceptual meanings that arise from the use of these metaphors. But they transformed these *dead* metaphors into *live* metaphors by redefining the notion of a dead metaphor. For Lakoff and Johnson, dead metaphors are those isolated metaphors such as the "leg of a table"; live metaphors are alive because they are used in ordinary language as parts of systematic metaphoric expression. Live metaphors are not only systematic; they are also extendable to new cases and appropriate for use in reason and use in behavior.

It is important to distinguish these isolated and unsystematic cases from the systematic metaphorical expressions we have been discussing. Expressions like wasting time, attacking positions, going our separate ways, etc., are reflections of systematic metaphorical concepts that structure our actions and thoughts. They are "alive" in the most fundamental sense: they are metaphors we live by. The fact that they are conventionally fixed within the lexicon of English makes them no less alive.[10]

This redefinition of life and death for metaphors seems to have the consequence of allowing Lakoff and Johnson no method of distinguishing between metaphoric and nonmetaphoric utterances. Instead, they distinguish between *literal* metaphors and *figurative* metaphors. Consider their description of metaphor: "The essence of metaphor is understanding and experiencing one kind of thing or experience in terms of another."[11] This description could fit any semantical meaning, the association of one word with another or the association of a word with an experience. One might be tempted to argue that all natural language is metaphorical by this definition and that the business of the analyst of language is to distinguish one kind of metaphor from another; one should develop criteria to understand the difference between literal metaphors and figurative metaphors. For example, "war" in *Webster's Third New International Dictionary* (1971) includes a lexical entry for "mental hostility" absent in Samuel Johnson's *A Dictionary of the English Language* (1755). At some time between the dates of these two dictionaries, the metaphor "Argument is war" became familiar enough to be entered into standard dictionaries as a lexical entry for "war."[12] Lakoff and Johnson would interpret this move as one from figurative metaphor to literal metaphor rather than from metaphor to ordinary language (as a dead metaphor).

Lakoff and Johnson employ a series of indirect arguments to support their interpretation of metaphor as pervading ordinary language. They attempt to demonstrate that alternative theories of metaphor that presume a literal language different from metaphors fail by assuming an improper objectivist account of the physical world and by constructing faulty abstract explanations based on an impossibly rigid set theory. Like Turbayne, Lakoff and Johnson believe that an objective account of the world remains impossible because such a theory is always metaphorical in the sense of presuming a basic metaphor. Objectivists who claim that ordinary language is literal necessarily adopt (often unconsciously) the conduit metaphor, which assumes that knowledge is objectlike and can fill the containers of our minds. Committed to this myth of objectivism, most theorists of metaphor ignore the metaphorical nature of ordinary language and the metaphorical nature of the theory that they invoke to explain metaphor. Refusing to bolt to subjectivism, Lakoff and Johnson attempt to steer a middle course by distinguishing between metaphorical and nonmetaphorical concepts rather than between literal and nonliteral language. They embed nonmetaphorical concepts in direct experience, which emerges through interaction of the agent with his or her environment. They do not seem to consider the possibility of admitting that all theories rest on metaphoric foundations, as Turbayne and I have suggested, and still maintain a difference between literal language and nonliteral language on the basis of semantic anomaly.

I will attempt to counter Lakoff and Johnson's arguments against employing a set-theoretical theory of semantic change as a basis for explaining metaphor, and then I will examine their notions of direct "emergence." This section of my argument merely clears the way for an account of the literal that follows; it does not serve as a substitute for that account so I ask the reader to be patient for just a few more pages before I turn to that task essential in my explanation.

Lakoff and Johnson claim that an abstraction theory fails as an explanatory account of metaphor because it seeks a single abstract concept general enough to fit the various meanings possible from a metaphor. They believe that no one concept can be stretched to include within it the different meanings of "war" found in the metaphors "Love is war," "Rational discourse is war," "Stopping inflation is war," and "Cancer is war."[13] They also believe that an abstraction view would prohibit the acknowledgment of the systematicity and partial metaphoric structuring found in ordinary language.

Finally, the abstraction hypothesis assumes, in the case of LOVE IS A JOURNEY, for example, that there is a set of abstract concepts, neutral with respect to love and journeys, that can "fit" or "apply to" both of them. But in order for such abstract concepts to "fit" or "apply to" love, the concept LOVE must be independently structured so that there can be such a "fit." As we will show, LOVE is not a concept that has clearly delineated structure; whatever structure it has it gets only via metaphors. But the abstraction view, which has no metaphors to do the structuring, must assume that a structure as clearly delineated as the relevant aspects of journeys exists independently for the concept LOVE. It's hard to imagine how.[14]

Lakoff and Johnson's attack on the abstraction hypothesis, however, fails to take into account the abstractionist's attempt to account for semantic change in metaphors. They have misrepresented the abstractionist position by treating it *as if* it proposed static general concepts that, in Lakoff and Johnson's view, cannot be legitimately stretched semantically to fit the various different metaphors involving the same concept. In fact, abstractionists devote most of their efforts to presenting complicated theoretical explanations of how semantic change necessary for metaphor is possible. In "Conceptual metaphor in everyday language," Lakoff and Johnson cite L. Jonathan Cohen and Avishai Margalit's "The role of inductive reasoning in the interpretation of metaphor" as an example of a wrongheaded abstraction theory. But these authors explicitly recognize that abstract concepts underlying metaphor, and even underlying ordinary language, cannot remain invariant.

Specifically from the requirement that an adequate linguistic theory should explicate the nature of the bond that links metaphorical to literal meaning within the structure of a natural language, it follows that such a theory *cannot assume that the meanings of lexical items are invariant* under the process of semantic composition.[15] (Italics added)

Abstract semanticists rarely if ever seek invariant general terms to "fit" or "apply to" various meanings for the same word. Samuel Levin, on whose work I draw in chapter 4, developed construal rules of adjunction and displacement of semantic markers to demonstrate the possibility of semantic change of meaning for metaphors within a theory of abstraction.[16]

Lakoff and Johnson also attack homonymy as an explanation of the relationship of the referents of metaphors. Under what they call the strong homonymy view the word attack in "They *attacked* the fort" and "They *attacked* my argument" would stand for two entirely different and unrelated concepts.[17] If the referents represent two entirely different concepts, then it is impossible to demonstrate a relationship between the two parts of the metaphor, and hence it is probably unintelligible. Admitting that no theorists hold this strong view, they next consider the weak homonymy view, which allows two referents with the same sound to be related. The word "attacked" in the above two examples can sound the same, have two different meanings, and yet have a similarity in meaning. Lakoff and Johnson find this view inadequate because no theory of similarity is sufficiently comprehensive to account for the numerous and strange forms of likeness that one encounters in metaphors.

> However, to our knowledge, no one has ever begun to provide a detailed account of a theory of similarity that could deal with the wide range of examples we have discussed. Although virtually all homonymy theorists espouse the weak version, in practice there seem to be only strong homonymy theories, since no one has attempted to provide the detailed account of similarity necessary to maintain the weak version of the theory. And there is a good reason why no attempt has been made to give such a detailed account of the kinds of examples we have been discussing. The reason is that such an account would require one to address the issue of how we comprehend and understand areas of experience that are not well-defined in their own terms and must be grasped in terms of other areas of experience. In general, philosophers and linguists have not been concerned with such questions.[18]

The absence of an explanatory theory, however, does not warrant rejection of a phenomenon. Just because no one has presented a full account of the so-called weak homonymy theory does not mean that it is wrong. Lakoff and Johnson argue that their theory of metaphor is a better theory not only because they have developed it more fully but also because their theory does not presume what they call the myth of objectivism. Both the abstraction theory and the weak homonymy view assume objectivism, an approach to language and the world that makes metaphor almost impossible.

Objectivism, according to Lakoff and Johnson, presumes an absolute truth in the world that can be accurately described by language. Objects in the world possess inherent properties that can be included in sets. Literal statements capture inherent properties and represent them in language. Metaphors juxtapose hitherto unrecognized similar inherent properties; when recognition of the similarity of these hidden features routinely occurs, the metaphor dies, becomes ordinary language, and a homonymous lexical entry is added to the dictionary.

Lakoff and Johnson offer four major objections to an objectivist account of metaphor, which I examine individually.

> *By definition, there can be no such thing as a metaphorical concept or metaphorical meaning.* Meanings are objective and specify conditions of objective truth. They are by definition ways of characterizing the world as it is or might be. Conditions of objective truth simply do not provide ways of viewing one thing in terms of another. Hence, objective meanings cannot be metaphorical.[19]

If objectivists can characterize the world as it "might be," then why can't they create diaphors, suggestive metaphors, that offer hypothetical possibilities about the world? In this objection, Lakoff and Johnson assume that all objectivists are literalists, a supposition far from the mark for poets and scientists; both the poet and the scientist want to speculate about the hidden features of human experience and the unknown aspects of physical reality. Both assume that they are speculating about something real and objective (even the poet in describing subjectivity assumes it to have a universal character). Objectivity for the scientist consists of events that are intersubjectively testable, not necessarily those that are absolute and obvious like "The cat is on the mat." Metaphorical meanings can be objective in the sense that they are experienced intersubjectively, not necessarily in the sense that they are literal.

> *Since metaphor cannot be a matter of meaning, it can only be a matter of language.* A metaphor, on the objectivist view, can at best give us an indirect way of *talking* about some objective meaning M′ by using the language that would be used literally to talk about some other objective meaning M, which is usually false in a blatant way.

Lakoff and Johnson are assuming that an objectivist must be committed to a controversion theory of metaphor in which the speaker intentionally utters a false statement when creating a metaphor. I have already argued that metaphors can have degrees of truth and falsity—an argument that I extend later in my treatment of the application of fuzzy sets and many-valued logic to metaphor. Lakoff and Johnson also seem to assume that in an objectivist view all metaphors must be epiphors, metaphors that are more expressive than suggestive and which eventually die and become part of ordinary language when lexical entries are added to dictionaries. If metaphor was not a matter of meaning, how could it be understood? Even objectivists must comprehend a meaning for a metaphor if they are to understand it. Certainly, some objectivists have argued for a context-free grammar with the meaning inherent in the language, but it is not necessary to hold such a position as an objectivist. The meaning of a metaphor can arise from the context of expression. I argued earlier that a theory of metaphor involves three aspects that can be set forth in interrelated levels of analysis: (1) a surface level analysis; (2) a semantical analysis of the linguistic deep structure; and (3) a deeper conceptual analysis that interrelates (1) and (2). Lakoff and Johnson arbitrarily limited the objectivist account to levels 1 and 2 and arbitrarily cut it off from level 3. The objectivist position that I am espousing in this book bears little resemblance to that denied by Lakoff and Johnson; I would claim that *both* literal language and metaphorical language express cognitive meanings.

Their next objection does characterize objectivism, although somewhat ambiguously.

> Again by definition, there can be no such thing as literal (conventional) metaphor. A sentence is used literally when M' = M, that is, when the speaker's meaning is the objective meaning. Metaphors can only arise when M' ≠ M. Thus, according to the objectivist definition, a literal metaphor is a contradiction in terms, and literal language cannot be metaphorical.

Those who hold that literal language can describe (not unambiguously) objects and events in the world agree that literal metaphors are a contradiction in terms. Metaphors arise from the juxtaposition of the referents of literal language. This does not imply that literal language is not conceptual, as Lakoff and Johnson assume in the objection presented just before this one. The ambiguity in this objection comes in the phrase "and literal language cannot be metaphorical." I have already suggested and observed in the case of Turbayne's position that any theory of explanation for metaphor as a theory is probably founded on a basic metaphor—my theory, which presumes a distinction (still to be shown carefully) between literal and metaphorical language, presumes a basic metaphor—that the world is conceptual (expressed in linguistic concepts and imagistic concepts). In the sense of assuming a basic metaphor, a theory that describes both literal and metaphorical language can itself be metaphorical. But this does not mean that every literal statement is a metaphor. Nor does it entail that dead metaphors (metaphors that have become literal language) cannot convey concepts without being metaphorical.

Objectivists are indicted as having accepted the conduit metaphor, which assumes that meanings are like objects and can be contained in sentences, in the mind, and in memory. Lakoff and Johnson follow Turbayne's procedure of demonstrating how we have been victimized by the conduit metaphor by showing the untoward consequences of accepting this metaphor.[20] As I show later they want to replace this metaphor by a nonmetaphorical concept of direct, physical interaction with the environment. I claim that such a move smuggles a basic metaphor back into the enterprise of trying to give a rational account of metaphor. But let me first consider the last crucial objection to objectivism.

Metaphor can contribute to understanding only by making us see objective similarities, that is, similarities between the objective meanings M and M'. These similarities must be based on shared *inherent properties* of objects—properties that the objects really have, in and of themselves.

But I have already argued, especially in the case of diaphors, that dissimilarities are often more important than similarities in proposing new meanings and new ways of looking at the world. Lakoff and Johnson seem to believe that objectivists can accept meaning only in epiphors; diaphors are not allowed to be meaningful in suggesting new hypothetical ways of conceiving of the world. Not all who believe in the existence of an external objective world assert that the properties of this world are inherent either in the objects and events or in the mind of the perceiver. The process of perception does involve mediation between the observer and the environment; the bodily perceptual apparatus, the cultural concepts, and the evolutionary biological heritage all combine in the knowledge process to produce an account of the world. These factors do relativize the knowledge that we possess, but they do not necessarily force us into either complete relativity or subjectivism. My subjectivism is built on tentative rather than absolute knowledge, on mediated rather than direct perception, and on tentative, interactive properties rather than absolute inherent properties. But Lakoff and Johnson do not think that one can remain an objectivist without retaining commitment to inherent properties.

In summary, the usual objectivist accounts of these phenomena (dead metaphor, homonymy with similarities, or abstraction) all depend on preexisting similarities based on inherent properties. In general, similarities do exist, but they cannot be based on *inherent* properties. The similarities arise as a *result* of conceptual metaphors and thus must be considered similarities of *interactional*, rather than inherent, properties. But the admission of interactional properties is inconsistent with the basic premise of objectivist philosophy. It amounts to giving up the myth of objectivism.[21]

They seem to conceive of the basic premise of objectivist philosophy to be that knowledge is a fixed, objective, absolute thing like an external, physical object. But as I have already noted, this premise rests on a basic metaphor. Furthermore, not all objectivists demand their knowledge to be absolute and unmediated. Lakoff and Johnson move in the direction of presenting a disguised objectivist (in my sense not theirs) account of how nonmetaphorical concepts emerge through physical interaction with the environment.

The conceptual system of Lakoff and Johnson finds its support in a direct bodily interaction with the physical environment. They select spatial concepts as a primary example of this form of direct emergence.

> The prime candidates for concepts that are understood directly are the simple spatial concepts, such as UP. Our spatial concept UP arises out of our spatial experience. We have bodies and stand erect. Almost every movement we make involves a motor program that either changes our up–down orientation, maintains it, presupposes it, or takes it into account in some way. In other words, the structure of our spatial concepts emerges from our constant spatial experience, that is, our interaction with the physical environment.[22]

Even the experiences of spatial orientation, however, involve cultural presuppositions so that one cannot have a purely physical as opposed to cultural experience. But Lakoff and Johnson distinguish between those experiences that are "more" physical and those that are "more" cultural. Emotional experiences are just as basic as spatial and perceptual experiences, but they "are much less sharply delineated in terms of what we do with our bodies."[23] We tend to conceptualize the non-physical in terms of the physical so that systematic correlations exist between emotional experiences and sensory-motor actions. Physical experiences produce emergent concepts, whereas concepts that arise from correlations produce emergent metaphors. The concepts "object, substance, and container emerge directly," whereas orientation metaphors like "The visual field is a container" emerge from "*systematic correlations within our experience*."[24] Lakoff and Johnson distinguish between experience and conceptualization in the following passage.

> Perhaps the most important thing to stress about grounding is the distinction between an experience and the way we conceptualize it. We are not claiming that physical experience is in any way more basic than other kinds of experience, whether emotional, mental, cultural, or whatever. All of these experiences may be just as basic as physical experiences. Rather, what we are claiming about

grounding is that we typically conceptualize the nonphysical *in terms of* the physical—that is, we conceptualize the less clearly delineated in terms of the more clearly delineated. Consider the following examples:

Harry is in the kitchen.

Harry is in the Elks.

Harry is in love.

The sentences refer to three different domains of experience: spatial, social, and emotional. None of these has experiential priority over the others; they are all equally basic kinds of experience.

But with respect to conceptual structuring there is a difference. The concept IN of the first sentence emerges directly from spatial experience in a clearly delineated fashion. It is not an instance of a metaphorical concept.[25]

Lakoff and Johnson are struggling valiantly to provide a basic experiential ground for conceptualization not too different from linguists who have attempted to construct a theory of language grounded in an experience of the literal. They seem to believe that the physical takes priority in conceptualizing because it can be "delineated" more easily than the emotional or social. Yet this delineation of the spatial, as Lakoff and Johnson have readily admitted, is also cultural. One cannot express even directly emergent spatial concepts without using language that has been culturally transmitted, and the ordinary language that we use, according to Lakoff and Johnson, is largely metaphorical. On what basis can one be sure that spatial concepts emerge *directly* rather than emerge as *mediated metaphorical concepts*? Does the language possess an implicit intuitive knowledge of the directness and nonmetaphorical character of spatial concepts? One must own this knowledge or some kind of similar insight if a justifiable distinction is to be made between direct emergence and metaphorical emergence. Lakoff and Johnson seem to have transformed the problem of distinguishing between direct and mediated experience. Direct emergence serves as the basis for nonmetaphorical experience on which metaphorical conceptualizations occur just as the nonphysical depends on physical concepts for its expression. But this nonmetaphorical direct experience also emerges in linguistic forms that are already culturally mediated and transmitted. Lakoff and Johnson present startling evidence of the cultural determination of spatiality when they cite the example of how the Hausas orient themselves to objects.

Given a medium-sized rock in our visual field and a ball between us and the rock, say, a foot from it, we would perceive the ball as being *in front of* the rock. The Hausas make a different projection than we do and would understand the ball as being *in back of* the rock. Thus, a front–back orientation is not an inherent property of objects like rocks but rather an orientation that we project onto them, and the way we do this varies from culture to culture.[26]

If some spatial concepts vary from culture to culture, how can we have any certainty that spatial concepts emerge directly? It seems more like a mediated, indirect emergence, which Lakoff and Johnson would call metaphorical. In seeking an unmediated, directly experienced ground for concepts, Lakoff and Johnson seem to be searching for a way to avoid linguistic relativity. They want to circumvent the consequence of their description of *most* ordinary discourse as metaphorical—that there exist no common experiential terms that give language a nonrelativistic basis. Discarding the words literal and objective as applying to aspects of ordinary language, they replace them with nonmetaphorical concepts and direct emergence. In their account, however, there seems to be no clear method of distinguishing between metaphorical and nonmetaphorical. The assertion that experience is primary over conceptualization does not suffice because both metaphorical and nonmetaphorical concepts emerge; the basis for judging concepts to be metaphorical is cultural mediation, the basis for nonmetaphorical concepts seems to be the same cultural mediation. Here we find a distinction claimed without a justified difference.

The notion of direct emergence similarly appears unclear; Lakoff and Johnson seem faced with a paradox similar to that which I found in the computational metaphor and also in my sketch of the nature of metaphor, namely, that to describe a theory of metaphor one must presume at least an underlying basic metaphor on which to construct the theory. Suppose that direct emergence is itself a metaphor for Lakoff and Johnson's theory of metaphor expressed in the form "The nonmetaphorical directly emerges." Then they are faced with the paradox that to describe the nonmetaphorical they must resort to a metaphorical description. Lakoff and Johnson admit that the concept of "emergence" in an entirely different context can be a metaphor when under a treatment of causation they observe that the emergence metaphor occurs when "a mental or emotional state is viewed as causing an act or event. . . ."[27] The use of emergence as a metaphor presumes in this case the metaphorical view that an act or event is an object that emerges from a container. Why can't we claim that the invocation of direct emergence for nonmetaphorical concepts (spatiality) similarly presumes the view that the world is a container from which objects (spatial concepts) emerge? Under this interpretation direct emergence no longer can stand opposed to metaphorical; it becomes a *metaphorical process* by means of which *metaphorical* concepts emerge.

Lakoff and Johnson attempt to bolster their notion of direct emergence by invoking the work of Eleanor Rosch on prototypical categories. Rosch claimed that humans describe the world in terms of paradigmatic prototypes that form categories defined by families of resemblance rather than by formal membership in sets. For example, a bird is better categorized by a robin than by a turkey. These prototypical categories combine attributes in an economy of purpose; the categorizing organism wants to generate as much information as possible with the least amount of energy expended in order to carry out a certain function.[28] The formation of these categories also links them together in a perceived structure of the world. Lakoff and Johnson explain their directly emergent concepts as prototypical experience similar to Rosch's prototypical categories. Causation, for example, has a directly experienced core, a prototypical gestalt—"the concept of causation is based on the prototype of direct manipulation, which emerges directly from our experience."[29] Again, the concept of direct manipulation, even if described as a prototypical experience, is determined by the cultural context in which it exists. The content that one gives to the concept of manipulating the environment depends on the assumptions that one inherits and invents about the nature of humanity, the nature of the environment, and the interrelationship between the two. Primitive peoples do not expect to manipulate the environment in the same manner as technologically sophisticated Western culture. From the historical perspective, an Aristotelian is expected to manipulate the physical world by directly pushing or pulling it, whereas men and women after the seventeenth century conceive of the legitimate possibility of action at a distance.

I applaud Lakoff and Johnson's efforts to find a method of distinguishing between the nonmetaphorical and the metaphorical, but I find them trapped by their own insistence that most ordinary language is metaphorical. Their rejection of the literal pushes them into the almost impossible position of trying to use language that they have shown to be metaphorical (conceptual in my sense) to describe language that they claim is nonmetaphorical (concepts that emerge directly). I applaud their efforts to explain metaphor as a cognitive device rather than as only a linguistic category, but they tend to assume that most conceptual language is metaphorical. Their efforts to explain the emergence of nonmetaphorical concepts in terms of experienced physical behavior fail because the expressions of this behavior are mediated by what they have described as culturally based metaphorical concepts. Contrary to Lakoff and Johnson, I claim that one can distinguish between literal and metaphorical on the basis of culturally determined, equivocal, tentative but objective (not in the absolute sense) experience. They are certainly correct in trying to ground metaphor in experience, but I would prefer that experience be described as mediated rather than claimed as direct, the latter being a mysterious and surreptitious use of metaphor.

The presentation of a distinction between literal and metaphorical does not escape the adoption of a basic metaphor to undergird my theory of metaphor. Lakoff and Johnson thought that they had avoided any resort to the metaphorical by acceptance of the notion of direct emergence, but even that concept depends on a metaphorical view of the world. What I argue is that admission of the use of a basic metaphor to construct a theory of metaphor does not eliminate the possibility of using literal language in contrast to metaphorical language. The admission of the use of a basic metaphor to construct a theory of metaphor does not require that every sentence within a language also be described as metaphorical. But this admission does require some consideration of the charge that the explicit use of a basic metaphor to form a theory of metaphor inevitably leads to a position of linguistic relativism.

Positions that view all language as metaphorical often support linguistic relativism by their rejection of literal statements on which there could be universal agreement as to meaning. Metaphoric expressions depend on the context of the hearer for their interpretation, and the context can vary from culture to culture.

Rejection of Linguistic Relativity

Linguistic relativity is most often associated with the works of Edward Sapir and Benjamin Lee Whorf in what has come to be known as the Sapir-Whorf hypothesis: the language of an individual partially determines the world view and the conceptual system of an individual.[30] Individuals who speak different languages, therefore, view the world differently with different conceptual systems. Whorf became convinced of this hypothesis through his study of the language of the Hopi. Many of their ways of understanding action are so different from English as to defy translation. The Hopi has no implicit or explicit concept of time and interprets the world as composed of events constituted objectively by perceived features, such as color and movement, and constituted subjectively as an expression of invisible intensity factors on which their stability and persistence depend. Complete translation from one language to the other remains impossible; to understand another language entails complete immersion in that other language with the concomitant change in thinking.

If all language is metaphorical, then even within the same language we may have a linguistic relativity among speakers because some adopt one metaphorical way of characterizing the world while others adopt another set of metaphors. Turbayne described how scientists and philosophers have been victimized by the mechanical metaphor and attempted to replace it with a linguistic metaphor. Lakoff and Johnson warned of the conduit metaphor, which assumes that the mind is a container that holds objectlike thoughts. Unless there is some commonly accepted literal language on whose meaning we can agree, a completely metaphorical language will allow linguistic relativity within a single language with the differing conceptual systems determined by the various metaphors adopted for expression by various individuals. Turbayne realized this possibility and sought to avoid it by allowing theories to be founded on basic metaphors while retaining an ordinary literal language. Lakoff and Johnson sought to avoid this kind of linguistic relativity by describing the direct emergence of nonmetaphorical concepts. But even these concepts in their account are expressed in ordinary metaphorical language, and so they come dangerously close to the position that all language is metaphorical and to the conclusion that individuals or cultures are beset by a cultural relativity according to their adoption of various metaphors.

Some of the most startling evidence against the Sapir-Whorf hypothesis has been uncovered in the discovery by Berlin and Kay that the color vocabularies of various languages form a fixed pattern:

1. All languages contain terms for white and black.

2. If a language contains three terms, then it contains a term for red.

3. If a language contains four terms, then it contains a term for either green or yellow (but not both).

4. If a language contains five terms, then it contains terms for both green and yellow.

5. If a language contains six terms, then it contains a term for blue.

6. If a language contains seven terms, then it contains a term for brown.

7. If a language contains eight or more terms, then it contains a term for purple, pink, orange, grey or some combination of these.[31]

Although Noam Chomsky and his fellow exponents of the transformational generative grammar proposed linguistic universals, these occupied the deep structure of abstract representation of language, and their empirical implications were not unequivocal in empirical testing.

Berlin and Kay's results were startling not only because they were unexpected by many but also because they were so carefully corroborated. This universal pattern of the use of color terms existed in widely disparate geographical areas and could not be explained by cultural contact and transmission. Berlin and Kay also tested various native speakers with Munsell color chips and mapped their identifications of colors in terms of their color vocabulary. Berlin and Kay concluded their study by noting that the addition of color terms follows a fixed pattern in languages, a process that they depict as an evolutionary one.

> The overall temporal order is properly considered an evolutionary one; color lexicons with few terms tend to occur in association with relatively simple cultures and simple technologies, while color lexicons with many terms tend to occur in association with complex cultures and complex technologies (to the extent that complexity of culture and technology can be assessed objectively).[32]

Eleanor Rosch tested the relativity hypothesis using color terms with the Dani of Indonesian New Guinea, a primitive, agricultural people possessing basically a two-color language.[33] Proposing perceptually salient colors that attract more attention and are more easily stored in memory, Rosch found that the Dani could more easily learn these focal colors (salient) and that the focal colors corresponded exactly to the colors that Berlin and Kay had concluded were universal.

> We began with the idea of color as the ideal domain in which to demonstrate the effects of the lexicon of a language on cognition, thereby supporting a position of linguistic determinism. Instead, we have found that basic color terminology appears to be universal and that perceptually salient focal colors appear to form natural prototypes for the development of color terms. Contrary to initial ideas, the color space appears to be a prime example of the influence of underlying perceptual–cognitive factors on linguistic categories.[34]

Rosch extended this notion of prototypicality beyond color to other categories, arguing that humans categorize according to natural prototypes rather than by analyzing the features of objects and classifying them abstractly. In her treatment of linguistic relativity, Rosch notes that facial expressions of emotion have also been discovered to be universal "only when an investigator thought to ask, not about all possible stimuli, but about the prototypes (best examples) of categories."[35]

The Notion of the Literal

Rosch's prototypical natural categories offer possible support for the literal. In her view, language arises from cognitive categorizing, a process that follows the natural contours of the external world, a process of mediation that is not unequivocal or precise but one that can be confirmed by the ways in which human beings universally do employ language. Lakoff and Johnson attempted to base their notion of direct emergence on the natural prototypical categories described by Rosch. They failed, however, to leave enough room in their description of language for the expression of these natural kinds in a literal rather than in a metaphorical language. Their omission may have arisen from their belief that to allow the literal would be to commit oneself to an objective myth that required an absolute certainty, a precision, and an unequivocality. I believe that none of these requirements need be fulfilled for an utterance to be properly called literal.

The belief that the literal must be precise and exact probably comes from the associations noted by various dictionaries, including the *Oxford English Dictionary*, that one sense of a translation is to be literal in the sense of verbally exact. Even though I am poised to join Rosch in a rejection of the linguistic relativity thesis, I contend that no translation can be exact; there are always nuances of difference between two languages. The differences between languages do not make effective translation impossible, a conclusion of linguistic relativity, but they prevent "exact" word for word translation. Dictionaries also include for their description of literal, "true to fact" and "not figurative or metaphorical." Ironically, what is true to fact depends on the categories that are used to describe facts, and my task here is to define the literal as different from the metaphorical; I cannot depend on an intuition of what the metaphorical might be in order to define the literal.

I define the literal as the use of ordinary language to express concrete objects and events. When we employ ordinary words in their ordinary dictionary senses to describe objects or situations that are publicly perceptible, we are speaking literally. This does not mean that literal sentences are precise or unambiguous. Like all language, to be understood, literal sentences must be interpreted in a context. If I say, "My house is cool in spite of the heat," you may interpret this to mean, "He has turned on his air conditioning," whereas I intend to convey the idea that my house is cool because I live among the trees. Even in acts of ostension where I point to a nearby blue chair and while still pointing say, "This is my favorite chair," you may correctly identify the chair and understand what I mean. But to a child learning a language or to a foreign speaker just beginning to encounter English, the act of pointing and uttering the statement may not be unambiguous. For a statement to be literal, however, it does not have to be completely free from ambiguity; under some contextual circumstances it may well be ambiguous. Nevertheless, under normal circumstances a literal statement can be understood and implicitly affirmed as a proper and normal utterance. By contrast, when I say, "My favorite chair takes me everywhere, across the ocean, to the moon, and even to places that exist only in the imagination," the hearer knows that I am not speaking literally because he or she can recognize the semantic anomaly that a chair literally does not possess those capabilities and could perform them only figuratively. Only as I read about faraway places or contemplate the moon or follow Don Quixote across La Mancha could my chair be said to be part of the instrumentality of reading and imagining.

I can agree with Rosch that the word chair as a natural prototypical category arose from the cognitive activity of men and women who picked salient features of an object and used them to form a mental paradigm of what a chair is. All other chairs bear a family resemblance to this prototype. But does this account of a natural category conflict with the earlier commitment to words as formed by associations of semantic markers located in fuzzy sets? Lakoff and Johnson believe that one must be committed to prototypical categories rather than to fixed abstract sets if one wants to avoid successfully the pitfalls of an absolute objectivism. Fuzzy sets, however, are not necessarily incompatible with prototypical natural categories because members of fuzzy sets are members to a degree; the prototype can be a full member defying the nature of the set, whereas other entities bearing a family resemblance to the prototype can have a membership function of a lesser degree.

My acceptance of the use of semantic markers seems to be at odds with the notion of a prototype as a gestalt. How can we contend that literal language finds support in natural categories and also contend that semantic change can be best explained by the membership of semantic markers of words in fuzzy sets? Does this commitment to a componential analysis of semantics contradict the acceptance of natural categories? When concepts such as "chair" are learned, they probably are learned by children as gestalt, natural categories. The category chair may extend far beyond chair in the mind of the child, and through a series of trial and error tests in which the word chair is mistakenly applied to other objects and then found to be incorrect after parental corrections, the concept comes to be fixed in language usage. But there is still a difference between the way in which a child learns a concept and the justification one gives for why the extension of a category applies to certain objects as prototypes and not to others. In language learning we are concerned with how a child comes to acquire a language; our account examines children's actual language of one-word and then two-word sentences and then speculates on the role of ostension, hypothesis testing, and the semantic association of words with other words.[36] In offering a justificatory account of how concepts "fit" the world, we are concerned with the scope of the extension of terms; why do we have two concepts, chair and table, subsumed under the superordinate category furniture? Why isn't it sufficient to have only the concept furniture? Probably, for functional reasons of conceptual economy, we have chair and table because if we did not have both when asked to sit in the furniture, we might not know which object was designed specifically for sitting.

For purposes of describing literal language, the acceptance of prototypical natural categories offers the language user a cognitive bridge to the physical world. I avoid an extended discussion of the ontology of these categories except to posit the existence of the external physical world as *there* and knowable through these natural kinds. The knowledge that these prototypical categories yields probably suffers from both imprecision and tentativeness. With the fallibility of our own perceptual systems, the limited nature of the categories as parts of those systems should not bother us unduly. There are many phenomena in the world, such as electromagnetic radiation, not directly picked up by our senses. Although our perceptual systems provide reasonably good guides for locomotion and survival in the world, they are limited in the scope of information they process and are sometimes erroneous. As parts of this perceptual system, natural categories are also good guides even though both limited and occasionally erroneous. The limits of these natural categories can be vividly demonstrated in the case of color terms. Berlin and Kay found that in languages with fewer than eleven basic color terms, when native speakers were asked to label color chips, some were left blank. Does this mean that they do not perceive these colors? Or that they do not perceive them *as* black, white, or red if they are users of only three colors? If the latter, then we have found further evidence of the limitations of the scope of natural categories. If primitive peoples are limited by their cultural context, perhaps we are similarly limited in the extension of our natural categories, even though we may be presently unaware of this limitation. Rosch was able to extend the categorical knowledge of the Dani by teaching them colors that were salient in the evolutionary development of color terms described by Berlin and Kay. Most scientists, however, do not have an instructor like Rosch who possesses a hypothesis about the evolutionary development of concepts and can instruct us along a path of salient categories. Seeking natural categories about the unknown requires extension of our existing categories, but how should we extend them? There exist almost infinite possibilities for extension. Metaphors that juxtapose often unassociated categories creating semantic anomaly offer one method of seeking the proper categories that might be prototypical and natural. Diaphors become epiphors when confirmation of a suggestive hypothesis is found. If the confirmation occurs over and over again and the metaphor becomes commonplace, then a new category of ordinary language occurs; this new natural category arises from the combination of two categories previously not associated.

The process of creating new concepts in metaphors differs from that of recognizing prototypical natural categories in that when confronted with a metaphor, the hearer must consider the ways in which the referents are similar and the ways in which they are dissimilar. This usually involves an implicit (or it may sometimes be explicit) conceptual consideration of the semantic markers of the referents. When we deal with natural categories in literal language, however, we understand them as gestalts and do not consider the semantic markers associated with the word. Metaphorical thinking differs from ordinary perceptions and understanding. Metaphors force us to wonder, compare, note similarities and dissimilarities, and then seek confirmation or disconfirmation of the suggestions posed by metaphors. Literal language rarely forces us to do any of these things. It would be surprising if there were no cognitive differences between consideration of metaphors and consideration of literal language. By claiming that most ordinary language is metaphorical and that knowledge of concepts is based largely if not completely on perception of prototypical natural categories as gestalts, Lakoff and Johnson have robbed metaphor of its distinctive cognitive feature, that of creating new categories through a complex cognitive process of change in the associations of words. By putting dead metaphors (conventional metaphors) on the same plane with imaginative metaphors, Lakoff and Johnson argue as if there was only one type of conceptual thinking—that involved in the recognition of natural categories. But they have ignored metaphorical cognition, the conceptual formation of new categories through juxtaposition of old categories in new ways.

In "Mohini Chatterjee," Yeats describes "birth" as a "cannon" that "thunders" time away.[37] One can easily understand birth to be like that of a cannon—in each a projectile emerges from a passage: in the one a baby is the projectile and in the other a cannonball. But what corresponds to the thunder of a cannon in birth? The screams of the mother or the screams of the baby or both? And how does this "thunder" eliminate time? Through eternal succession of biological reproduction or through the creation of an eternal religious soul? The semantic anomaly of birth being a cannon produces hypothetical consideration of similarities and differences. It produces speculation not only about the meaning of these phrases but also about the events in life to which these words refer. Ironically, cannons kill the very things that birth brings, namely, life.

Suppose now that I uttered the ordinary sentences about birth, such as "Birth is a stage of biological reproduction" or "Birth is often painful to the mother." In these utterances I do not have to worry about how "birth" as a natural category is related to the other parts of the sentence. Without semantic anomaly I am not forced to imagine how birth, a natural category, can be combined with some other natural category, a cannon, to form a new speculative category, "birth as the thunderous firing of a cannon."

I resort to fuzzy sets, sets in which members are partial members, as an explanatory conceptual device that can include both natural categories and concepts that are undergoing semantic change. By doing so, I do not claim that the recognition of objects or events in literal sentences is the same conceptually as the comprehension of a metaphor. Metaphors involve conceptual comparison and contrast, and that can be possible only when the referents of a metaphor are considered in terms of their attributes (semantic markers) and the differences and similarities found among those attributes.

Finally, in my discussion of the literal and metaphorical I must observe that the line between the two is not clear-cut. Since many metaphors are in the process of dying and becoming part of ordinary language, everyday discourse includes many metaphors with only a flicker of metaphorical life. Familiarity and context determine just how metaphorical ordinary language is. But when metaphors become so commonplace that one or more of the referents adds a lexical entry in a dictionary, then we can be sure that the metaphor has completely died and is now literal rather than metaphorical.

The line between literal and metaphorical language may also be fuzzy for another reason—the fact that metaphors draw on literal language to form their unusual juxtapositions. After a metaphor has been comprehended, the individual referents through interaction may change their meanings. For example, after Yeats's suggestion that births are cannons, we may not be able to think of a birth without also thinking of it as a cannon. Through the interaction of referents, ordinary language may become partially metaphorical before the metaphor actually dies and becomes an established and literal way of viewing the world.[38] Even though the line between literal and metaphorical usage is blurred, the conceptual processes of each are different enough to warrant a distinction. My argument in favor of a distinction between literal and metaphorical language does not rest on the need of a theory of metaphor to have such a distinction nor on demands for an objective account of the world; instead, I base my argument on the different processes of thinking involved in both and the different functions performed by each. Literal language seeks to use established categories (including those derived from dead metaphors) to describe the natural world in common terms that can be universally comprehended. Metaphorical language seeks to create new suggestive ways of perceiving and understanding the world and involves a conceptual process different from that of literal description. Certainly, I would argue that literal language offers a possible way of constructing an objective though fallible view of reality. I also find that by distinguishing between literal and metaphorical, I can construct a more intelligible and comprehensive theory of metaphor than one which denies the distinction.

Finally, I admit that my theory of the literal presumes a basic metaphor—that the physical world is composed of natural categories. This presumption undergirds my confidence that ordinary talk about objects describes, not in an absolutely infallible manner but in a pragmatically useful way, what we encounter in the world. This theory of the literal finds corroboration in the universality of certain conceptual categories—color and motion, for instance. It also finds corroboration in our ability to manipulate the world successfully and thereby to survive.

4
The Semantics of Metaphor

The Problem of Change in Semantics

The possibility of semantic change allows metaphors to transform the meaning of seemingly odd juxtapositions of words into novel perceptions and hypotheses. I have noted that semantic anomaly serves as an important, necessary but not sufficient condition for metaphor. From what seems to be an unusual combination of referents, a person confronting a vibrant metaphor comprehends new analogies and disanalogies. Such an encounter often produces emotional tension; the hearer is discomfited by an association of referents so strange that at first he or she may even think that the juxtaposition is wrong. If the meanings of the referents were permanently fixed, then the unusual junction of referents would be unintelligible. How can one understand the tendency to avoid facing difficult problems through a rhetorical defense in the metaphor "The semantic fumigation of a problem"? To fumigate means to disinfect by means of smoke or fumes; in the *Oxford English Dictionary* it also means to perfume. Words cannot be physically transformed into smoke or fumes; a device for fumigating, such as a fire or a spray gun, cannot take words and either burn them or force them through a nozzle. Unless the meaning of the verb fumigate can be changed, the metaphor "The semantic fumigation of a problem" is incomprehensible. Yet when we utter the metaphor, most people, especially those used to the tactics of politicians, comprehend it at once. They may even imagine a decision maker spraying words onto a physical problem of where to locate a highway in a city. Or we may conceive of the manager making a rotten problem smell good by carefully choosing pleasant words to mask unpleasant aspects. We live in the age of the euphemism; limited nuclear war is called a "surgical strike"; a garbage collector, a "sanitary engineer"; an undertaker, a "funeral director"; to be fired becomes "not rehired"; and an accident, an "unforeseen event."

Words in our language undergo changes in meaning almost constantly and metaphor serves as one of the instruments for accomplishing those alterations in meaning. That the meaning of language changes is little debated, but much debate rages over how these changes can be explained. The purpose of this chapter is to develop an account of changes in semantic meaning that is sufficient to explain the construction of metaphors, both epiphors and diaphors. Although I call my explanation a theory of semantic change, I recognize that semantics cannot be completely separated from syntax. The position of a word in a sentence and its syntactical function contribute to an understanding of the meaning of the word. One cannot determine semantic meaning solely by the construction of a lexicon and of semantic rules that select lexical meanings and apply them to a syntactical deep structure. Interaction between the syntactical structure and the lexical entries determines the meaning of individual words. Among metaphors, simple utterances of the form "A is B" might lead one to think that the semantical meaning of metaphors could be understood solely by considering the juxtaposition of the referents of A with those of B, but as I noted in considering the work of Brooke-Rose in chapter 2, verb metaphors and genitive metaphors integrate syntactical function with lexical entries of their referents to produce meaning. One can say, "The senator semantically fumigated the problem of nuclear proliferation by emphasizing the strict security measures undertaken by producers of plutonium." Here the metaphor stands as a transitive verb metaphor with the object of the transitive verb specified.

Throughout my analysis of metaphor I presume a three-level analysis: (1) surface language, (2) semantics, and (3) cognition. Let me remind the reader that these levels are not mutually exclusive and that in considering the semantics of metaphor I recognize that the surface context affects the meaning. At the deepest level cognitive processes select the salient features of referents that are similar to form an analogy as well as identify those dissimilar features that produce the disanalogy. My account of the semantics of metaphor offers a rational reconstruction of how changes in meaning can occur at the level of linguistics. I do not contend that such a description generates a full account of metaphor; the discussions in chapters 5 and 7 add analyses of lower and higher levels. The semantics of metaphor is an interactive mechanism that relates surface language to cognition.

To develop a semantics of metaphor I examine how words are associated with one another, adopting the notion of semantic markers as the basis for constructing a pattern of association. At the heart of this account is the claim that semantic markers can be represented as fuzzy sets and that in metaphors whose unlikely markers are juxtaposed, the degrees of membership of one semantic marker in the fuzzy set representing the other semantic marker can be successfully developed in a four-valued logic that avoids direct contradiction and allows the conveyance of partial truths.[1] I explore the benefits and deficiencies of earlier attempts to explain semantic change by means of (1) hierarchies of trees, (2) matrices like those of Osgood's semantic differential, and (3) rules of semantic change like those of Levin.[2] Finally, I attempt to combine my claims about metaphors as partially explained by fuzzy-set theory into a hierarchy of matrices that avoids the problems previously encountered in attempting to utilize these devices to explain semantic change.

The meaning of a word can be understood either by means of ostension—the utterance of the statement "This is an X" accompanied by the act of pointing to X—or by means of association with other words. Ostension plays a large role in the learning of language by children when they learn to identify objects in their presence by imitating the sounds spoken by an adult to represent that object.[3] Mama points to herself and says, "Mama," and her twenty-month-old child repeats the word. The infant may think of the term "Mama" as representing any person present or any woman present. Through a trial-and-error process of testing the range of meaning of this word with proper corrections from adults, the child comes to identify the term consistent with adult usage. Note that this process of ostension is not unambiguous; the child does not know the exact reference of the word spoken and the thing pointed at by the speaker. Even an adult learning a second language may not be exactly sure what the instructor means when pointing to a dog and saying, "Aqui esta un perro." The English speaker may guess that the Spanish instructor means "dog" by "perro," but the instructor could well have used another word, "una cola," used the same act of pointing, and meant "tail." The student might have wrongly surmised "dog" instead of "tail." After a language has been learned, except in unusual situations such as learning a new language or coining new specialized words, most semantic meaning depends on association of the target word with other words to achieve comprehension. Uttering the word woman brings with it the associations of female and adult. From semantic memory we recall the identifications of woman with female and adult. The term semantic feature or semantic marker has been used to designate these forms of association with the target word.[4] Much contemporary semantic theory called componential analysis employs contrasts among semantic markers as the basis of its analysis. I briefly examine componential analysis, note its benefits and limitations, and adapt some of its notions for a semantics of metaphor.

Componential Analysis

Componential analysis assumes a system of contrasting semantic markers, such as Animate/Inanimate, Organic/Inorganic, Male/Female,

Singular/Plural, Adult/Young, Tall/Short.[5] The applicability of each term of the contrastive pair to the target word can be indicated by a plus (+) or a minus (−). For example, a componential analysis of man, woman, boy and girl can be presented as follows:[6]

man:	+Human	+Adult	+Male
woman:	+Human	+Adult	−Male
boy:	+Human	−Adult	+Male
girl:	+Human	−Adult	−Male

Geoffrey Leech calls these formulas componential definitions.[7] Interestingly, in this scheme the same words can be defined by their opposites in each contrastive pair of semantic markers with the application signs (+ or −) reversed. For man we would have: −Inhuman −Young −Female. One wonders whether the contrastive pair of semantic markers without the applicability signs would be sufficient for a componential analysis. Is there a difference between saying that a man is a human, adult male and that a man is not an inhuman, young female? Componential analysts seem to assume a symmetry between a positive application of a marker and the negative application of its contrastive opposite. Consider, however, the term young adults, often used to signify men and women in their early twenties. Such a combination destroys the absolute contrastive opposition between the markers Young and Adult. The category of young adults combines the further semantic associations of Vigor and Near-Teenage with Having-achieved-majority (past age 21) to make the line between Young and Adult fuzzy. Leech acknowledges the fuzziness of componential boundaries but believes that this objection to contrastive analysis can be overcome by considering the areas of common intersection of such terms as Young and Adult as a legitimate use of the category young adults.[8]

Semanticists use the term hyponymy to indicate "meaning inclusion," such as inclusion of man or woman in the classes defined by the semantic markers Human and Adult. From this definition hyponymy is an asymmetric relationship; the meaning of neither Human nor Adult can be included in that of man or woman. In talking of meaning inclusion and of the classes defined by semantic markers, I have introduced a possible confusion between intension and extension. Some theories of semantics claim that meaning can be successfully achieved only through reference (extension). Although I have admitted that through ostension reference plays a role in the meaning of words, for the moment I treat hyponymy solely in intensional terms, leaving the question of how to relate extension and intension to chapter 7.

To establish synonymy in componential analysis one has to show that two words have identical semantic markers. But how many identical semantical markers suffice to demonstrate that two words are synonyms? If one takes the three semantic markers +Animate, −Human, and +Four-legged for both cat and dog, one might wrongly claim that cat and dog are synonyms. To show the difference, additional semantic markers would have to be added *based on prior knowledge* of the distinguishing features between cats and dogs. Not only is this a circularity but it also comes close to Quine's claim that synonymy cannot be established without resorting to perception.[9] In a strictly formal sense, circularity cannot be avoided; to present a semantic analysis of a word we must already know the meaning of that word. The process by which we learn the meaning of words, however, may be quite different from the abstract account that we give of theoretical semantic meaning. Thus the circularity may be genetic rather than a full, formal petitio principi of logic.

Synonymy may be possible between two words only in a carefully defined and delimited way. If one took into account all the semantic markers of the words boat and ship one could hardly establish them as synonyms since each has so many different meanings and nuances. One could not substitute ship for boat in the expression "to be in the same boat" nor could one make the opposite substitution in the idiom "when my ship comes in." A ship is usually considered to be larger than a boat (*Oxford English Dictionary*), although as nouns they can be synonyms in the sense of vessels that float and as transitive verbs they can be synonyms in the sense of placing an oar in the proper position. Using words as synonyms requires knowing not only which similar semantic markers to include but also which semantic markers to eliminate. For two words to be synonyms their semantic markers must be identical, and the various different semantic markers that the two words might possess in other meanings or nuances must be inappropriate.

Metaphors both depend on and produce polysemy—the multiple meanings associated with a *single* word. Unless a word can be taken in more than one sense, metaphor is impossible. And metaphors juxtapose normally unassociated referents, thereby creating new meanings. Polysemy exists not only as different grammatical functions of the same word but also as different collections of semantic markers within the same grammatical function. As a noun, ship includes the semantic meanings of, "1. a vessel, esp. a large ocean-going one propelled by sails or engines; 2. a sailing vessel . . . ; 3. the crew of a vessel . . . ; 4. an airship or airplane; and 5. when one's fortune is assured . . . ."[10] The third, fourth, and fifth meanings may have arisen from metaphoric usage of the term ship. If one considers a ship to be only a fabricated device that floats on water, then to call the crew the ship juxtaposes the semantic markers Animate for crew with Inanimate for ship, and we have a metaphoric usage. Under my theory of metaphor, however, when through usage the metaphor becomes commonplace enough to warrant a new lexical entry in the dictionary, it becomes a dead metaphor and part of ordinary language. If one considers a ship to include the sailors who run it, then to use the word ship to stand for crew is an instance of synecdoche rather than of metaphor. Describing objects that fly rather than float does illustrate metaphoric usage, since the semantic marker of the original meaning of ship included the semantic marker Floating-on-water; ships in the original sense could not float on air since they were too heavy. Balloons changed that limitation because they are lighter than air—filled with hot air, helium, or hydrogen—and analogous in the principle of fluid displacement to ships that float on water. Airplanes do not find support by displacement, but they are designated airships since they, like balloons, move through the air. On receiving a large amount of money and exclaiming, "My ship has just come in," we are using ship to represent fortune—originally a metaphoric usage derived from the arrival of trading ships laden with goods that provided their owners with vast fortunes.

The clash of semantic markers occurring in the juxtaposition of the referents of a metaphor produces semantic anomaly. Unless the same referent can have both an ordinary literal meaning and a hypothetical possible meaning, metaphors are not possible. By examining the semantic markers associated with the referents of a metaphor, one can locate the source of semantic anomaly as well as discover possibilities for analogy. Some linguists propose that in addition to syntactic markers and semantic markers each lexical entry for a word should include selection restrictions that show the limits of applicability of the word.[11] The word woman, for example, would have the selection restriction of male. This seems obvious, but the proposers of selection restrictions had less obvious words in mind, like American football, which does not apply to female, or even more obscurely gringo, which in Mexico applies only to non-Mexicans, especially North Americans. Nevertheless, if there is a relatively complete list of semantic markers, these markers should by their very definition exclude those other semantic markers with which the target word cannot be associated. Since metaphors often accomplish their tasks by associating semantic markers that are not normally combined, if selection restriction was accepted as absolute and a legitimate part of semantic analysis, much semantic anomaly necessary for metaphor would be eliminated.

From componential analysis I accept the notion that words are defined in meaning by a series of semantic markers formed in an association.

These associations of semantic markers can form different lexical entries for the same word, hence polysemy. Not all semantic markers need form contrastive pairs; the boundaries between these pairs are often likely to be fuzzy rather than discrete. Finally, in my account I consider only semantic markers and do not resort to the specification of selection restrictions.

Metaphor and Fuzzy Sets

To begin the analysis of the semantics of metaphor, consider a quasi-componential analysis of the metaphor "The locomotive is in bed."[12] Let us agree to take this as a metaphor and not as a literal description of a child's toy resting in her bed. Two of the metaphoric possibilities for interpretation are (1) that a dynamic person whom we call a "locomotive" has gone to bed or (2) that a literal locomotive used in railroading has gone to the roundhouse, which we call a "bed." In the first case the two referents of the metaphor are a dynamic person and a literal locomotive. In the second case, we have the juxtaposition of an ordinary bed with a roundhouse. Two of the semantic markers for the first interpretation are Animate for the dynamic person and Inanimate for the literal locomotive. How can we combine these two semantic markers that when taken together produce semantic anomaly? In the second interpretation, a bed, itself an inanimate object, is used by animate human beings for sleep. Here we have the reverse juxtaposition of semantic markers, Animate for the bed taken in its functional sense and Inanimate for the imagined roundhouse. Again we are faced with the semantic anomaly of combining seemingly contrasting and perhaps even contradictory semantic markers. The opposition of semantic markers, such as Animate and Inanimate, led proponents of the controversion theory to assert that metaphors necessarily produce false statements. But if the relationship of meaning inclusion, hyponymy, is not excluded absolutely for locomotive and roundhouse in Animate, then a contradiction need not take place. This would mean that the boundary between Animate and Inanimate is not discrete but rather is fuzzy. As a basis for semantic change in metaphor, I begin by establishing the sets of members defined by semantic markers as fuzzy sets. I argue that the concept of a fuzzy set is not incompatible with the way in which classes of objects are perceived in the world as prototypical classes. Finally, I attempt to construct formal but flexible relationships among semantic markers defined as fuzzy, prototypical classes that alter semantic features of the referents of a metaphor.

Intuitively, we use the notion of a fuzzy set in everyday language when we speak of a beautiful painting or the fact that a whale is a mammal or that John is a tall man. The membership of a painting in the set of beautiful paintings is relative to the other paintings included within that set and a function of whether we consider it more or less beautiful than others. Similarly, we often think of whales as fish since they, like fish, swim in the sea, but our knowledge of biology reminds us that they really are mammals. Our classification of them as mammals, however, finds less security than our assignment of lions, apes, and humans to that category. Membership of men in the class of tall people also depends on relative comparison. Realizing the ambiguity of these types of class membership, L. A. Zadeh defined fuzzy sets in his classic paper as follows:

> Let X be a space of points (objects), with a generic element of X denoted by x. Thus, $X = \{x\}$.
>
> A *fuzzy set* (*class*) A in X is characterized by a *membership* (*characteristic*) *function* $f_A(x)$ which associated with each point in X a real number in the interval $[0,1]$, with the value $f_A(x)$ at x representing the "grade of membership" of x in A. When A is a set in the ordinary sense of the term, its membership function can take on only two values 0 and 1, with $f_A(x) = 1$ or 0 according as x does or does not belong to A. Thus, in this case, $f_A(x)$ reduces to the familiar characteristic function of a set A.[13]

By using this definition, one can construct algorithms to represent the degrees of membership of things in sets as Zadeh has done for concepts such as age—young, middle-aged, and old—based on mapping linguistic concepts to numerical formulas.[14]

Consider the notion of tallness. One can present, as George Lakoff showed, a subjective linguistic intuition of how height relates to "tallness" in the population of contemporary America[15] (table 4.1). Suppose that John is tall to the degree of 0.7 according to Lakoff's linguistic intuition; therefore he is not tall to the degree of 0.3. Consider the statement "John is tall and not tall," which normally seems to be a contradiction but under this interpretation of his membership in the fuzzy set of tall people may not be a contradiction at all. Relative to some people John *is* in fact *tall* and relative to others *not* tall. Recognizing that one need not assign the value of only true or false to the statement

Table 4.1

Height	5'3"	5'5"	5'7"	5'9"	5'11"	6'1"	6'3"
Degree of Tallness	0	0.1	0.3	0.55	0.8	0.95	1.0

"John is tall," Zadeh noted the possibility of establishing a three-valued logic within the bounded relationship $0 < \beta < \alpha < 1$ such that

(1) "x belongs to A" if $f_A(x) \geq \alpha$; (2) "x does not belong to A" if $f_A(x) \leq \beta$; and (3) "x has an indeterminate status relative to A" if $\beta < f_A(x) < \alpha$.

This leads to a three-valued logic (Kleene, 1952) with three truth values: $T(f_A(x) \geq \alpha)$, $F(f_A(x) \leq \beta)$, and $U(\beta < f_A(x) < \alpha)$.[16]

My strategy is to explore the semantic markers of the referents of metaphors and to interpret them in terms of the semantic truth values of Zadeh's notion of a fuzzy set. The truth values of these attributes express the degree to which each attribute of the referent of the metaphor can be a member in the set of attributes defined by a literal reading of that referent. The interpretation of the metaphor determines which attribute of the referent must be measured in terms of membership in the set defined by the literal meaning of that referent. I am forced to compare two kinds of attributes for the same referent: (1) those presented by the metaphorical interpretation and (2) those presented by a literal interpretation.

Recall the metaphor "The locomotive is in bed." One might construct a scale of membership for persons in the sets of "locomotives" and "roundhouses" in the set of "beds." On the surface it seems as if a "person" could not be a member of the set of "locomotives" unless one separates the attributes of both "locomotives" and "persons" and compares those that are similar and those that are dissimilar. Perhaps the less likely the membership of "person" in the set of "locomotives," the more diaphoric the metaphor. Assume that in ordinary language "locomotives" are a proper subset of the semantic marker Inanimate and that "persons" are a proper subset of Animate. In ordinary circumstances, an individual locomotive seems to be a paradigm example of an entity with a membership $f_A(x)$ value of 1 in the set Inanimate. But in the metaphor the membership function shifts to a value less than 1 as one begins to see the similarity between the dynamism of a person and the obvious dynamism of the locomotive engine. The metaphor may become less diaphoric. If we set the value of β low enough on Zadeh's scale, $0 < \beta < \alpha < 1$, and if an individual person has a degree of membership greater then β for the metaphor "The locomotive is in bed," then no contradiction need be produced. Let me extend Zadeh's three-valued logic to a four-valued logic based on the interval $0 < \beta < \gamma < \alpha < 1$. The truth values are now T ($f_A(x) \geq \alpha$), F ($f_A(x) \leq \beta$), D ($\beta < f_A(x) < \gamma$), and E ($\gamma \leq f_A(x) < \alpha$). As α approaches 1 and β approaches 0, if there are no members of the set with intermediate values, we have the situation of a classical two-valued logic.

But for metaphors whose referents have values in the ranges of D and E, we can speak of diaphors and epiphors. Under this description of a range of likely and unlikely association, metaphors yield degrees of truth, falsity, diaphor, and epiphor.

My four-valued logic (T, F, D, and E), defined by membership in a fuzzy set, offers the possibility of eliminating the contradiction between the semantic markers of the referents of a metaphor. The clash of Animate and Inanimate need not produce an outright contradiction in the metaphor "The locomotive is in bed." If considered as a person, "locomotive," an inanimate object, is a member of the fuzzy set Animate to a degree within the range D. We have produced a diaphoric suggestion rather than a false statement. If "roundhouse" can be thought of as functionally a member of Animate of degree D or E, then considering a "roundhouse" to be a "bed" generates a legitimate metaphor. By allowing the semantic markers of the referents of a metaphor to admit degrees of membership, it is possible to have unusual and creative juxtapositions of semantic meanings.

One may question whether any metaphors are produced in the ranges of T and F in the semantic markers of the referents of a metaphor. Because one can probably imagine at least some minimal analogy between any two or more juxtaposed referents, would the likelihood be great of producing falsity for the membership of one of those referents in the fuzzy set defined by a pertinent semantic marker? Probably not, for we usually discard those word combinations that do not produce at least enough similarity of features to warrant calling them diaphors. Similarly, could one produce a metaphor whose referents existed in the T range of membership in the fuzzy set defined by a pertinent semantic marker? Again probably not because referents so similar that they produce almost full rather than partial membership in the fuzzy set defined by the pertinent semantic marker would produce a combination of words that was no longer a metaphor but an analogy. If few metaphors have referents that fall into the T and F ranges of membership of the fuzzy sets defined by pertinent semantic markers, then why construct a four-valued range of membership? Why not define membership in fuzzy sets in terms of two values—diaphor and epiphor? Such a move would deny that metaphors can be true or false; rather, they would be epiphoric or diaphoric. I resist that move because I believe that there are juxtapositions of referents that are most unlikely and therefore false and juxtapositions of referents that possess so many similarities that they are analogies rather than metaphors. I have already described metaphor as possibly traversing a path from diaphor to epiphor to ordinary language. As the referents of a metaphor move from E to T in their range of membership of a referent in the fuzzy set of a semantic marker, the metaphor becomes a well-recognized analogy and finally, when commonplace, a dead metaphor and part of ordinary language. The four-valued logic of membership of a referent in a fuzzy set defined by a semantic marker allows metaphor to be a part of a general theory of semantics rather than a special case. By locating D and E between T and F, I am not claiming that metaphors are completely excluded from considerations of truth and falsity but rather that they are between the two; a metaphor may be close to T or F and through usage become T or through the falsification of a hypothetical scientific metaphor become F.

Through continued use a metaphor such as "The locomotive is in bed" may change the value of the function $f_A(x)$ that associates "person" with "locomotive." If we speak of a specific person as a locomotive, we may become quite comfortable with an association that seemed at first startling and diaphoric. We may even begin to speak of a class of "persons" as "locomotives," for example, football linemen or dynamic business executives. By using a metaphor repeatedly, we fix the association of the referents and may change a diaphor into an epiphor, and if the metaphor becomes common enough, finally drive it into ordinary language. At the last stage, the metaphor dies and exists no longer as a metaphor. Not all metaphors go through all or even part of this process; some diaphors are so suggestive that they remain diaphors and are not transformed into epiphors. Metaphors that are transformed by usage can be described as having referents whose membership in classes of attributes move along the scale $0 < \beta < \gamma < \alpha < 1$.

So far I have argued that by locating the attributes of the referents of a metaphor in fuzzy sets, I can avoid the charge that metaphors are illegitimate linguistic entities that produce contradictions. I have not, however, explained how these new associations of referents (including the new association of the attributes of the referents) can generate new semantic meanings. To explore this problem, I return to Zadeh and examine his characterization of meaning in terms of fuzzy sets.[17]

Zadeh begins his quest for a definition of meaning by defining a kernel space K as a prescribed set of objects that could be almost anything—lines, numbers, smells, objects in the world, etc.[18] He lets A be a fuzzy subset of K, where μ_A is a membership function (similar to $f_A(x)$) that associates each element w of K with its grade of membership $\mu_A(w)$ in K. Like $f_A(x)$, $\mu_A(w)$ is a number in the interval $[0,1]$. Zadeh next defines a universe of discourse as "a designated (not necessarily proper) subset of E," giving the following informal description of universe of discourse and formal definition of E:[19]

Informally, the "universe of discourse" is a collection of objects, U, that is rich enough to make it possible to identify any concept, within a specified set of concepts, with a fuzzy subset of U.

One way of constructing such a collection is to start with a kernel space K and generate other collections by forming unions, direct products, and collections of fuzzy subsets. Thus, let $A + B$ (rather than $A \cup B$) denote the union of A and B, let $A \times B$ denote the direct product of A and B; and let $\mathcal{F}(A)$ denote the collection of all fuzzy (as well as nonfuzzy) subsets of A. Then, with K as a generating element, we can formally construct expressions such as

$$E = K + K^2 + \ldots + K^r,$$
$$E = K + K^2 + \mathcal{F}(K),$$
$$E = K + K^2 + K \times \mathcal{F}(K),$$
$$E = K + K^2 + \mathcal{F}(\mathcal{F}(K)),$$
$$E = K + K^2 + (\mathcal{F}(K))^2.$$

The universe of discourse U can be much richer and more definite than the original kernel space K because U is a subset of E, where E can represent any number of different relationships and subsets.

Again let me apply Zadeh's theory to my analysis of metaphor. Consider the metaphor, "The telephone is my umbilical cord to the world," similar to the earlier example, "The locomotive is in bed." Here we have the problem of juxtaposing the inanimate attributes of a telephone with the animate attributes of an umbilical cord, which is similar to combining attributes of locomotives with beds. In the example of "The telephone is my umbilical cord to the world," K is the set of all physical objects in the world, A is "telephone," B is "human bodies," $\mathcal{F}(K)$ includes the combination of A and B, K^2 includes the product $A \times B$, and K^3 includes the relation of a line of communication for knowledge for B. The universe of discourse U is written as

$$E = K + K^2 + K^3 + \mathcal{F}(K).$$

Now consider Zadeh's approach to defining meaning in terms of fuzzy sets to see if this development can be extended to metaphors. Zadeh defines meaning as follows:

> Consider two spaces: (a) a universe of discourse, U and (b) a set of terms, T, which play the roles of names of fuzzy subsets of U. Let the generic elements of T and U be denoted by x and y, respectively. Our definition of the meaning of x may be stated as follows.
>
> *Definition* 5. Let x be a term in T. Then the *meaning* of x, denoted

by $M(x)$, is a fuzzy subset of U characterized by a membership function $\mu(y|x)$ which is conditioned on x. $\mu(y|x)$ may be specified in various ways, e.g., by a table or by a formula, or by an algorithm, or by exemplification, or in terms of other membership functions.[20]

Zadeh intended to keep y as a variable and measure the degree to which y was an x as the meaning of x, $M(x)$, by constructing an algorithm or table or intuition for the function $\mu(y|x)$. He presents the example of defining red from the sets of colors (T) that include red and the examples of defining young, middle-aged, and old in terms of algorithms operating on the set of integers from 0 to 100. But consider what happens when x is not a name to be defined in terms of y but another term other than x. Instead of trying to define the name red in terms of the meaning of red, $M(\text{red})$, let us attempt to define red in terms of the degree to which it represents something other than the color red. Consider red in "The reds crossed the border," where "red" means "communist." In a metaphor we seek to define a name in terms of some other name rather than in terms of the meaning of itself.

Consider the metaphor, "Thoughts are prisons," taken from the line, "Make not your thoughts your prisons" (Shakespeare, *Antony and Cleopatra*, Act V, Scene II, line 184). If "prison" is taken figuratively as a conceptual limit, then we are faced with the partial membership of a nonphysical entity, a conceptual limit in the fuzzy set defined by the semantic marker Physical. The membership of "conceptual limit" has to be within the range greater than β on the four-valued scale of membership in the fuzzy set defined by the semantic marker Physical in order to produce at least a diaphor. The selection of "conceptual limit" for "prison," however, involves choosing from a myriad of possible interpretations for prison. The actual selection is a psychological process and awaits further development, but Zadeh does allow for a semantical hierarchy in this process of choosing a meaning for a referent.

Let us analyze the association of "prison" with "thought," holding the latter constant and searching for a figurative meaning for the former. The meaning of "prison" under Zadeh's scheme is defined by the subset $M(x)$ of U that is determined by the membership function $\mu(y|x)$, a measure of the association of the degree to which "prisons" can be identified with "thoughts." The set T could be the set "buildings with bars" or "conceptual limits." These sets are subsets of each other, and for a metaphor the selection of a particular T becomes crucial to the question of how the element x in T can be mapped to $M(x)$ in U identified with a different y. If we choose T to be "buildings with bars," then it becomes difficult to see how to relate a "thought" (y) with a "prison" (x). One has to select T in such a manner that the attribute of "prison" that defines T allows an association with the y in U that produces $M(x)$. I have varied T and could also vary U because I want to define "prison" in terms of "conceptual limit" and not in terms of "buildings with bars."

Zadeh defines a hierarchy of subsets of U to establish the possibility of levels of meaning.

> *Definition* 9. Let K be the kernel space of U, the universe of discourse. Then a term x and the corresponding concept $M(x)$ are at *level* 1 if $M(x)$ is a subset of K or, more generally, K^n, $n = 1, 2, \ldots$, for some finite n; x and $M(x)$ are at level 2 if $M(x)$ is a subset of $\mathscr{F}(K)$ or $(\mathscr{F}(K))^n$ for some finite n; and, more generally, x and $M(x)$ are at level l if $M(x)$ is a subset of $(\mathscr{F}^{l-1}(K))^n$ for some finite n, where $\mathscr{F}^{l-1}(K)$ stands for $\mathscr{F}(\ldots \mathscr{F}(\mathscr{F}(K)))$, with $l - 1$ $\mathscr{F}$'s in the expression. Equivalently, and recursively, we can say that $M(x)$ is a concept at level l if $M(x)$ is a collection of concepts at level $l - 1$.[21]

This definition generates a hierarchy of concepts that defines sets of objects correlating an increase in abstractness and generality with an increase in level. The concepts white, red, brown, etc. are at level 1; the concept color at level 2; and the concept visual object at level 3. If one insists that the x and y that define $M(x)$ be at the same level, then my account of metaphor as possessing two referents that are members of fuzzy sets might fail, for the level of one referent might be different from that of the other. The fuzzy subset of T, "conceptual limit," that allows a "prison" to be interpreted as a "thought" might indeed be different from the "nonphysical" or "mutual" of the set U that defines "thought." Further, fuzzy relations for metaphors at a lower level may change membership at a higher level. When the word "prison" can be understood as a "thought," the value of the membership of "prison" in the fuzzy set defined by the semantic marker Physical changes, for to some small degree we may after comprehending the metaphor "Thought is a prison" come to understand "prisons" as nonphysical. The conflict of levels of meaning often occurs in diaphors, whose referents are suggestive and hypothetical.

When Zadeh defines $M(x)$ as a "fuzzy concept, or simply a concept,"[22] he raises the question of whether he has really defined the meaning of x as $M(x)$. In picking out $M(x)$ in U, how do we know what to look for unless we already have some notion of the attributes of x? If we want to know the meaning of red, how can we find $M(red)$ without already knowing intuitively the color of a red object? If red is an uninterpreted term in T and $M(x)$ is a concept, then the best that we can have is an intensional definition of the meaning of red. But Zadeh might reply that $\mu(y \mid x)$ maps x to an object in the universe of discourse and that U can be composed of either conceptual or physical objects. If the latter holds, then by assigning the membership of x to U, we are ostensively mapping the term x to an object. But how do we know what object to put into a subset in U so that when we assigned an x to it, it turns out to be red? In this problem, Zadeh stands no worse off then anyone else who has attempted to present a completely adequate and noncircular definition of meaning. His claim that $M(x)$ *is* a concept might be modified to the claim that $M(x)$ *defines* a concept to avoid the interpretation of u as solely intensionally defined.

If $M(x)$ *defines* or *characterizes* a concept rather than being one, this move allows enough leeway that when $M(x)$ changes as it does in metaphors, our concepts change similarly. To further investigate just how meanings can change in the context of fuzzy sets, let me present a definition of metaphor as an extension of Zadeh's definition of meaning. Although it was possible to interpret an x in T different from the y in U to achieve an $M(x)$, in many metaphors, as Max Black claimed long ago, there exists an interaction and both $M(x)$ and $M(y)$ change.[23] Using Zadeh's definition I note only a change in $M(x)$:

> *Definition of Metaphor:* Let U be formed from K as an E; let A and B be subsets of U, where $x \in A$ and $y \in B$; let $M(z)$ be the subset of U formed by $\mu(x|y)$ $A \times B$ and $\mu(y|x)$ $B \times A$. Let $M(z)$ define the metaphor z, where $z \in T$.

$A \times B$ maps each x in A into a y in B; $B \times A$ maps a y in B into an x in A. $M(z)$ is defined as the union of these two maps with $\mu(x|z)$ and $\mu(y|z)$ defined by the minimum value of $\mu(x|y)$ and $\mu(y|x)$, respectively. In this definition of metaphor, both A and B can be fuzzy, and the series of relationships that define $\mu(x|y)$ and $\mu(y|x)$ can be fuzzy. This definition of a metaphor allows the computation of the values of $M(x)$, $M(y)$, and $M(z)$, namely, the values of each of the two referents of the metaphor and a new meaning, $M(z)$, for the metaphor itself.

Because Zadeh allowed K to be defined either intensionally or extensionally, metaphors can compare entities in the physical world with each other, an entity in the physical world with an imaginary thing, or two imaginary things with each other. By defining U to include both sets of physical entites and sets of fictional things, diaphors can be produced. Let us return to the example of "The locomotive is in bed" to see how this definition of metaphor actually operates:

K_1 = objects,
A = locomotives,
B = persons,
C = beds,
N = animate objects,
I = inanimate objects,

$U_1 = E_1 = K_1 \times K_1^2 \times \mathscr{F}(K_1)$, where $\mathscr{F}(K_1) = A \times B \times C \times N \times I$ and $K_1^2 =$ persons that sleep in bed.

$\mu(x|y)$ is defined by the degree to which locomotives are persons; $\mu(y|x)$ is defined by the degree to which persons are locomotives. $M_1(z)$ is defined by the set defined by the union of $\mu(x|y)$ and $\mu(y|x)$.

This interpretation yields both a dynamic person resting in bed *and* the ambiguous possibility that a locomotive rests in a bed, a piece of furniture. If $\mu(x|y)$ is small, a value less than β in the earlier scale, then we can rule out this possibility as false.

Now consider a second interpretation of "The locomotive is in bed":

$K_2 =$ objects,
$A =$ beds,
$B =$ roundhouses,
$C =$ locomotives,
$N =$ animate objects,
$I =$ inanimate objects,
$U_2 = E_2 = K_2 \times K_2^2 \times \mathscr{F}(K_2)$, where $\mathscr{F}(K_2) = A \times B \times C \times N \times I$ and $K_2^2 =$ locomotives that are located in roundhouses.

$\mu(x|y)$ is defined by the degree to which beds are roundhouses. $\mu(y|x)$ is defined by the degree to which roundhouses are beds. $M_2(z)$ is defined by the set defined by the union of $\mu(x|y)$ and $\mu(y|x)$.

Here we have a locomotive in a literal bed if a bed can be a roundhouse with a value greater than β and a locomotive in a roundhouse if a bed can be identified with a roundhouse.

Suppose now that we want to leave the metaphor "The locomotive is in bed" ambiguous as to interpretation: the "dynamic person in bed" or the "locomotive in its roundhouse." Without a context in which to locate this metaphor, both and even perhaps other interpretations might be possible. The ambiguous meaning can be represented by

$$M_{\text{amb}}(z) = M_1(z) \times M_2(z).$$

Zadeh's fuzzy-set theory offers a possible theoretical interpretation for metaphors that avoids the charge that metaphors produce contradictions and generate impossible meanings. Modifications of Zadeh's theory allow me to claim further that we can construct a range of truth values that includes the traditional true and false and also diaphor and epiphor ($0 < \beta < \gamma < \alpha < 1$). We can even construct metaphors that remain ambiguous in their interpretation when no context exists to aid us in selection of a particular meaning.

The analysis of semantic markers of the referents of a metaphor by fuzzy sets not only applies to metaphors of the form "*A* is *B*" (noun metaphors) but also succeeds with verb metaphors. As Brooke-Rose noted, verb metaphors tend to be much more complicated but they can be examined in terms of semantic markers because they change nouns "implicitly rather than explicitly."[24] In the metaphor "You must try to root out your faults one by one," quoted by Brooke-Rose, the verb "root" (pulling out plants or weeds) has Physical as one of its semantic markers, whereas "faults" (character traits) has Nonphysical as one of its semantic markers. "To root" can be taken figuratively as meaning the elimination of an undesirable trait, and thus a nonphysical activity has a partial membership in the fuzzy set defined by the semantic marker Physical. Or one can take "faults" to be physical in the sense of being "weeds," and physical activity has a partial membership in the fuzzy set defined by the semantic marker Nonphysical. An analysis for "root" and "faults" in terms of my adaptation of Zadeh's definition follows the lines of that presented for "locomotive" and "bed."

The analysis of the semantic markers of the referents of a metaphor in terms of fuzzy sets provides the opportunity for semantic change to occur without the charge of contradiction. I have yet to present rules for these changes; I have given no description of how words are organized in their normal association and how changes of these associations can occur. Before proceeding to that task, let us question whether fuzzy sets do in fact describe the ways in which people classify entities in the world. Is the adoption of fuzzy-set theory so abstract as to be unrealistic for a description of how metaphors operate semantically in ordinary language? To justify my adoption of fuzzy-set theory, I attempt to demonstrate that it is compatible with the work of Eleanor Rosch on the categorization of terms in language.

Prototypical Categories

Eleanor Rosch, as I noted in chapter 3, developed a theory of categorization that explored the formation of categories in cultures and found universal adherence to certain prototypes that describe a basic category in terms of a family of resemblance rather than defining that category by means of a series of attributes.[25] Membership in a category is determined by the perceived distance of resemblance of the entity to the prototype. Robins, for example, serve as a prototype for the category bird, whereas turkeys and penguins, although birds, are not considered to be as representative of that category as robins, sparrows, or blue jays are. Turkeys and penguins seem to the average language user to stand further away from the concept of being a bird.

Thus, in the sentence "Twenty or so birds often perch on the telephone wires outside my window and twitter in the morning," the term "sparrow" may readily be substituted for "bird" but the result turns ludicrous by substitution of "turkey," an effect which is not simply a matter of frequency.[26]

Basic categories formed by prototypes have a level of abstraction that presents the maximum information with the least cognitive effort. Rosch also believes that the world provides structured information, basic objects that have salient features presenting the perceiver with natural categories. Above these natural categories stand superordinate categories, which are more abstract and more comprehensive. Superordinate to the category bird is the category of animal. Below natural categories stand subordinate categories that are less abstract and less comprehensive, for example, robin and turkey. Relationships among natural categories, superordinate categories, and subordinate categories present a structured hierarchical organization of language used in the description and interpretation of the world. Natural categories are of crucial importance to this hierarchy and derive their existence from basic objects. Basic objects are the ways in which nature is perceived to cut itself at its own joints.

A working assumption of the research on basic objects is that (1) in the perceived world, information-rich bundles of perceptual and functional attributes occur that form natural discontinuities, and that (2) basic cuts in categorization are made at these discontinuities. Suppose that basic objects (e.g., chair, car) are at the most inclusive level at which there are attributes common to all or most members of the category. Then both total cue validities and category resemblance are maximized at that level of abstraction at which basic objects are categorized. That is, categories one level more abstract will be superordinate categories (e.g., furniture, vehicle) whose members share only a few attributes among each other. Categories below the basic level will be bundles of common and, thus, predictable attributes and functions but contain many attributes that overlap with other categories (for example, kitchen chair shares most of its attributes with other kinds of chairs).[27]

One might wonder whether Rosch's natural categories really do derive their character from basic objects in the world or whether, instead, so-called "natural" categories are projections of cognitive categories onto the world.[28] Rosch denies both the strong and weak forms of the linguistic relativity thesis by citing the evidence of the universality of the use of color terms in languages. Berlin and Kay demonstrated in their classic study of color terms that languages that vary widely in nature and location use the same sequential pattern of eleven basic color names.

Rosch's theory poses a serious challenge to my account of the semantic aspects of the referents of metaphors as defined by fuzzy semantic markers on two counts: (1) If categories arise from prototypes, then why should one worry about semantic markers as forming the basis of semantic meaning? (2) Even if one could justify the use of semantic markers as compatible with prototypes, then isn't the intrusion of fuzzy-set theory, because of its abstract nature, antithetical to the notion of "natural" categories? Rosch objects to the componential analysis of semantic categories, elements of which I have presumed for the assignment of semantic markers to the referents of a metaphor, on the grounds that this is a "digital" presentation of categories that may obscure the "analog" approach presuming prototypes.

In a number of fields, the semantic categories of natural languages are treated in a manner similar to the concept formation paradigm. A major trend in linguistics (cf. Katz and Postal, 1964) is to treat semantic categories as bundles of discrete "features" which determine how the words can be used in sentences. Features, loosely speaking, are those characteristics of nouns we can describe with adjectives. In these terms, the meaning of "girl" might be represented by such features as +animate, +young, −male. These features clearly differentiate the category from all others and also render each category instance logically comparable to all others, in that instances are alike in possessing the combination of features. . . .

Undoubtedly, some categories and some kinds of processing of categories do involve digital codes. The "technical" criteria for membership in those categories that have technical criteria (explained below) are probably a case in point. However, the model of categories provided by artificial concept identification research may be pernicious in that researchers have, thereby, tended to neglect other types of categories and category codes which may be more appropriate to the way natural categories are formed and coded in cognition and more appropriate for cross-cultural comparisons.[29]

Rosch's task and mine are different, for she wants to describe how categories emerge in cultures and I wish to reconstruct rationally a process by which individuals can comprehend metaphors. This latter task involves an abstract, theoretical description of how the mind processes a metaphor at the semantic level sufficiently to understand it.

Rosch, on the other hand, wants to see how the categories that we employ in language emerge from the world as natural categories. She may be largely correct in her description; the language that we speak may to a large degree be determined by how we perceive nature to be cutting itself at its joints. I do not claim in opposing her theory of categorization that linguistic concepts arise from the mental reification of features that have been perceived in the world. I do claim, however, that when we utter the word chair, we possess conceptual knowledge of its semantics: that a chair is Inanimate, a piece of furniture, used to sit on, etc. When we use the word girl we associate with it +Animate, +Human, +Female, and +Young. Within Rosch's own theory, room exists for the existence of these semantic markers as superordinate and subordinate categories. Rosch's presumption of a structured hierarchy of categories above that include categories below corresponds to hyponymy in componential analysis. Claiming prototypes for natural categories builds a bridge from the hierarchy to the physical world. Centering her attention on these bridges, Rosch reminds us of the natural and cultural aspects of language as having been overlooked in widespread concerns to the construction of rational reconstructions of the syntax and semantics of language. To explain how semantic change operates to permit the comprehension of metaphors requires a return to abstraction; I am concerned legitimately with the semantic features of words, the referents of metaphors. If one attempts to construct a theory describing the semantics of metaphor solely on the basis of natural categories or on the basis of ordinary language, such an explanation will be extremely limited. Although metaphor does occur as a *natural*, creative human process, it does not follow that it can only be explained in terms of *natural* language. That conclusion wrongly follows from an equivocation on the word natural. Chemical reactions are quite natural in the sense that they occur in nature, but that does not mean that an explanation of such reactions must be confined to nonabstract *natural* descriptions.

Now to the second question, which I rephrase as: Can fuzzy sets be introduced to represent both semantic markers (the superordinate and subordinate categories of Rosch's hierarchy) and natural categories? Rosch finds no objection to the fuzziness of the boundaries of natural categories because the distance between a target word and its prototype remains vague. She states, "Most, if not all, categories do not have clear-cut boundaries."[30] Rosch also cites the work on "hedges" by Lakoff that I have already partially presented as an illustration of fuzzy-set theory as applied to language. Natural categories as well as superordinate and subordinates categories can be better represented by fuzzy sets than by classical sets with discrete boundaries.

Although logic and psychology may treat categories as though membership is "either–or" and all members have a full and equal degree of membership, natural languages themselves possess linguistic mechanisms for coding and coping with gradients of category and membership. In English there are qualifying terms and phrases which Lakoff (1972) calls "hedges" (terms such as "almost," "virtually"). Lakoff pointed out that even people who insist that statements such as "A robin is a bird" and "A penguin is a bird" are equally "true," would have to admit that different hedges were applicable to statements of category membership for the two birds. Thus, it is correct to say that a penguin is "technically" a bird but not that a robin is "technically" a bird because a robin is more than just "technically" a bird; it is a bird par excellence.[31]

Thus my use of fuzzy sets to represent the semantic markers of the referents of metaphor is not disputed in Rosch's theory. And my adoption of semantic markers can be subsumed in her theory as subordinate and superordinate categories derived from natural categories. Rosch's task and mine with respect to semantics are quite different however; where she deals with culture, I develop an abstract description of a linguistic process that eventually will be related both to the natural categories and to a cognitive process.

Semantic Trees

The discovery that the semantic markers of the referents of a metaphor can be represented as fuzzy sets and that semantic markers can exist in a hierarchy of categories does not describe how these markers are related in that hierarchy. The semantic markers of a metaphor's referents are not only fuzzy categories but also words. The problem of how disparate semantic markers can be combined meaningfully is also the problem of how to link words together that are not normally associated. Fuzzy sets that allow degrees of membership offer the possibility of varying truth values according to the degree of membership; I have proposed a four-valued logic ($F,D,E,$ and T) as a method of avoiding outright contradictions in metaphors. The tree diagram has been a favorite method of organization for many semanticists wishing to represent relationships among words in a hierarchical structure.[32] As one moves down the branches of the tree, words become less abstract and their generality diminishes. Nodes above a word dominate the nodes (and words) below it. Consider the tree diagram (figure 4.1) for the word boy.

At the level of $+$Male$/-$Male, one can question whether $+$Young$/$ $-$Young should be above or below $+$Male. Is the consideration of

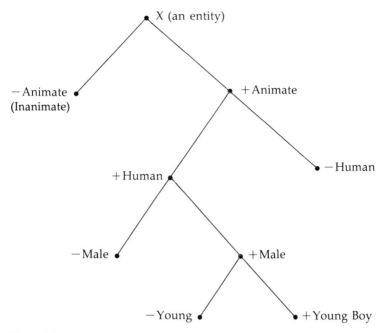

Figure 4.1
Tree diagram for the word boy.

being young or old more or less general than that of being male or female? One might be tempted to argue that saying all humans are either male or female is more general than saying many people are at the borderline between youth and old age. But because I have represented all semantic markers, including those of sex and age, in fuzzy sets, the degree of membership has little to do with the range of generality. One might argue that there are males who are not young, and therefore +Male should be above +Young, but one could conversely argue that there are those who are +Young and are not Males, and therefore +Young should be above +Male. No decisive answer to this question seems possible. But is this question important?

If one constructs a tree diagram for the semantic meaning of two words and the same semantic markers appear at different levels in each tree, then one can wonder whether the degree of generality of semantic markers varies according to the word described rather than according to a hierarchical pattern found in the linguistic world. One can also wonder whether there exists a minimum number of semantic markers that describes all the words in a language in an interrelated pattern. If one constructs a tree diagram for every word in the English language, can one superimpose these trees onto a massive supertree of more than two dimensions since the same semantic markers would have an incredibly large number of branches radiating from a single node? Conceptually this seems at least possible; envision the supertree as having n dimensions, where n is defined by the maximum number of branches emanating from a single node. (Later, I will challenge the possibility of a fixed hierarchical pattern for this conception of a supertree.) The number of nodes necessary for this supertree would be enormous because so many specialized words require esoteric nodes with few branches. Consider the word haversack, which would have to be differentiated in a tree from closely related words such as knapsack and backpack. Being "canvas" and having a "single shoulder strap" would distinguish it from knapsacks and from backpacks, which are usually carried on the back. But the function of a haversack would also have to be presented in order to differentiate it from women's pocketbooks that also can be "canvas" and have a "single shoulder strap." The degree of specialization for so many words becomes so minute that one may wonder about the usefulness of the supertree. One might reply, however, that at least something similar to the supertree exists in our semantic memory, and it prevents us from making egregious mistakes in associating phrases such as "He entered the hospital and underwent an abortion."

Some critics of language believe that interpreting semantic meaning in terms of the associations of words in trees can produce a method of preventing unintentional ambiguity. Among those who have tried to untangle semantic ambiguity is Fred Sommers, who attempted to employ tree diagrams as "logical maps" that "enforce ambiguity."[33] Sommers approached the problem of ambiguity by adopting the notion of a linguistic map in which the location of an expression determines its sense.

> We must therefore keep in mind that a map of sense relations giving the locations of a group of expressions does not tell the whole story of "their use in the language," i.e., their meanings. Nevertheless, we shall see that such a map removes ambiguity, ensuring univocity for the expressions located on it. For this reason we shall identify the sense of an expression with its location on a map. This entails a distinction between *sense* and *meaning*, a distinction which we shall enforce rather than justify. The *sense* of an expression will be its location with respect to other expressions, its semantic range. It is what it "makes sense" with as contrasted with what it fails to make sense with. Its *meaning* is governed only in part by sense rules. "Tall" and "short" may have the same

"sense"; it is because of other rules governing their use that they diverge in meaning. Thus, giving the sense of an expression is not yet the same as giving its meaning. One who wishes to know more about the meaning of a given located expression will enquire at that address.[34]

To construct the map, Sommers begins with an analysis of how various terms in subject–predicate relationships can be associated. Expressions that can be properly related are said to have the sense relation U. Examples of U-related sense-pairs are (tall, tree) and (sensation, itch). To expression-pairs that cannot be related, such as (anger, tree), (mood, itch), and (anger, valid), Sommers gives the designation of N for their non-sense value. For pairs for which one cannot give the value U or N, Sommers assigns the value D. Euipped with the values U, N, and D, Sommers then extends the applications of these relationships to triads of expressions. From U (bench, new), U (theorem, new) one cannot infer U (bench, theorem), but rather N (bench, theorem). Similarly, from U (game, lasts all winter) and U (toothache, lasts all winter) one obtains N (game, toothache). From these and many other triads, Sommers derives the relationship of $U(AB)$ and $U(AC)$ produces $N(BC)$ as defining what it means to say that a term is "higher than" other terms on a map. Figure 4.2 shows the origin of the basic element of the linguistic map, namely the *tree*. Defining a term as being higher than others, however, does not tell us whether it is related to the terms below it univocally or equivocally. "Lasts all winter" is related univocally to "game" and "toothache," whereas "circular" is higher than "apple" and "argument" and yet remains equivocally related to them. To identify equivocality, Sommers makes the following assumption:

If A occurs as higher than B and C then there is no expression D such that either B or C occurs as higher than A and D. Thus, if $U(AB)$ $U(AC)$ $N(BC)$, then there is no D such that either $U(DB)N(AD)$ or $U(CD)N(AD)$.[35]

From these assumptions, he derives a rule $R(U)$ as necessary to prevent an expression A from being both above B and C and yet also below B or C due to equivocality:[36]

$$R(U): N(AD)[U(BD) \lor U(CD)] \supset \neg [U(AB)U(AC)N(BC)].$$

This rule "enforces ambiguity" by splitting the sense of words such as "circular" into two different locations on the language tree when applied to "apple" and "argument."

The notion of a series of language trees, each with a univocal sense, forms the heart of Sommers's program for disambiguation. Whenever one faces the problem of semantic ambiguity, one should determine

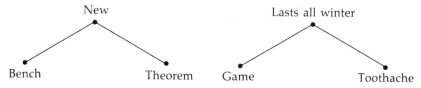

Figure 4.2
Two tree diagrams demonstrating linguistic maps.

the nodes of the tree by word associations involving the U(AB)U(AC)N(BC) rules and determine equivocality by considering further associations with terms like *D, E, F*, etc. to see if *R(U)* holds, and if it does not, then a second and perhaps a third tree will have to be constructed to handle the equivocal senses.

When confronted with equivocity, Sommers, as I have noted, splits the sense of a word and gives it two locations on the language tree.[37] He considers the pairs (human, reasonable) and (argument, reasonable) and decides that there must be two senses of "reasonable" and thus two nodes on the tree for that word. If one pursues this line of reasoning, then words with many senses will have many nodes, and questions arise as to whether these nodes should be on the same level or some above others and whether the various uses of a word produce new senses that make the tree proliferate so rapidly that a single unified tree becomes impossible.[38] If one allows a metaphoric use of words, then the tree seems to grow in a complicated and even perhaps contradictory manner. Sommers allows for metaphor but enjoins against letting metaphors express contradictions.

> If, metaphorically, I wish to speak of an itch as a mood or a mood as an itch, then to be consistent in my metaphor I must also allow for the sense of "My mood was on my chest" or any other place on the body. Carrying a metaphor through consistently is nothing more than giving it those sense relations which the data sentences of ordinary language have. . . .[39]

> Inconsistency is therefore an added prohibition dependent upon the non-violation of category rules defined by the tree structure.[40]

The latter restriction severely limits the range of metaphor since many do express contradictions and not just category mistakes if taken literally. By contending that "univocity is locatability" and by assigning each univocal sense of a word to a different location on the tree, Sommers produces either a whole series of separate trees in which each tree is given its character by the context of the expression or a single tree that is so snarled and tangled with its new growth of metaphor that it no longer guarantees that the nodes of one expression are always higher than others.[41] Both productions are disastrous for Sommers's program of giving sense to language and enforcing ambiguity by the rules of a linguistic map.

Metaphors, however, may yield even more dire results for the language tree than those just noted above, for the very distinction between the U-relationship and the N-relationship rests on the notion of a grammatical category mistake. When we allow expressions to stand together in a U-relatedness, we are recognizing their usual juxtaposition, and when we deny their association in N-relatedness, we base our decision on the observation that they are not normally associated. But a metaphor juxtaposes expressions that are *not* normally related, namely, those that are N-related, and gives them a sense that may be meaningful. A metaphoric interpretation, therefore, can change an N-relationship into a U-relationship. Sommers acknowledges this possibility but then seems to pass over its consequences as he develops his language tree.[42] Sommers might resort to the distinction that he makes between sense and meaning claiming that, although the former influences the latter, meaning also derives from the context of utterance. But this distinction seems to collapse when one probes the basis on which one initially learned that there are several senses of an expression which are equivocal and which should be located at different nodes or on different trees. The different meanings in the various contexts, such as those of a "rational argument" and a "rational human," generate the different senses of the word rational. Only if we know the various meanings of a word can we determine whether it is used univocally or equivocally. The distinction between meaning and sense collapses under the need to determine equivocity.

Vagueness also presents problems for Sommers's attempt to decide whether expressions are U-related or N-related. A. G. Elgood produced several counterexamples demonstrating that terms can be U-related in one way and N-related in another.[43] Consider (trousers, 40-inch waist) and (high-heeled, shoe), which possess U-related terms, and (40-inch waist, shoe) and (high-heeled, trousers), which have N-related terms. The term waders, however, can have both "40-inch waist" and "high-heeled" as predicates so that these terms can be N-related with respect to one context and U-related in another. One wonders why there cannot be more than two branches from each node; certainly, Sommers's rules $R(U)$ would have to be changed, but such obvious counterexamples might be handled if that were possible.

Before abandoning trees altogether, let me examine more explicitly the difficulty that metaphors present for explaining ambiguity in a tree diagram. Consider the representation (figure 4.3) of the literal sense of "locomotive" from the metaphor, "The locomotive is in bed." If one

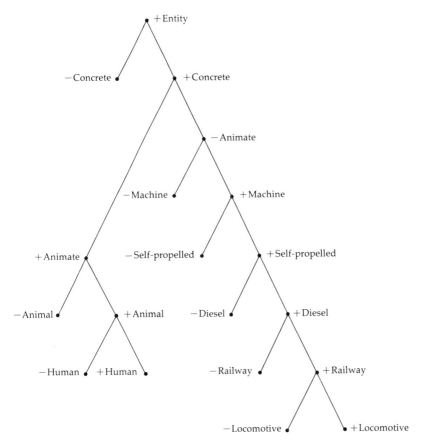

Figure 4.3
Tree diagram of the literal sense of the word locomotive.

adopts the tree diagram for locomotive then one is faced with the impossibility of juxtaposing +Locomotive with +Human, since they exist on different branches dominated by the node +Concrete. This means that a locomotive could be like a person or a person like a locomotive only in the sense of both being "concrete" objects. In the metaphor, I considered the locomotive to be a dynamic human being; I also could have considered the locomotive to be like a person, hard to start running in the morning after a long night's rest in the roundhouse (bed). In the tree diagram, because +Animate does not dominate +Locomotive, the two semantic markers cannot be juxtaposed. Sommers's solution to this problem was to develop another tree diagram with +Locomotive dominated by +Animate. Such a solution seems ad hoc and demolishes the possibility of constructing a single supertree. If one allows a new tree with rearranged semantic markers for each new metaphoric usage, then the semantic forest may become so thick as to prevent comprehension of any generality at all. We might also have two different kinds of +Animate, one when used to refer to animals and plants and another when used to refer to locomotives. Since personification occurs so often metaphorically in literature and poetry, there would be a large number of senses of +Animate. Semantic trees present definite hierarchies and a formal method of relating words with other words. That some words are related in a treelike hierarchy to other words (semantic markers) seems conclusive. The limitations of the tree for semantic ambiguity result from the rigidity of trees; if one multiplies the number of trees, then their power of generalization becomes greatly diminished. If one insists on a single supertree, then semantic change becomes difficult if not impossible.

The Semantic Differential

Among many psycholinguists the semantic differential provides the primary method for deriving semantic meaning from the association of words with other words.[44] This method, formulated by Osgood, Suci, and Tannenbaum in their widely used book, *The Measurement of Meaning* (1957), establishes a measurement scale of fifty polar adjectives: good–bad, large–small, beautiful–ugly, yellow–blue, etc. Subjects are offered a seven-point scale on which to rank the test word in relation to its perceived closeness to either polar adjective. In the ranking scale, the middle point indicates indifference between the polar terms. When the task is completed by indicating the relationship of the target word to the fifty polar pairs of adjectives, a composite relationship, called the semantic differential, can be computed for the target, and that can be called the affective meaning of the word.[45]

Selection of the fifty polar adjectives determines the very nature of affective meaning; Osgood et al. chose what they believed to be the fifty most representative polar terms taken from the 289 pairs of adjectives in *Roget's Thesaurus*. Their choice was guided by empirical tests of the frequency of normal associations of words. Cluster analysis of many semantic differentials indicated that three groups of polar pairs of adjectives entered into the majority of determinations of meaning. These groups of polar pairs, called factors, are (1) an evaluative factor, including the polar terms good–bad, optimistic–pessimistic, positive–negative, complete–incomplete, and timely–untimely; (2) potency, including hard–soft, heavy–light, masculine–feminine, severe–lenient, strong–weak, and tenacious–yielding; and (3) oriented activity, including active–passive, excitable–calm, and hot–cold. The experimentally measured associations that words have with these polar terms can be presented in a semantic space, where the number of factors used in correlation determines the dimensionality and where the distances between words and clusters of words measures in part semantic differences in meaning among those words. Not only do relative semantic meanings exist among words but also the origin point of the multidimensional space offers a point to which all meanings (semantic differentials) can be referred. The assignments of differing weights to the relation of the target word to each polar pair can be used as membership functions indicating the degree of membership in each term of the polar pair considered as a semantic marker and represented by a fuzzy set.

The semantic differential technique offers a possible way of organizing the interrelationship among words that explains affective semantic meaning—how many people organize the meaning of a term in relation to a fixed set of representative polar adjectives. In their earlier research, Osgood and his associates were severely criticized for assuming that their technique measured a more comprehensive and objective form of meaning rather than affective or subjectively perceived meaning.[46] Osgood's more recent report on his extensive study of semantic differentials in various cultures acknowledges that "affective meaning" was measured in his method.[47] The newer studies still retain, however, the concept of a semantic field derived from matrices of associations of words measured among paired polar adjectives (the semantic differential).[48]

I find two major objections to this method of ascertaining the association of words as a semantic basis for a semantics of metaphor. First, the measurements of the associations of a target word with fifty polar adjectives do not necessarily represent the normal semantic markers with which the test word is associated in ordinary language. Second, the semantic differential technique measures how people associate words under test conditions and leaves almost no room for changes in semantic meaning necessary for the intelligibility of metaphors.

By reducing the number of paired adjectives in *Roget's Thesaurus* from 289 to 50, Osgood hoped that he had produced a representative way of testing words. In componential analysis, however, the linguist attempts to associate target words with semantic markers that usually are nouns rather than adjectives. As modifiers, adjectives serve to enhance descriptions (the "yellow" dog), to evaluate objects and actions (that was a "good" play), and to make judgments (the "happy" boy (both a description and an evaluative judgment that the boy is happy)).

It is not surprising, therefore, that the most common factor selected by subjects for association with test words was evaluation. When we think of a dog, for example, we may be interested in whether he is good or bad and whether he is wet or dry, but these adjectives do not reveal what we know about the dog in terms of its semantic meaning. We know that a dog is an animal with four legs and fur, is usually domesticated, barks, and possesses a tail. Asking whether a dog is yellow or blue, or the polar pairs of adjectives of the semantic differential, does little to illuminate the semantic meaning of "dog." Because some dogs are yellow and few if any dogs are blue (some Huskies have an almost steel-blue gray), the subject can probably locate "dog" closer to yellow than blue on the semantic scale of measurement. Many associations with polar adjectives seem arbitrary and irrelevant to semantic meaning as the subject is forced by the semantic differential technique to associate target words with other words not normally associated with that word in the semantic memory. Why not associate words on the basis of lexical meaning, their semantic markers, which is a much more natural association than that of paired adjectives? Proponents of the semantic differential technique would reply that such an association would be almost impossible to measure because the number of words associated would be enormous and one would have no means of relating words distant from one another in the semantic space. The semantic space would be so vast and the number of matrices so numerous as to make the problem of measuring meaning virtually impossible. This answer resembles the problem of creating a single diagram of a supertree to represent all semantic relationships; the supertree would have to be multidimensional and hierarchical. At the ends of its branches, to account for individual nuances of words, there would have to be so many final nodes that the tree would almost topple from the weight of the ends.

The second objection to the multidimensional semantic space defined by the semantic differentials also resembles a problem encountered in considering tree diagrams as a basis for semantics: how to allow for semantic change within the theoretical semantic model. To account for semantic change, either the number of trees has to be multiplied almost endlessly or the branches of the tree have to be bent and broken to allow for the association of disparate semantic markers existing on widely separated branches. Similarly, after one has measured the semantic differential, how can one propose a new and creative association of words that violates the established affective meaning relationships? Until a metaphor had become widely enough accepted to measure a different association among words than the one normally used, no alteration in perceived meaning using the semantic differential technique would be detected. The meaning of the most vibrant, diaphoric metaphor might appear to have a null meaning or at least a strange meaning on the scale of fifty contrastive terms. This assumes, however, that one could even test a metaphor on the scale. Since only one word at a time can be measured, metaphors that are combinations of two words, not just one word, could not be measured. Even the measurement of a one-word metaphor would be different, because metaphor derives its suggestive meaning from the juxtaposition of more than one referent. The word tachyon exists as a metaphor, invented by physicists in the 1960s to embody the hypothetical meaning of a particle that travels faster than the speed of light. How does one rate "tachyon" on the semantic differential scale? Is "tachyon" closer to "good" or to "bad"? If you deny the possibility of particles traveling faster than the speed of light, you may rate it nearer "bad"; if you hope for an overthrow of the constancy of light in relativity theory, then you undoubtedly place it closer to "good." In the semantic scale many different forms of reasoning and association may occur in the subject's mind. When asked to rate a "dog" as yellow or blue, I may remember reading a story entitled "The Yellow Dog" and therefore identify "dog" closely with yellow. The subjectivity involved in rating leads to the recognition that the semantic differential technique measures *affective* rather than semantic meaning. Componential analysis seeks to avod measuring affective meaning by relying on the lexicon, a device for explaining how words are associated at any one given time. Certainly the lexicon depends on the collective usage of individuals, but these associations are ordinary, and they are used intersubjectively in communication. Objectivity in science consists in the intersubjective testability of data. A lexicon possesses this kind of objectivity. But one might argue that if lexicons are standards of objective semantic meaning, then how can metaphors that alter those forms of meaning produce creative meanings that are intersubjectively accepted as meaningful? Since metaphors seem to violate the semantic markers found in lexicons, why do we accept them? A successful reply to this challenge depends on the development of a legitimate theory of semantic change. Lexicographers readily admit that words change in meaning; if they did not, we would have little use for new dictionaries. By considering semantic markers as fuzzy sets and by constructing both a hierarchy of these markers that is not so rigid that semantic change becomes impossible and a description of how semantic change occurs according to general rules, I hope I have presented such an account.

Tree diagrams and multidimensional semantic spaces described in semantic theories do not seem to permit semantic change readily. I will argue that a much more general conception of semantic space than that offered by Osgood et al. can provide a general structure for a theory of how words are associated and how these associations can change over time. I will also argue that a much more general hierarchy exists than the strict one enforced by standard tree diagrams. Before proceeding to the development of a semantic theory that is adequate for metaphor, I need to review another necessary ingredient in the semantics of metaphor—the proposed rules for specific semantic change.

Rules for the Semantics of Metaphor

Rules for semantic change often describe how new semantic markers are added to and how old semantic markers are deleted from the list of semantic markers ordinarily associated with the semantic meaning of a word. The descriptive aspect of these rules makes them seem ad hoc because they attempt to portray semantic change after it has taken place and been comprehended. When we comprehend a metaphor such as "The locomotive is in bed," the construction of semantic rules explaining how a locomotive can be Animate or a bed Inanimate involves adding the feature Animate to Inanimate (locomotive) or Inanimate to Animate (bed), where each of the semantic markers is represented by a fuzzy set. Deeper than semantic rules for change in meaning lies a psychological account of cognition. Viewed as a knowledge process, metaphoric comprehension requires identification of both similar and dissimilar salient features accompanied by the imaginative combination and rearrangement of these features. I consider these cognitive aspects of metaphor in a later chapter; for now I am content to acknowledge the possibility of developing semantic rules that are descriptive of the change of association of semantic markers in metaphors.

Samuel Levin proposed a series of relationships of adjunction and displacement to account for change of semantic meaning in metaphor.[49] Either relationship can apply to the sample metaphor "The locomotive is in bed"; but to fit Levin's model better, modify the metaphor to "The locomotive sleeps."[50] If we interpret the metaphor ambiguously, with "locomotive" being both an "inanimate object with traction" and a "person" with degrees of membership in the fuzzy sets Animate and Inanimate representing semantic markers, then the following relationship results:

$$N(+a, +\delta, +b)/V(((+c, +d, +e)X)\langle(+\lambda)\rangle) \Rightarrow$$
$$N(+a, [+\lambda \ \& \ +\delta], +b),$$

where N is a noun (locomotive), V is a verb (sleeps), a, b are features of a locomotive, δ is Inanimate and another feature of locomotive, c, d, e are features of sleeps, λ is Animate and another feature of sleeps, and X is the element of V transported to N. In this relationship, the imagination takes the semantic marker Animate of "sleep" and juxtaposes it with the semantic marker Inanimate of "locomotive." This produces a contradiction only if "locomotives" cannot be Animate to a certain degree in a fuzzy set. In a sense, by moving λ into conjunction with δ, the membership of "locomotives" in the sets of Animate and Inanimate becomes fuzzy. Before this metaphor if one had always thought of locomotives as inanimate objects, then the occasion of the metaphor changes the membership value of "locomotive" in the set Inanimate.

Levin's relationship of displacement applies when the "locomotive" is interpreted as "person," $M(z)$ finds a value greater than α in my scale of measurement ($0 < \beta < \gamma < \alpha < 1$), false attributions are located in $\mu_A \leqslant \beta$, diaphors in $\beta < \mu_A < \gamma$, epiphors in $\gamma \leqslant \mu_A < \alpha$, and true attributions in $\mu_A \geqslant \alpha$:

$$N(+a, +\delta, +b)/V(((+c, +d, +e)X)\langle(+\lambda)\rangle) \Rightarrow N(+a, [+\lambda], +b).$$

Here Inanimate (δ) is replaced by Animate (λ). If we reverse the metaphor and claim that a literal "locomotive" rests in a roundhouse, then we can write a similar relationship of displacement in which the Animate (λ) of "sleep" is replaced by the Inanimate (δ) of "locomotive."

Levin's feature-change relationships demonstrate more precisely just how the process of moving features from one word to another occurs. These relationships, however, do not explain how we modify membership functions of words in classes. How do we shift the value of membership of "locomotive" in Inanimate or Animate? Certainly, without the possibility of membership in fuzzy sets, Levin's relationships, especially those of conjunctive adjunction, might produce contradictions. Somewhere within the brain, an imaginative process of feature modification takes place that sometimes displaces and sometimes juxtaposes. This allows us to create fuzzy sets by altering membership functions.

Levin's account of semantic change allows for only simple addition and simple displacement of semantic markers. Many semantic markers, however, find association through a complex, often hierarchical conceptual relationship. Lakoff and Johnson observed numerous conceptual relationships involved in the juxtaposition of the referents of a metaphor.[51] Among them they noted the conceptual relationships of "war" in metaphors that expressed arguments as battles and a coherence in metaphors that presumed a spatial orientation.

There is an overall external systematicity among the various spatialization metaphors, which defines coherence among them. Thus,

GOOD IS UP gives UP orientation to general well-being, and this orientation is coherent with special cases like HAPPY IS UP, HEALTH IS UP, ALIVE IS UP, CONTROL IS UP. STATUS IS UP is coherent with CONTROL IS UP.[52]

Recognizing that semantic markers may be related in an ordered function, Uriel Weinreich distinguished between semantic features (markers in my sense) that were unordered, calling them clusters, and semantic features that were ordered, calling them configurations.[53]

> We wish to distinguish sets of semantic features which are ordered and unordered. Let us call an unordered set of features a *cluster*, and an ordered set a *configuration*. We will use parentheses to symbolize both types of sets, but the symbols for features in a cluster will be separated by commas, while those in a configuration will be separated by arrows. Letting *a* and *b* be semantic features, we introduce the following definitions:
>
>   Cluster: $(a,b) = (b,a)$
>   Configuration: $(a \rightarrow b) \neq (b \rightarrow a)$
>
> Suppose the meaning of *daughter* is analyzed into the components 'female' and 'offspring.' Anyone who is a daughter is both female and an offspring; we represent the features 'female' and 'offspring' as a cluster. But suppose the meaning of *chair* is represented in terms of the features 'furniture' and 'sitting.' Whatever is a chair is 'furniture,' but it is not 'sitting': it is 'to be sat on.' We would represent this fact by saying that the features 'furniture' and 'sitting' form a configuration.
>
> A configuration (ordered set) of features is our way of formally representing a syntactically transitive expression in the definition of a concept. It would be easy to demonstrate that componential analysis in semantics has so far been restricted almost entirely to clusters (unordered sets) of features.[54]

Weinreich then sets out rules of relationships to demonstrate how changes in clusters and configurations can take place. The relationship of "linking" results in the formation of new clusters. "Nesting," a nonlinking construction, attempts to represent the intuitive feeling of transitivity, as when the verb "fix" operates on the object noun "teeth." A configuration rather than a cluster represents the combination of "fix" with "teeth." Quantification and deixis can be interpreted as a nonlinking relationship of "delimitation," restricting the class of referents rather than associating referents in clusters. "Modalization" offers the possibility of suspending belief about the truth or falsity of a juxtaposition of referents.

The variety of nonlinking relationships resulting in different kinds of configurations seems so great as almost to defy enumeration. Weinreich indicated only a few such relationships, but he extended semantic theory by suggesting that there exists more to the juxtaposition of semantic markers than simple association; his proposal for configurations moves semanticists immediately into the conceptual level, for they must now ask about the nature of the configuration: are the two semantic features related by spatial orientation, by historical tradition, by imagery, etc.? One might ask whether all clusters in metaphors can be reduced to configurations, the association of referents by means of an imagined relationship. Even in the most hypothetical diaphor, the interpretation of that metaphor as meaningful rests on recognition of some analogy; there must be some perceived relationship between the two referents of the metaphor for it to be intelligible. On the semantic level, we might properly distinguish between linking relationships forming new clusters, the mere juxtaposition of referents, and nonlinking relationships producing new configurations arising from relationships conceived of in the hearer. Legitimate metaphors usually result from configurations rather than from linking relationships. In semantic theory it would be wise to retain the notion of linking relationships, the invention of new clusters without configurations to allow for nonsense and unsuccessful metaphors. In other words, not all the juxtapositions of referents produce successful metaphors; some are so strange as to prevent comprehension of relationships of similarity. On the other hand, if the configurations produced by association of the referents of a metaphor are so explicit and obvious, then the metaphor is an analogy rather than a metaphor because semantic anomaly is one of the necessary characteristics of a legitimate metaphor.

When applied to metaphor, Weinreich's careful assessment of how semantic change occurs through the rearrangement of semantic features in linking and nonlinking relationships pushes one to an analysis of cognitive relationships capable of generating configuration. And Weinreich's position, like that of Levin, can be mated to the representation of semantic markers by fuzzy sets. I will not repeat that application but rather move on to the development of a full theory of semantics adequate to produce metaphors. This theory includes the following elements: (1) the assumption of a conceptual semantic space represented in an n-dimensional matrix, (2) the semantic meaning of words generated by semantic markers represented as fuzzy sets, (3) the organization of semantic associations in quasi-treelike hierarchies of clusters (not to be confused with Weinreich's notion of cluster), and (4) a method for producing semantic rules of change of meaning grounded in cognitive processes rather than the invention of essential universal semantic rules of change.

A Hierarchical Semantics of Metaphor

As a representation of the almost infinite number of ways in which words can be associated with other words to generate meanings, imagine a semantic space in which words can be linked with each other by means of vectors. Since all the words of a given language exist in this space, the number of associations that a target word may have need not be limited. Each link with another word produces an additional vector, and the number of dimensions possessed by a word is determined by the number of vectors (associations generating different meanings). This semantic space is potentially infinitely large so that the number of semantic dimensions of a word may also be large. The length of the vector between two words determines how closely they are related. Words closely associated in meaning will have short vectors and can be imagined to exist in subspaces or clusters. Within this semantic space, both words and their semantic markers—other words—are related by vectors. Thus the semantic marker Inanimate will have relatively short vectors to words such as "automobile" and "locomotive" but a much longer vector to "human being." Similarly, Animate will have relatively short vectors to "dog" and "human being" but a much longer vector to "locomotive." The possibility of constructing relatively long vectors between usually unassociated words allows for the creation of metaphors. By linking words not normally associated (the referents of a metaphor), one can create new meanings. If the new vector produces enough analogy between the words to allow for comprehension and enough disanalogy for suggestion of a novel hypothesis, then a new, legitimate metaphor is born. The imaginative cognitive process that creates new meanings by associating referents not normally associated, thereby producing concurrent semantic anomaly, exists at the semantic level as the construction of lengthy vectors between normally unassociated words. To imagine more concretely just how this semantic space might operate, consider a limited group of words, and look at their actual and possible associations.

Our limited lexicon is composed of "chair," "table," "boy," "move," "the," and "to." Lexical entries for the nouns and verbs are[55]

Chair, noun: (a) an article of furniture used for sitting
            (b) the leader of a meeting
      verb: (a) to lead a meeting

Table, noun: (a) a flat piece of furniture on legs
             (b) an assembled group at a meeting
             (c) a list of words or numbers
      verb: (a) a parliamentary action
             (b) to put into a list
Boy, noun: (a) a male child below the age of puberty
             (b) all lads still at school
      verb: (a) to act as a boy in dramatic productions
             (b) to have a boy play a woman's part
Move, verb: (a) to change position
             (b) a parliamentary action

From this lexicon, one can see that there are several clusters of closely related words with relatively short vectors connecting them. These clusters are derived from their vectorial relations to the words "furniture," "parliamentary procedures," "person," and "physical object." Further removed are "acting" and "list." This lexicon abridges severely the extensive possibilities of meaning for these words, but the shortened list illustrates my suggested vectorial relationships. Nor can one adequately represent n dimensions in two dimensions, but perhaps figure 4.4 can give some sense of the semantic space. The cluster of closely related words for "parliamentary procedures" is shown by the dashed line. The summation of the vectors for "chair" includes those to "chair-

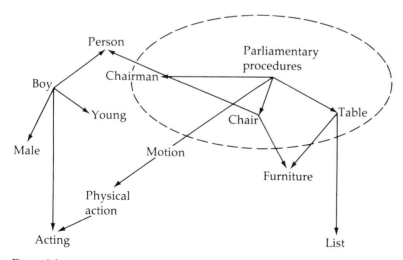

Figure 4.4
Semantic space for the limited lexicon of chair, table, boy, and move.

man," "parliamentary procedures," and "furniture." One could similarly construct the summation of vectors as the meaning of "physical object" or for "person." Now in relation to this representation, consider the following sentences:

(1) The chair moves to table.
(2) The chair moves to the table.
(3) The boy moves to chair.
(4) The boy moves to the chair.
(5) The boy chairs the table.
(6) The boy tables the chair.
(7) The chair boys the table.
(8) The table boys the chair.

The syntactical construction of sentence (1) identifies "chair" and "table" as words of parliamentary procedure, whereas inserting "the" in sentence (2) before "table" changes the possibilities for semantical interpretation. Although in (2) "chair" could be an object of furniture and the sentence could be descriptive of the motion of one object or another, more often "chair" would mean a "chairman" either who changed position toward an object or toward an assembled group of directors or toward a list as a "table" on the wall. The ambiguities of "table" in (2) can be seen by looking at the three vectors from "table" to other words. Only a knowledge of a larger context in which (2) was uttered could offer a clue as to which reading was proper.

In sentences (3) and (4) we encounter a pair of sentences similar to sentences (1) and (2) in which the insertion of "the" introduces the ambiguity, for in (3) it remains quite clear that the "boy" is offering a parliamentary motion, whereas in (4) we do not know whether he is changing his location in reference to a "chairman" or to a piece of "furniture." The discovery that a change in syntax affects semantic interpretation should not be surprising since a complete separation of syntax and semantics is not possible. These two aspects of grammar are intimately entwined, for one cannot recognize syntactic parts without a knowledge of the semantic meaning of those constituents; nor can one reconstruct semantic ambiguities without a knowledge of syntactic structure as in the two cases just noted, in which the introduction of "the" completely changes the possibilities for semantic interpretation.

Sentences (5) and (6) offer an interesting pair with (5) the less ambiguous of the two. In (5) we normally have a young male presiding over a meeting of a group, whereas in (6) we have a young male putting either a piece of furniture or the name of a presiding officer into a list. One would have to possess more vectorial relationships than those in figure 4.4 in order to know also that only "parliamentary acts" and not "chairmen" can be "tabled" in a parliamentary procedure.

There exists another possible metaphoric interpretation of sentences (5) and (6) not provided by the lexical interpretation listed for these words. We could interpret (5) metaphorically as a young male transforming one piece of furniture normally used for placing objects on it into another piece of furniture used for sitting. Imagine a youngster nailing a framed back to a table and saying to his mother or friend, "Now I have chaired the table." Similarly in (6), one could take a saw, cut off the back of the chair, and call it a table. In fact, there are medieval pieces of furniture that serve as both chairs and tables with the back of the chair rolling over to become the top of the table, and in such cases it makes good sense to speak of "chairing" a "table" and "tabling" a "chair." But when such usage becomes common and well understood, these locutions lose their tension and also lose their metaphoric quality. Then a new lexical entry can be added for each word with concurrent additional vectors added in our semantic field. The new vectors connect "chair" and "table" with the physical activity of transforming furniture.

Sentences (7) and (8) appear to be anomalies, for in (7) it is difficult even to imagine how either a "chairman" or a "piece of furniture" could employ another "piece of furniture" or a "list" or "an assembled group at a meeting" as a "young male child" or as a "woman" in a dramatic performance. Sentence (8) seems equally implausible; yet we can conceive of the remote possibility that a "list" puts a "chairman" into the role of either a "young male" or a "woman" in a play. The other possibilities of a "piece of furniture" or a "parliamentary procedure" that is dedicated to *inaction* creating an actor do not follow because these subjects are not agents for such a change.

These few examples from our limited lexicon demonstrate that, within a semantic space where meanings are determined by vectors linking words, ordinary sentences are possible, ambiguities can be represented, and anomalies recognized, and there always remains the possibility of metaphoric construction by the addition of new vectors. Whether one can recognize as meaningful two words associated in an unusual juxtaposition still depends on an act of cognition by the interpreter. An n-dimensional semantic space offers a linguistic theory in which semantic anomaly and semantic change of meaning becomes possible; this apparatus, however, does not guarantee that semantic meaning will be achieved, for that depends on comprehension by the person confronting the metaphor. Even though the creation of a metaphor is a cognitive act, it is accomplished by means of a linguistic procedure.

My proposed semantic space can also be represented as an n-dimensional matrix, where the rows and columns represent the vectors.

Summation of each of the rows and columns for a word associated with another word generates the vectors between the two words. A single target word will have numerous vectors as it relates to other words, and these vectors can be represented in mathematical relationships within the matrix. The n-dimensional matrix representing vectorial relationships of word association in a semantic space differs from the matrices of Osgood's semantic differential technique by linking words with their semantic markers taken from normal associations in lexicons rather than by associating a test word with fifty adjectival parts of polar opposites. In my matrix, meanings emerge from already established cultural practices. But this traditional usage is not so rigid as to prevent innovative juxtapositions of referents as in the creation of metaphors.

Earlier, I argued that the semantic markers of the referents of a metaphor could be represented by fuzzy sets allowing the juxtaposition of seemingly unrelated or opposed terms without producing an outright contradiction. "Locomotive" had partial membership not only in the fuzzy set representing the semantic marker Inanimate but also in the fuzzy set representing the semantic marker Animate. One can properly ask how my use of fuzzy sets to represent these semantic markers of the referents of metaphors is related to my conception of words finding their meaning through vectorial associations with each other in an n-dimensional matrix as the computational device for a conceptual semantic space. I have claimed that the degree to which two words are associated can be expressed as a function of the length of the vectors between the words and that these vectors can also be tabulated in a matrix. The lengths of these vectors are also an expression of membership in fuzzy sets representing semantic markers. If all the vectors are normalized, then their lengths will be between 0 and 1. I have defined the distance between words as a measure of the degree of association in meaning of the words; the longer the vector between the words, the further apart in meaning. I have also defined degrees of membership of words in fuzzy sets in an opposite fashion: the greater the value between 0 and 1, the closer the relationship in meaning. Since the lengths of vectors through normalization and membership in fuzzy sets by definition are on the same scale of measurement between 0 and 1, measuring the same association but in opposite ways, subtracting the length of the vector from 1 gives the degree of membership in the fuzzy set. This follows my intuition that a vector with infinite length expressed by the value 1 under normalization would have a degree of membership of 0 in the fuzzy set of a semantic marker. In other words, two completely unrelated words would have the maximum vector between them and the least degree of membership in fuzzy set of a semantic marker that futilely attempted to associate the two in meaning.

Subtracting from 1 the normalized length of the vector between "locomotive" and "animate" in the conceptual semantic space yields the value of the degree of membership of "locomotive" in the fuzzy set representing the semantic marker Animate. If "locomotive" and "animate" are related by a vector of length 0.9, then "locomotive" has a degree of membership of 0.1 in the fuzzy set representing the semantic marker Animate. Since Animate and Inanimate are a pair of polar semantic markers, if "locomotive" has a degree of membership of 0.1 in Animate, then it has a degree of membership of 0.9 in Inanimate. The length of the vector between "locomotive" and "inanimate" in the semantic space is 0.1. Normalizing the vector expressed in a row or column of a matrix arbitrarily reduced the values of the distances between words in the semantic space to an interval between 0 and 1, the same interval of measurement for the degree of membership in fuzzy sets. Both the degree of membership in fuzzy sets and the length of vectors in semantic space would be measured on different scales, but the fact that they can be reduced to the same scale provides us with a convenient mapping algorithm.

Conceptually, the variability of the length of a vector between two words is similar to membership of those two words in a fuzzy set representing a semantic marker related to both. To make this relationship more comprehensible, consider the metaphor employed by Wallace Stevens in "On the Manner of Addressing Clouds": "Finest philosophers and ponderers,/Their evocations are the speech of clouds."[56] Philosophers are often thought of as having their heads in the clouds, but this metaphor suggests that they are clouds speaking, a form of personification. Again, we have the problem of relating inanimate objects, "clouds," to animate beings, "philosophers." But on reflection, through interaction this metaphor may also be suggesting that philosophers are clouds in the sense of being so aloof that they are dehumanized abstractions. In this second sense, we have the opposite problem of relating animate beings, "philosophers," to inanimate objects, "clouds." The similarity between "philosophers" and "clouds," however, may also derive from the analogy between the noise-making activity of both, the speech of philosophers and the thunder of clouds. Yet these activities occur only under certain circumstances, when philosophers make pronouncements and during thunderstorms. Philosophers can just as readily be silent during meditation or when they are listening similar to silent clouds floating in the sky. Stevens suggested the mode of noise by linking "speech" with "clouds" in the poem. The vector between "philosophers" and "clouds" results from the summation of a number of other vectorial relationships with other semantic markers, where the length of each vector expresses the degree of membership of the two words in a fuzzy set defined by relationship to a semantic marker. For example, consider the associations between "clouds" and "humans" and between "philosophers" and "humans" in figure 4.5. The vector between "humans" and "philosophers" is extremely short since "philosophers" are usually thought of as a subset of "humans." But if one takes this metaphor seriously, then there may be some philosophers, namely clouds, who are to a minute degree not humans. Conversely, one might assume that "clouds" are an infinite distance from "humans," but through the personifying function of the metaphor, some clouds do imaginatively speak as philosophers, and so the vector has a finite length. These vectorial distances express the degree to which both "clouds" and "philosophers" are members of the fuzzy set representing the semantic marker "humans." Consider now the associations of "clouds" and "philosophers" with "speech." These associations depend on further associations of both with "noise," and "noise" can be decomposed into the association of "clouds" with "thunder" (figure 4.6). One can ask if any thunder occurs that does not produce noise; probably not, although perhaps one can imagine metaphoric silent thunder so that the vector length between "noise" and "thunder" is almost 0. Subtracting 0 or an extremely small number from 1 to obtain the membership value of "thunder" in the fuzzy set "noise" produces a value

Figure 4.5
Diagram of the associations of clouds, philosophers, and humans.

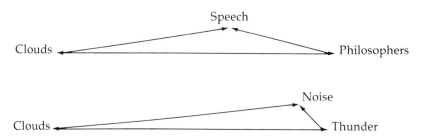

Figure 4.6
Diagrams of the associations of clouds with speech and philosophers and with noise and thunder.

close to 1 in accord with our intuitions that "thunder" is a proper subset of "noise." The fuzziness of "noise," however, leaves open the possibility that one could invent a metaphoric usage of thunder such that silent thunder occurred. This is one of the great advantages of mapping fuzzy-set theory onto my model of semantic space.

The relationship between words like "noise" and "thunder" or "humans" and "philosophers" again raises the question of subordination and hierarchy that we encountered in dealing with Rosch's contention that there exist natural categories that are bridges to the real physical world. Within my conceptual semantic space numerous hierarchical arrangements exist, but it seems doubtful that a single tree structure can be constructed for all the associations. My examination of Sommers's attempt to formulate strict rules of proper and improper association of words based on the dominance of nodes in a tree structure indicated the impossibility of a single tree, because new associations, especially metaphors, violate the traditional associations of an existing hierarchy. Nor can one resort to a different tree for each new usage, for that would destroy the generality of word associations in a *single* semantic space. Instead of these extremes, a single hierarchy or an infinite number of trees, I propose the existence of a finite number of relativistic, interrelated hierarchies that are loosely related. The relativism of these hierarchies can be achieved by relaxing the notion of a single node dominating the branches beneath it. Consider the hierarchical network shown in figure 4.7.

Suppose that nodes A and B are superordinate semantic markers for C and D and for E and F, respectively. Under the usual tree diagram node A would dominate nodes C and D because "noise" dominates

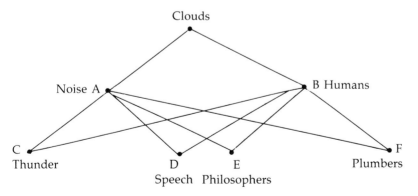

Figure 4.7
Hierarchical network for associations of noise, humans, thunder, speech, philosophers, and plumbers.

"thunder" and "speech." If node B represents "humans," E "philos-ophers," and F "plumbers," then under the standard tree structure, we would be prohibited from relating C to B; we would wonder how philosophers could be clouds that thunder. Allowing all the subordinate nodes to be related to any of the superordinate nodes solves this prob-lem. The cost of doing this is the diminution of dominance. Instead of having a single node dominating only those branches below it, we now understand dominance to be by levels. Words on level AB dominate those on level CDEF. One can immediately question whether these levels are fixed, and I must deny their stability; different metaphoric contexts establish some words as subordinate in this case and super-ordinate in another case. This is where relativism enters into the hierarchical network. Before despairing at the looseness and relativity of this shaky hierarchy, however, a considerable general stability does hold the edifice together; rarely if ever will "humans" not dominate "philosophers." I agree with Rosch that natural categories serve as bridges from language to the real physical world. Perhaps in this case "men" and "women" are the natural categories and "humans" is a superordinate category derived from the combination of the natural categories. But the point remains that these hierarchical relationships are stable and even under extreme metaphoric usage rarely change. Natural categories not only provide semantic space with points that anchor this conceptual construction in the bedrock of the physical world but also serve as the girders from which various relativistic interpre-tations can be hung. My hierarchy is somewhat relativistic: it does not possess the rigor of logical dominance found in the usual tree structure, but it does possess sufficient stability not to collapse, and it does possess a hierarchical character so that it makes sense to talk about levels of categories. Flexibility is the greatest advantage of my conceptual model over the usual logical tree structure; sufficient semantic change can generate legitimate metaphors within this relativistic but stable structure.

Crucial to this model of semantic space is the notion of measuring the length of vectors between words as an indication of how closely the words are related in meaning. When normalized and subtracted from 1, these values can be mapped to fuzzy sets representing semantic markers (words). I now present a sketch of how such values can be explicitly measured even though most such assessments are usually implicit and cognitive.

Thomas Saaty developed an elaborate procedure in decision theory, called the analytic hierarchy process, for the assessment of hierarchical priorities.[57] Saaty made pairwise comparisons of two entities with respect to the degree of their importance relative to a third superordinate item. If we have A_1 and A_2, we compare them with a higher goal B. We can then arrange these comparisons in a matrix in which the importance of A_1 to A_2 relative to B is the inverse of the importance of A_2 to A_1 relative to B. Saaty proved that the relation between the size of the matrix and the value of the maximum eigenvector is a measure of the consistency of the choices (if the value of the maximum eigenvector $= n$, where n is the size of the matrix, then the choices are consistent). Consider the matrix (figure 4.8) in which A_1 and A_2 are the items to be compared with respect to a superordinate category B; w_1 and w_2 are the weights given to A_1 and A_2, respectively. Saaty measured the weight ratios w_1/w_2 and w_2/w_1 on a preference scale of the following five ranks: 1, equally important; 3, weakly more important; 5, strongly more important; 7, demonstrably more important; and 9, absolutely more important.

Now consider A_1 and A_2 to be words, such as "philosophers" and "clouds," and compare them with respect to their relationship to a superordinate word, such as "human." Priority vectors for A_1 and A_2 can be constructed by summation of their respective rows, thus providing measurement of the vectors relating A_1 to B and A_2 to B. A value for the characteristic vector (eigenvector) relating A_1 to A_2 can also be constructed. For the computation of these values, Saaty first normalized the values for each column. Thus his procedure is consistent with my contention that if the vectors are normalized and subtracted from 1, a value for the degree of membership of A_1 and A_2 in the fuzzy set representing B is obtained. Saaty and others recognized the desirability and the possibility of relating this form of decision theory to fuzzy-set theory.[58] Edward J. Lusk contended that "conditioned sets of fuzzy variables may be used to provide priority weights" for Saaty's analytic hierarchy process.[59]

One may object that when average people confront a new metaphor, they do not construct a conceptual semantic space composed of relativistic hierarchical levels; they do not then compute vector lengths or degrees of membership in fuzzy sets by forming matrices of pairwise comparisons of associations of words relative to a superordinate category. Critics of my abstract theory of semantics might argue that the

	A_1	A_2
A_1	w_1/w_1	w_1/w_2
A_2	w_2/w_1	w_2/w_2

Figure 4.8
Matrix comparing items A_1 and A_2 according to weight ratios.

average person either understands or does not understand the suggestion or insight posed by the metaphor. I agree entirely with the criticism about the description of what happens *explicitly*. When encountering a new metaphor, the average person does not consciously construct semantic spaces, hierarchies, or matrices to comprehend the metaphor. But I have never contended that this process must occur *explicitly*. Rather I have attempted to offer an explicit rational reconstruction of what occurs *implicitly*. With respect to his own theory Saaty acknowledges this point.

> The theory reflects what appears to be an innate method of operation of the human mind. When presented with a multitude of elements, controllable or not, which comprise a complex situation, it aggregates them into groups, according to whether they share certain properties. Our model of this brain function allows a repetition of this process, in that we consider these groups, or rather their identifying common properties, as the elements of a new level in the system. These elements may, in turn, be grouped according to another set of properties, generating the elements of yet another "higher," level, until we reach a single "top" element which can often be identified as the goal of our decision-making process.[60]

Although I am not necessarily interested in the reduction of an n-dimensional matrix to a single goal for semantics—I am much more interested in the relationships between words at various levels in the hierarchy—I agree with Saaty that any such decision procedure for choosing words and associating them relative to associations with other words in a hierarchy *occurs* implicitly as a cognitive process within the brain. This leads to my final contention about the semantics of metaphor—that the associations of words found in the understanding of metaphors depends on cognitive processes.

The relations by which words change their semantic meaning can be simply described as those of (1) the addition of a semantic feature, (2) the deletion of a semantic feature, (3) the inversion of a semantic feature, and (4) the transformation of a semantic feature. I have already noted that the addition or deletion of features may be partial; "clouds" add the feature of being human to a certain degree, and "philosophers" add the feature of being inanimate to a certain degree, whereas they diminish the degree to which they have membership in the fuzzy set of animate beings. These partial additions and deletions are a form of inversion; the degrees of membership that "philosophers" and "clouds" have in the fuzzy sets representing the semantic markers Animate and Inanimate become inverted. In the case of "The locomotive is in bed," if we interpret this metaphor to speak about a dynamic person resting, then "locomotive" adds the feature of personhood through the personifying metaphor. I have shown that the degrees of membership that "locomotive" has in the fuzzy sets representing the semantic markers Animate and Inanimate change. Although deletion and inversion are involved, the dominant aspect of semantic change in meaning involved in this interpretation of the metaphor requires the addition of a semantic feature—that of an inanimate object taking on the character of being a live human being. By transformation as a relation of semantic change I mean to convey the notion of the creation of new semantic features through cognitive processes such as synaesthesia, image formation, and abstraction. Many metaphors depend on moving from one form of sensation to another to achieve their meaning; others depend on a visual picture expressed in words, and still others depend on a process of abstract analogy. In Tom Robbins's mixed and complicated metaphor, stars "are pimples of consciousness"; one cannot escape the visual pictures of stars as dots of light and pimples as eruptions on the skin.[61] Consciousness becomes transformed into a cosmic skin stretched across the sky with stars as glowing pimples. The relations of addition, deletion, and inversion are all involved in the semantic change in meaning of "consciousness," but I describe this process as one of *transformation* because, in addition to those relations, one must resort to a visual picture to complete the change in semantic meaning.

The relations of addition and deletion of semantic features can be expressed in formal rules similar to those proposed by Levin or in clusters and configurations as proposed by Weinreich, but these semantic formalizations are not the end of the story. Although some semanticists believe that formally expressed semantic rules, such as those describing semantic change of meaning, are universal and innate within the mind, I hold rules to be mediational between deep cognitive processes and the expressions of surface language. In my account, the presentation of semantic rules or of a semantic model like my n-dimensional semantic space does not end the question of how change in semantic meaning occurs. The underlying cognitive processes that produce these semantic changes must be found. Metaphor is a knowledge process usually presenting its insights in language (there may be visual metaphors, which are treated in a later chapter). An account of the semantics of metaphor offers a rational reconstruction of how the mind translates its cognitive processes into linguistic expression. A semantics of metaphor offers a reconstruction of a mediational device; the mediation takes place within the mind, mapping deep cognitive intuitions to cultural linguistic expressions. In the next chapter I move into an account of metaphor as a knowledge process, to probe more deeply into an explanatory account of metaphor. After descending further, however, I will attend to some further linguistic aspects of metaphor that occur closer in level to surface language, namely, the function of metaphor as a speech act (chapter 6).

5

Metaphor as a Knowledge Process

A Sketch of Cognition and Knowledge

Metaphors appear as linguistic devices in surface language, but the intentional ability to produce a semantic anomaly that suggests a new meaning originates in a cognitive process. The human mind combines concepts that are not normally associated to form new concepts. This cognitive activity operates consciously and unconsciously in the wider context of the functioning of the human brain in the physical world. When we speak of metaphor as a knowledge process, we include in that knowledge process the cognitive activity of the mind, the activities of the brain on which the mind depends for its operations, and the interaction of the mind with its environment. I describe the latter as a form of interaction between biological and cultural evolution brought about by the formulation of new metaphors.

Throughout this book I have distinguished among three explanatory levels relevant to metaphor: (1) a surface level in which metaphors appear in linguistic form, (2) a deeper level of linguistic explanation, and (3) the deepest level of cognitive activity. Whereas in the preceding chapter I was concerned largely with the second level, in this chapter I treat this third, deepest level. The cognitive activity described here makes possible the linguistic expression of metaphor, a rational reconstruction of which was presented in chapter 4. Here, I attempt to demonstrate that legitimate cognitive processes underlie semantic change described in terms of an n-dimensional hierarchy of words with the nodes of the hierarchy defined as fuzzy sets.

By including metaphor within the framework of a knowledge process that describes a form of evolutionary epistemology, I move the considerations of metaphor from the third back to the first level of explanation. The mental formation of metaphors constructs a linguistic bridge from the embodied mind to culture. New metaphors change the culture in which we live, thereby affecting the ways in which humans interact with their environment. These changes in the culture are a form of cultural evolution, and the interaction of the human body (including the brain) with a changed environment in turn affects biological evolution. This movement from the mind, which employs the activity of the brain, to culture marks a movement from level 3 to level 1. This does not destroy my construction of three levels of explanation for metaphor because I have consistently asserted that these three levels of explanation are not mutually exclusive and because they have been introduced primarily to provide heuristic clarity.

In most of this chapter I am concerned with providing an account of cognitive activity, which is described best at level 3. Only after I have presented an account of metaphor as a proper cognitive activity will I turn to metaphor as a mediating device between biological and cultural evolution. To establish metaphor as cognition I deal with (1) memory, (2) creativity, (3) imagery, and (4) features of similarity and dissimilarity. Before turning to these topics, first consider the issues for cognition raised by the preceding account of semantic change by attending to a specific metaphor.

Thomas Hardy writes in *Tess of the D'Urbervilles*, "The drops of logic Tess had let fall into the sea of his enthusiasm served to chill its effervescence to stagnation."[1] The "drops of logic" refer to the arguments against religion that Angel Clare had given to Tess, and the sea of enthusiasm refers to Alec D'Urberville's conversion to evangelical Christianity. What enabled Hardy to retrieve from his memory the concepts of "drops of water," "logic," "a sea," and "religious enthusiasm" and to juxtapose them into a striking metaphor—the drops of logic falling into a sea of enthusiasm? Certainly this metaphor conjures in the mind of the reader a visual image of raindrops falling into a large body of bubbling water, but the drops are arguments, and the sea consists of beliefs reinforced by emotional feelings.

Metaphor and Memory

Undergirding such a creative formulation must be a semantical organization of concepts in the long-term memory that does not prohibit such a juxtaposition. Suppose that the retrieval mechanism was such that one could not possibly *remember* both "raindrops" and "logical arguments" at the same time. If one imagined the human memory to be a series of filing cabinets such that one could open and close one cabinet at a time without removing any of the contents, and, further, if the concepts for "raindrop" and "logic" were in separate cabinets, then the very organization of memory would prevent the creation of this metaphor. Since Hardy did formulate this metaphor, one can argue that this supposition is incorrect and that the organization of the memory must be such that "raindrops" and "logic" can be retrieved and then combined by a creative process. In the case of a new metaphor, a new combination of words has not been uttered previously and cannot therefore be remembered. To understand better the role of metaphor as a cognitive process let me speculate briefly on what the nature of the semantic long-term memory might be. In doing so, however, I do not attempt to occupy the position of a psychologist justifying a particular theory of memory but rather draw elements from several psychological theories of memory that are compatible with the semantic theory of metaphor already developed in chapter 4.

I begin by avoiding the question of whether there exists a separate short-term memory because I am primarily concerned not with how information is acquired and stored but rather with the problem of how to draw on information already found in the memory. I agree with psychologists who envision the long-term memory as composed of concepts and words and not just words alone.[2] Long-term memory can be envisioned as composed of concepts in one section and of names in another section. Many of the names are names of concepts, but some of the concepts stored are nonverbal, as in the case of feelings and images. Painters rarely retrieve words when they draw on past experiences as the basis for creating a new work of art. A poet attempting to express an event passionately experienced searches through his lexicon of words stored in his memory as the proper expression of the vividly remembered emotional experience (a nonverbal concept in the long-term memory). Conceiving of the semantic memory in terms of *both* concepts and words, not just in terms of words, allows the production of artistic metaphors.

Psychologists also suggest a division within the long-term memory between episodic memory, the personal remembrances of each individual, and semantic memory, the general information including the semantic meaning of words remembered in common by all individuals. Metaphor production, however, suggests that a strict division between the episodic and semantic memories in the long-term memory should not be enforced. The inventor of a metaphor retrieves from the long-term memory combinations of words that are not normally associated, and the motivation for doing so may arise from particular experiences etched in the episodic memory. If retrieval from the semantic long-term memory operated in the same fashion for everyone, then the possibility of creating novelty would seem unlikely. How can a poet create a new metaphor if he retrieves combinations of words in the same way that everyone else does? The distinctive aspect of a poet like Dylan Thomas in his handling of words comes from his unusual, rather than usual, usage. Although the semantic memories of various individuals may differ according to what they have learned—one person's vocabulary may be greater than another person's—an even greater divergence of experiences can be found in the episodic memory. By allowing the episodic memory to fuse with the semantic memory in long-term memory storage, the origin of metaphor creation may lie in personal experience and not just arise from the semantic aspects of language learning fixed in the memory.

To explain how metaphors can be created from concepts stored in long-term memory, reconstruction as a method of recall seems favored over a process of recall that reads off each of the concepts. The more variability in the recall process, the greater the leeway for the production of metaphors. If poets could recall perfectly only those concepts stored in memory, then they would be robbed of the serendipitous strange combinations of referents that might arise from mistakes in memory. If the recall mechanism is that of reconstruction rather than that of making exact copies of the items stored, then mistakes become possible and even likely. Despite the difficulty of specifying how the reconstructive process actually operates, the fact that some such procedure does occur finds some corroboration in psychological experiments.[3]

Within the long-term memory, if the organization of concepts in memory depends on fixed, rigid relationships, then semantic change necessary for the generation of metaphors becomes difficult if not impossible to explain. The structure understood to underlie the organization of concepts within the semantic memory must allow for the possibility of change or else the meanings of the concepts will be permanently fixed. In Hardy's descriptive metaphor, "raindrops" must be capable of being understood as "logical arguments," and "logical arguments" capable of being understood as "raindrops." This interaction between the referents of a metaphor creates new word associations; hence the relationships among concepts and the words designating those concepts in semantic memory must not limit the meanings only to the meanings that we have experienced in the past.

Two of the prime candidates for an organizational structure of semantic long-term memory are the network model and the set-theory model. The widely discussed semantic network model of Collins and Loftus envisions the semantic memory as a vast network of concepts interrelated through propositional relations.[4] Some of the nodes (concepts) are superordinate to a particular node, whereas other nodes are subordinate. One can enter the network at the point of naming a concept; memory activation spreads from that node to adjacent nodes such that when one utters the word robin, one immediately also knows that a robin is also a bird (superordinate) and possesses wings (subordinate). These ordered relations can be arranged in a hierarchy. Confirmation of this hierarchy arises from the discovery that the reaction times of subjects are usually longer as the category size increases. It takes longer to answer the question, "Is a robin an animal?" than it does to answer the question, "Is a robin a bird?" The larger the category, the more relations that have to be considered, hence the longer reaction time. Collins and Loftus noted what they called "priming" in memory—the activation of the members of a category when a concept is mentioned. If the category fruit is activated, one can recall apple, pear, banana, etc. rather quickly, but if one is asked to name the first word that one can think of that is a fruit and begins with P, a longer time is required because the category P ranges over many more categories than just fruit. And it makes a difference in what order the question is asked— subjects asked to find a fruit beginning with P respond more quickly than those asked to find a word beginning with P that is also a fruit.[5] Collins and Loftus also used their hierarchy of concepts based on super-ordination and subordination to explain typicality—the typical concept (e.g., robin) exists in the memory between the superordinate (bird) and the subordinate (wing).

The major motivation for the construction of structures for semantic memory arose from the experimental evidence that subjects can re-member organized information more easily than they can recall random lists of words. The propositional network hierarchy offers a plausible solution to these well-established data with some experimental support of its own. For a theory of metaphor, however, one must raise the question of how activation can occur at nodes that are not primed— they are not normally related through a categorical relationship of subordination. How does the poet activate two nodes widely separated in memory? When T. S. Eliot writes in *The Waste Land*, "I will show you fear in a handful of dust,"[6] the activation of "fear" as a conceptual node in the Collins and Loftus semantic network would not normally activate the node for "dust." Further, it seems unlikely that Eliot had been frightened by dust as a child and had that experience stored in his long-term episodic memory. Rather, Eliot developed the metaphor of the aridity of modern society as a frightening sterility, and the jux-taposition of "fear" with "dust" serves as a basic metaphor for the entire poem. It is unlikely that Eliot experienced and stored in memory the combination of "fear" and "dust," so how can this juxtaposition be explained? From the perspective of metaphor creation, the semantic network theory as just sketched seems too rigid.

Proponents of a set-theory model, which is based on a comparison of semantic features, similarly find the network model too rigid.

Moreover, the evidence presented thus far is somewhat problematic for previous models of semantic memory. First, consider network models in relation to the results on hedges and typicality. These results point to the conclusion that category membership is a matter of degree, with typical instances being better members than atypical ones, and this conclusion is not in keeping with the salient, structural aspects of network models.[7]

We should observe first that the network model of Collins and Quillian mentioned above was a predecessor of Collins and Loftus. Smith et al., the authors of the quotation, came to the same conclusion that I arrived at in my semantic theory of metaphor, namely, that the boundaries of the semantic categories of words are not rigid but fuzzy. As an alternative to a network theory, they propose a model for semantic memory based on the semantic features of a word. Their structure is composed of a series of semantic concepts defined as sets that include defining features and accidental or characteristic features. For retrieval, a two-stage process takes place. In the first stage the set instance and the target category are compared with respect to both defining and characteristic features; in the second stage, only agreement between the defining features is considered. Smith et al. provide a mathematical formulation of their theory and experimental evidence to support it. One of their experiments shows clearly that in a large number of cases an increase in category size decreases rather than increases the reaction time necessary for recall contrary to the findings of supporters of the network theory.[8] Smith et al. explain this phenomenon by demonstrating that the increase in reaction time when one moves from a smaller to a larger semantic category occurs when the larger category has fewer common features. When the reaction time decreases in the move from smaller to larger, the larger target category possesses more features in common with the test case. They claim that their two-stage set-theoretical feature model predicts this phenomenon because if more features are found in common in the comparison between the test case and the category, less time is required for identification; in their theory one finds so many features in common in the first stage of the process of retrieval that one does not have to resort to the second stage. When the test category possesses fewer features in common with the target category, then one has to move beyond the first stage, in which one compared both defining and characteristic features with the target category, to the second stage, where one locates only the similarities between the defining features of both categories (test and target). Smith et al. claim that this evidence warrants acceptance of their theory over the network model as an explanation of semantic memory.

This feature model for semantic decisions fits well with my development of fuzzy sets as the basis for an explanation of semantic change.

I employed a componential analysis of the referents of metaphor and located these referents in fuzzy sets with a four-valued logic of T (true), F (false), D (diaphor), and E (epiphor) applied to an interpretation of these sets. The two-stage process of semantic decision proposed by Smith et al. might well describe the method by which a formulator or comprehender of metaphor comes to identify the semantic features of a new metaphor. First, the creator of a metaphor compares the features of the referents; next, those analogous features, which Smith et al. call the defining features, are identified in the second stage. My account demands one further cognitive process, that of identifying the disanalogous features, for those may produce not only the semantic anomaly but also the suggestive hypothesis of a diaphor. In a diaphor the comprehender is challenged to consider an almost impossible juxtaposition of referents. In the diaphor of the "colored quark," the scientist knows the impossibility of considering them to be colored, yet one must think of color as a property that distinguishes one quark from another even though one remains unsure of the nature of this property. The second stage of Smith et al. can be modified to include not only agreement of the defining features but also disagreement of the semantic features. If one does this, the distinction between defining and characteristic (accidental) features becomes fuzzy. I have noted that as some metaphors make a transition from diaphor to epiphor to ordinary language, semantic features that may have been considered accidental when the metaphor was a diaphor may become essential as the metaphor becomes an epiphor.

The set-theoretical feature model for semantic memory, while accounting for semantic change, does not account for the hierarchical nature of semantics. The notion of prototypicality investigated by Rosch does fit my intuitions, especially with subordination and superordination demanding a hierarchical relationship. Intuitively, we do perceive some objects, such as robins, as more typical of birds than others, like turkeys, which although they are birds, seem less typical of what it means to be a bird. And in terms of generality, we do have knowledge that birds, snakes, and dogs are animals, but we do not perceive the category animal as prototypical in the world. Similarly, we abstract wings, feathers, feet, and beaks from our prototypical robin.

The semantic explanation of metaphor described in chapter 4 demands a long-term semantic memory that combines aspects of both the network and the set-theoretic models. But is this possible? Although my semantic explanation locates fuzzy sets as nodes in the hierarchical network, can one make a parallel assertion in describing semantic memory? James D. Hollan claims that the network models and set-theoretic models are mathematically compatible.[9]

A more general question is whether set-theoretic and network models are isomorphic. In the case of current psychological models, I contend the answer is affirmative. One can map any set-theoretic model onto a network model by following the procedure exemplified with the Smith et al. (1974) model. The sets associated with a given concept need only be transformed into a collection of ordered pairs in which the concept serves as the first element and the elements of the sets associated with the concept serve as second elements. One then has a relation, specified by the collection of ordered pairs, and any relation can be represented by a digraph. The function associated with the digraph would assign a value or identifier to each edge to indicate which original set it was derived from. By reversing this procedure, one can map network models onto set-theoretic models. It is important to note that this argument is not meant to apply as the term is used in computational linguistics.[10]

I avoided Hollan's caveat in the last line of the quotation by moving the semantic features of computational linguistics into fuzzy sets and by denying the exclusivity of the network hierarchy in which I locate the fuzzy sets as nodes. I defined both the concepts named by words and the concepts of semantic features of those words as fuzzy sets; then I located both concepts (words and features) in a relatively flexible hierarchy (as developed by Thomas Saaty in the analytic hierarchy process), noting that this hierarchy can be represented further in an n-dimensional matrix.

The ACT model of semantic memory developed by John Anderson offers an example of a network theory of long-term memory avowedly compatible with a set-theoretic model.[11]

> Networks would be controversial and wrong if they claimed that all possible connections among ideas could be specified by a *finite* network. Such a claim would be wrong because there is a creative component to associative thought such that ideas are capable of entering into relations with an unlimited variety of other ideas. However, modern network theories have conceded this point by permitting procedures of elaboration, deduction, induction, etc., to operate on these network structures and to create new connections in the network. Productions in the ACT model give the system a capacity to generate new connections beyond those in any initial network. Given this liberalized conception of a network it is hard to see what strong empirical claims it makes. . . . Network presentations just amount to convenient notations for representing knowledge. Whether networks will remain with us will depend

on how convenient they prove to be—that is, whether or not they turn out to be cumbersome in some applications. So far, they seem to be serving psychology rather well.[12]

In ACT, Anderson proposed a distinction between declarative knowledge and procedural knowledge, locating the former in a vast semantic network with proposition as the basic relation. Procedural knowledge is represented by a "production" composed of a condition–action pair specifying a set of features that, if they exist in the activated portion of the memory, allow a particular action to take place, thereby altering the memory. Propositions are composed of subject–predicate and relation–argument associations, allowing a greater variability and flexibility in the structure of semantic memory than that postulated by Collins and Loftus. Finally, Anderson simulated ACT in a series of computer programs.

The importance of ACT for the semantics of metaphor arises from the flexibility of this theory of long-term semantic memory. It is compatible with set-theoretical considerations of semantic features, and it allows for the generation of new relations. This is just the kind of theory of memory that we need to account for the production of metaphors through a process of semantic change represented by a flexible hierarchy of semantic nodes in which the concepts at the nodes are represented by fuzzy sets. To see more clearly how the creation of a metaphor can be understood in ACT, consider the following metaphoric usage from Wallace Stevens's poem "Man and Bottle." Stevens identifies "mind" with the "great poem of winter" and "man" and then describes mind/man as one who "Destroys romantic tenements/Of rose and ice."[13] The "mind" is not normally associated with a "great poem of winter," nor are "romantic tenements" normally composed of "rose and ice." "Tenements" are usually considered to be anything but "romantic." Let us consider, however, only the first metaphor, that which associates a "mind" with a "poem of winter." The procedural knowledge of a metaphor creator consists of a two-stage production in ACT with the first stage devoted to testing whether enough features exist in the memory to make the association and the second stage allowing a modification of the memory. The first stage might, therefore, explore the semantic features of "mind," "poem," and "winter" to see if there exist enough similarities of features to allow a meaningful juxtaposition. If sufficient similarity is found, then the metaphor "great poem of winter" can enter the semantic memory, altering the propositional relations among concepts. Seen from the perspective of fuzzy sets, the coining of a new metaphor changes the degrees of memberships of the features of these concepts in various sets. "Poems" may become members of the set Animate, whereas "minds" may become partial members of the set of items that make audible sounds (spoken poetry). ACT may not be the final version of a theory of memory, but it possesses enough scope and depth to allow for the creation of metaphors through a process that alters relations in semantic memory.

In examining several theories of semantic memory I have found a cognitive structure in which my theory of semantic change for metaphor can find a comfortable and compatible home. I have not, however, described sufficiently the creative process by which metaphors are generated. Although ultimately this process may remain largely mysterious, a number of characteristics of this creative activity can be outlined, and to this task I now turn.

The Creative Act of Metaphor

The creation of a new metaphor occurs when an individual juxtaposes conceptual referents never before combined, producing both a semantic anomaly and a new conceptual insight. This new metaphoric expression surprises us by both its strange grammatical form and its suggestion of a new possible way of looking at an event or at the world. The mark of a creative poet, scientist, or theologian arises from the individual's ability to step outside of the normal way of conceiving of things and to reconceive them in a new conceptual system expressed in highly suggestive metaphoric language. Describing how this process of reconceiving through the creation of new forms of language takes place remains almost inexplicable. Somehow the creative person reaches into the long-term semantic memory and activates widely separated parts of the network, putting together concepts in a new and vibrant fashion that illuminates a problem or experience. The motivation for this act may be to suggest a new hypothesis or to express a deeply felt experience. Even though I cannot describe in detail how this creative process takes place, I can speculate on some of the necessary features of metaphor formation.

Arthur Koestler describes the cognitive process underlying the act of creation as that of *bisociation*, a process that differs from *association* by moving human expression from the normal literal communicative mode to one with more than one dimension of meaning.[14] In creative acts of humor, discovery, and art, bisociation results from an excess of human energy. Koestler compares the development of new conceptual insights to the process of biological evolution claiming that "new ideas are thrown up spontaneously like mutations; the vast majority of them are useless, the equivalent of biological freaks without survival-value."[15] Unlike biological evolution, however, the evolution of ideas is an ever-repeated process that does not end in ecological niches. Although Koestler may be correct in describing the creative process as something like a series of trial-and-error tests of the various combinations of possible concepts, I am much more interested in some account of how one can select the successful outcomes. How can one decide which particular combination of which referents produces the new insight that the author of a metaphor wishes to express? In sketching this decision process I claim that at least three considerations are involved: (1) the seeming transgression of the normal semantic rules of association, (2) the cognitive exploration of both the features of similarity and dissimilarity of a metaphor, and (3) a motivation to undertake (1) and (2), or stated more simply, a motivation to create a new cognitive insight through a metaphor.

To sketch how these considerations operate, consider one of Shakespeare's metaphors. In *Antony and Cleopatra*, Thyreus brings the following message to Cleopatra from Caesar:

> Shall I say to Caesar
> What you require of him? for he partly begs
> To be desir'd to give. It much would please him
> That of his fortunes you should make a staff
> To lean upon.[16]

Shakespeare reached into his semantic memory and drew on "fortunes" and a "staff" and combined them in a metaphor. The reader almost immediately comprehends the similarity between a "fortune" and a "staff"—both provide *support*, the first financial support and the second physical support. Semantic anomaly is produced by the seeming violation of the normal semantic rules that limit "fortunes" to money and land, which only in the strangest sense could provide physical support for someone about to fall. The production of metaphors such as "Fortunes are a staff to lean upon" seems to require the violation of the usual rules of semantic association. Yet metaphors paradoxically seem to provide the means by which the rules of semantic association change. The cognitive process that identifies similarities of the referents of the metaphor provides the justification for a change in the rules. The prevalence of metaphor in all endeavors, scientific as well as poetic, warrants my claim that the production of metaphors is not a deviant form of rule breaking. Instead, I argue that semantic rules are fluid and depend on cognitive justifications for their status.

One may rightly ask, however, whether there can be a semantic rule, or for that matter a cognitive rule, that describes the process of selecting those attributional features of referents that allow enough similarity for the production of a successful metaphor. Probably not! Metaphors are so varied in their juxtaposition of referents and the cognitive basis for recognizing similarity are so multifaceted that the formulation of a single discovery rule for metaphor production seems unlikely. I have already noted that if the normal rules of semantic association were rigid, metaphor creation would be impossible, for a metaphor seems to violate ordinary rules of association. Similarly, if the semantic memory could be activated by only one node in the hierarchical network, then metaphors could not be produced, for the juxtaposition of two widely different referents depends on activation of nodes in the semantic memory widely separated from one another. If one had a single rule for metaphor production, this would seem to imply that one could establish a definite method of identifying cognitive similarities and dissimilarities among referents. This seems extremely unlikely because of the wide range of cognitive properties that allow both identification and contrast among referents in the formulation of metaphors. Compounding the problem of searching for a single cognitive rule of metaphoric association is the changing nature of that association, as I discovered in my analysis of semantic change occurring in fuzzy sets. The degrees of membership which the semantic features of the referents of a metaphor may possess in a semantic set may change as the metaphor becomes used more often. "Beds" may become more usually identified with "locomotives" or "fortunes" with "staffs" as these metaphors find repetition in everyday language.

The cognitive exploration of the similarity and dissimilarity of the features of a metaphor resembles in part the process involved in mnemonics. I have already noted that items organized in the memory are easier to recall than unorganized items. Professional mnemonists learn to associate widely disparate items with other items based on a previously established and organized list in the memory. The prior list may be organized on the basis of rhyme, number, or location. The last has an ancient origin:

> One of the oldest and best-known mnemonics was used by the ancient Greek orators to aid them in giving their speeches. According to Yates (1966) the mnemonic received its name in a most unusual fashion. The Greek poet Simonides was attending a banquet when he was called from the banquet hall. During his absence from the hall the roof collapsed killing all who had remained inside. The bodies of the individuals were so mangled that their loved ones were unable to identify the remains. Simonides was able to recall each person by the place at which he sat at the banquet table. Hence the name *method of loci*.[17]

By using this method, one can learn an established pattern of locations, such as the rooms of one's house, and then when called on to learn a new list of items, can associate each of the new items with the locations already learned. One could accomplish the same thing in memory by learning rhymes or by learning a fixed pattern of letters or numbers. The importance of mnemonics for metaphor arises from its illustration of the possibility of intentionally activating widely separated parts of memory. If one had to learn the names of chemical elements, one could place each new name in a different physical location based on a list of locations already stored in the memory. There would be little relationship between the nature of the element and the location. In a metaphor, however, there *is* a definite relationship between the referents located in different parts of the memory. Later in this chapter, I will speculate on just how similarities and dissimilarities of features can be recognized. For the moment, I am content with the discovery that, at least in an ad hoc manner, one can intentionally activate different parts of the semantic memory to produce mnemonic effects.

Motivation provides the stimulus for both the ad hoc process of mnemonic identification of referents in the memory and the identification of the referents of a metaphor based on relations of similarity and dissimilarity. Mnemonics involves intentionality on the part of the person wanting to remember, whereas metaphor formation is sometimes intentional and sometimes unintentional. Often the scientist or poet intends to produce a suggestive expression but may not explicitly intend to produce a metaphor. Reaching into the memory and striving to convey a new insight or a deeply felt emotion, the creator expresses an idea in the form of a metaphor. Without motivation to express a new feeling or insight, the juxtaposition of unusual referents would never occur. For activation of two or more different nodes within the semantic memory to take place, something more than just the desire to remember must occur. The creator of a metaphor must strongly desire to proclaim a new insight or feeling, and knowledge of this desire may be conscious or unconscious. Here I enter one of the most mysterious questions about metaphor: what enables some people to create metaphors so readily, whereas others rarely engage in metaphor formation? I have already noted that the contents of both episodic and semantic memories affect the ability to produce metaphors. The richness of personal experience and the extent of vocabulary determine the possible range of metaphoric expression. But what brings about the creative and new juxtaposition of referents? Motivation must provide the stimulus, but can a person who has a conscious motivation to engage in metaphor production learn to create metaphors? Can people receive training in learning how to see one thing in terms of another?

Those who have coined the term synectics contend that people can learn to conceive of one concept in terms of another in order to solve problems.[18] By becoming aware of the metaphoric process, one can explicitly learn how to produce metaphors, but the conceptual richness and fruitfulness for explanation or expression of experience is not thereby guaranteed.

Although I cannot probe the depths of the creative process much further, I can note that emotion often plays the largest role in providing the motivation for metaphor creation. Even the conscious intention to suggest a new insight finds roots in a strongly emotion-laden desire. Koestler quite rightly identifies the creative act as a release of excess emotional energy. This discovery, that emotions become intimately tied to cognition, should not surprise us because long ago David Hume made a good case for the identification of reason with the "affections" (broadly equated with "emotions") in his famous *Treatise of Human Nature*.[19]

Although I have not explained the nature of the creative process of metaphor formation, I have discovered that cognitive rules of the association of concepts must be viewed as fluid and changing, that somehow the inventor of metaphors must be able consciously or unconsciously to identify the similarities and dissimilarities of metaphors, and that motivation rooted largely in emotion provides the driving force underlying the production of metaphors. I must now turn to the ways in which the referents of a metaphor may be linked, considering first propositions and images and then the saliency of features.

Metaphor and Images

A debate about whether images are stored in the long-term memory has raged among psychologists during the past decade. Many psychologists dealing with this problem have come to the conclusion that if images are stored in the memory, these images are not like pictures or photographs and that the metaphor of the mind visually seeing a mental picture is misleading.[20] Psychological evidence seems to indicate that images are not read off a mental picture by the mind. Although there exist many positions on images in the memory, I briefly sketch three: (1) Zenon Pylyshyn's contention that images can be better explained by a system of propositions, (2) Allan Paivio's development of a dual storage system, and (3) Stephen Kosslyn's development of the cathode ray tube metaphor as an explanation of the production of images.[21]

Images offer an alternate method of relating the features of the referents of metaphors to that of propositions. Sometimes the comprehension of a metaphor depends on a visual image rather than on a linguistic understanding of the referents. Is this visual recognition of similarity compatible with the account of the semantics of metaphor embedded in the modified network theory of long-term memory (Anderson) that I have presented? Recall Thomas Hardy's metaphor cited previously: "The drops of logic Tess had let fall into the sea of his enthusiasm served to chill its effervescence to stagnation." Many readers encountering this metaphor form the mental image of drops of cold rain falling into a warm, bubbling sea. How does this mental image combine with the combination of features stored as nodes (fuzzy sets) in a propositional network found in the semantic memory?

Pylyshyn contends that such a mental image can be better understood not as an alternative or as a parallel form of mental representation in memory but as a form ultimately reducible to propositions.[22] The main argument of Pylyshyn's widely discussed paper "What the mind's eye tells the mind's brain" seems to be an argument of economy of explanation based on the contention that since the information recalled from mental images can just as readily be recalled from propositions, there must exist an underlying interlingual (between images and propositions) language, and that could be only propositional. The latter conclusion arises from the contention that not all propositional relations, especially abstract ones, can be represented in recall from memory by images, but all images can be alternatively expressed by a series of propositions. Pylyshyn does not deny the existence of mental images; rather, he denies that images are "primitive explanatory constructs."

Paivio avoided such a reduction of images to propositions by postulating a dual system of process and memory, one for verbal processing and a second for nonverbal processing (images).[23] Although not reducible, these two systems interact, accounting for the fact that the same information can alternately be recalled from either an image or a series of propositions. In what follows Paivio outlines his theory:

> Images and verbal processes are viewed as alternative coding systems, or modes of symbolic representation, which are developmentally linked to experiences with concrete objects and events as well as with language. In a given situation, they may be relatively directly aroused in the sense that an object or an event is represented in memory as a perceptual image and a word as a perceptual-motor trace, or they may be associatively aroused in the sense that an object elicits its verbal label (or images or other objects) and a word arouses implicit verbal associates or images of objects. In addition, it is assumed that chains of symbolic transformations can occur involving either words or images, or both, and that these

can serve a meditational function in perception, verbal learning, memory, and language.[24]

For Hardy's metaphor of the "drops of logic," under Paivio's interpretation we may form an image through one process and comprehend the semantic similarities and dissimilarities of the features of the metaphor's referents in another process. These two processes can combine through a mediational process to form a single interpretation of the metaphor. But even this account leaves us dissatisfied with the relation of image processing and the semantics of metaphor that I have developed. In Paivio's account, the formation of a mental image seems more akin to a perceptual process, whereas his verbal process fits better my account of semantic change. One consequence of accepting Paivio's dual account might be that there exist two processes of metaphoric comprehension (or creation, if viewed from the point of view of the formulator of a new metaphor) rather than one. If this is so, then my account of semantic change would account for only one process.

Kosslyn disagrees with Pylyshyn, stating that images can be reduced to propositions alone in memory, and goes beyond Paivio by specifying the development of a computer program as a simulation of the mediational process between propositions and other data necessary to produce images. Kosslyn uses the metaphor of the cathode ray tube as the core of his explanatory theory. Like Paivio, he finds "spatiality" as one of the prime characteristics of images. In contrasting images with propositions, Kosslyn describes the following as *privileged properties* of images:

> 1. Images occur in a spatial medium that is functionally equivalent to a (perhaps Euclidean) coordinate space. . . .
>
> 2. Images are patterns formed by altering the state of local regions in the internal spatial medium. . . .
>
> 3. Images not only depict information about spatial extent, but also depict information about the appearance of surface properties of objects such as texture and color. . . .[25]

Although this information about the surface appearance might also be reducible to propositional information, it seems difficult to understand just how one could project the experience of spatiality into a set of propositions other than just the assertion that "experience took place in space." Although Kosslyn refuses to reduce images to propositions, he does claim that images possess a "propositional" component in addition to what he calls a "literal memory component."

> In summary, we assign the following characteristics to the long-term memory representations underlying images: The medium is

not structured spatially, but stores units of information corresponding to files on a disk in a computer. These encodings are accessed by name. The names indicate the contents and the format of the encodings. The units are specialized to represent either literal encodings of appearances or lists of facts. Lists of facts are searched serially from the top. The actual data-structures have the following properties: (1) They have both "propositional" and "literal memory" components. (2) The literal memory component contains representations that underlie the quasi-pictorial experience of imaging; they produce an internal depiction of the appearance of an object or scene. A skeletal shape is always encoded, and representations of local regions may also be encoded. The literal representations may be easily adjusted prior to producing a surface image to alter the subjective size of images, and to alter the relative locations of imaged parts or objects. (3) The "propositional" component consists of list-like structures. These lists contain the various types of information described above. (4) The underlying structure is loosely hierarchical, propositions indicating how images of parts ultimately are related to positions on a "skeletal" shape. Lists of propositions may also be organized into hierarchies and other graph structures.[26]

Kosslyn's assumption that images are at least closely but not exclusively tied to propositions allows me to retain my semantic account of metaphor based on the comparison of semantic features with concurrent changes in the membership of fuzzy sets defining those features. This does not mean that metaphors cannot express nonverbal nuances like those found in visual images or sounds or smells. In my description of concepts in long-term memory, I admit that many of these concepts may be nonverbal. But metaphors are *linguistic* expressions of cognitive processes, and it should not be surprising, therefore, that the primary cognitive mode of both the formation of a metaphor and of its comprehension should rest in a cognitive account of semantics—a hierarchy of fuzzy concepts embedded in a network theory of memory. Not all the parts of the mental image of Hardy's drops of logic falling into a sea of enthusiasm can be reduced to propositions found in the long-term memory, but enough of that linguistic expression can be found in the propositional network to allow me to explain the comprehension of that metaphor in semantic terms. I contend that one need not necessarily invoke *special* cognitive relationships to understand the phenomenon of metaphor; any semantic theory worth its salt should be able to explain metaphor just as any cognitive theory of memory should be able to account for images in metaphors.

Before leaving the topic of images and metaphors, I should note that Robert Verbrugge and Nancy McCarrell conducted a series of experiments on metaphoric comprehension in which a statement of the implicit resemblance prompted the recall of its related metaphor.[27] They claimed that their results could not be "attributed to the activation, transfer, or additive combination of pre-existing properties of the topic and vehicle terms or to pre-existing associations between grounds and sentence terms."[28] They argued that metaphoric comprehension required a novel schematization of the topic domain and the development of an abstract relationship between topic and vehicle that constitutes the "functional memory unit." They left for further research the description of the exact nature of this relationship, noting that "metaphor invites pretending, imagining, reasoning by analogy; in its more powerful forms, it requests a perception of resemblances by means of an unconventional reshaping of identities."[29] I agree with this last statement but contend that a refined description of semantic features embedded in a cognitive hierarchy of concepts with a mechanism for semantic change (fuzzy sets) goes a long way in explaining how metaphors can be understood as normal rather than abnormal linguistic expressions of cognition. My treatment of mental images argues that the formation of mental images in metaphor creation or comprehension does not present a process so far removed from the cognitive account of semantic change that I have offered thus far that it warrants abandonment of my scheme.

Features of Similarity

Creating or comprehending a metaphor depends on recognizing the similarities among semantic features of a metaphor's referents. I have assumed that individuals can both reidentify objects as being of the same type or fitting into the same category and recognize objects or features that are similar. These assumptions rest on both the human perceptual system and the long-term memory network that combine to allow the human being to comprehend the similarity of patterns. My account of metaphor as a cognitive process stops short of presenting a physiological account of perception but I will explore further the nature of the similarity of semantic features at the cognitive level of explanation.

Amos Tversky presented an account of the features of similarity, which rejects the geometric representation of similarity and replaces it with a set-theoretic approach to similarity.[30] Tversky undermined the geometric model by presenting counterexamples to the assumption of symmetry between features seemingly presumed by "essentially all theoretical treatments of similarity" (especially the geometric model).[31]

> Similarity judgments can be regarded as extensions of similarity statements, that is, statements of the form "*a* is like *b*." Such a

statement is directional; it has a subject, *a*, and a referent, *b*, and it is not equivalent in general to the converse similarity statement "*b* is like *a*." In fact, the choice of subject and referent depends, at least in part, on the relative salience of the objects. We tend to select the more salient stimulus, or the prototype, as a referent, and the less salient stimulus, or the variant, as a subject. We say "the portrait resembles the person" rather than "the person resembles the portrait."[32]

Tversky replaces the geometric model with a set-theoretic model for the similarity of features based on the following matching relationship:

$$s(a,b) = F (A \cap B, A - B, B - A).$$

The features of *a* are represented by the set *A* and those of *b* by *B*. This relationship defines the similarity of *a* to *b*, $s(a,b)$, as an expression of the intersection of the features of *a* and *b*, $A \cap B$; of the features that belong to *a* but not *b*, $A - B$; and of the features that belong to *b* but not *a*, $B - A$. Tversky then proceeds to define the relations of monotonicity and independence for his set-theoretical model of similarity.

Tversky presents experimental evidence that not only shows the asymmetry of the relations of similarity but also demonstrates that the context of juxtaposition affects which features are considered to be similar. Sweden, Poland, and Hungary were compared with Austria; 49% of the subjects found Sweden more similar to Austria than the other two, 15% found Sweden more similar to Poland, and 36% found Sweden more similar to Hungary.[33] When the group was changed to Sweden, Norway, and Hungary in comparison with Austria, the percentages of similarity became: Sweden, 14%, Norway 26%, and Hungary 60%. Tversky vividly demonstrates that how similar Sweden and Hungary are to Austria depends on the context in which the comparison is made. In the first group, Sweden seems to be more similar to Austria, whereas in the second comparison, Hungary seems more similar to Austria. The salience of similarity features changes according to the context.

Based on the results of this experiment and others, Tversky defined the saliency of a feature in terms of not only its intensity but also its diagnosticity. He also related saliency to focus by developing his matching relation into a metric called a contrast model. He states his "representation theory" as follows:

Suppose Assumptions 1, 2, 3, 4, and 5 [matching, monotonicity, independence, solvability, and invariance] hold. Then there exist a similarity scale *S* and a nonnegative scale *f* such that for all

a, b, c, d in Δ

(i) $S(a, b) \geq S(c, d)$ iff $s(a, b) \geq s(c, d)$,

(ii) $S(a, b) = \theta f(A \cap B) - \alpha f(A - B) - \beta f(A - B)$ for some $\alpha, \beta,$ $\theta \geq 0$,

(iii) f and S are interval scales.[34]

The function $f(A)$ measures the salience of feature a. The parameters $\alpha, \beta,$ and θ are used to change the relative values of saliency determined by the context. If, for example, α is greater than β, then the features of a are weighted more heavily than b, and we are said to focus on a. This would be the case in which Sweden is considered to be more like Austria when compared with Poland and Hungary. When Norway is substituted for Poland in the comparison, the value for Sweden diminishes, and the focus changes. Tversky noted that his notions of focus and asymmetry of features coincide with Rosch's work on categories if "prototypicality" is interpreted in a relative rather than in an absolute sense.[35]

In my analysis of the comparison of the semantic features of the referents of metaphors I locate the features in fuzzy sets and then embed those sets in a geometrical feature space with the fuzzy sets as nodes of a nonexclusive hierarchical network. Do Tversky's arguments against a geometrical model largely based on the asymmetry of features undermine my model? Probably not, for I do not presume that feature a is symmetrically like b; in fact, in the fuzzy sets, I assume that a is like b to a degree, but that does not mean that b is like a to the same degree. A person can be like a locomotive to a certain degree through finding partial membership in the fuzzy set of Inanimate objects, but a locomotive does not become like a person to the same degree. The interaction in the metaphor "The locomotive is in bed" between the semantic features Animate and Inanimate does not have to be the same for the two referents locomotive and person (as related to bed). If locomotive became Animate to degree 0.11, its membership in Inanimate might diminish to $1 - 0.11$, but the degree to which bed has membership in Animate and Inanimate might very well be different from the hypothetical 0.11 value. Within my model asymmetry can be expressed through weighted memberships in fuzzy sets similar to Tversky's weighting of the saliency of a feature $f(A)$ by the use of x, a partial determinant of the asymmetrical focus of a comparison of features a and b.

Carol Krumhansl claims that Tversky's attack on geometrical models can be mitigated by modifying the notion of semantic space to contain the notion of spatial density.[36] I agree with Krumhansl that Tversky's objections to the spatial model can be overcome by modifying the traditional rigid semantic spatial model, which I attempted to accomplish in chapter 4 by constructing a more flexible hierarchical model and by incorporating the characteristics of fuzzy sets into the structure. I believe that the latter incorporation meets Tversky's challenges to present a theoretical model that does not presume symmetry in the referents of a metaphor.

Tversky's work on similarity extends the notion of saliency beyond the concept of intensity alone; the features of similarity considered to be salient among the referents of a metaphor depend on the context in which they are juxtaposed. Tversky contends that notions of prototypicality are relative rather than absolute. Here I must disagree on the grounds that at least some of Rosch's prototypical categories seem to be firm; they are natural in the sense that this seems to be the way nature cuts itself at its joints. Color seems to be one of those genetically programmed evolutionary categories that appears among all humans in all languages in a prototypical fashion. Other categories seem to possess the same firmness but do not depend on either cultural context or the context of juxtaposition for their universal employment as cognitive categories. If I agreed with Tversky that all categories are relative to context, I would have to reformulate my contention that one can distinguish between literal and metaphorical language. If all conceptual categories were relative in their presentation of saliency, we could never be sure that what we talked about in ordinary language rested on literal conceptions of the world. I have already admitted that these literal conceptions are not unambiguous; hence my thesis is weak in the sense of not resting on an absolute distinction between literal and metaphoric or between prototypical and relative categories.

I am now at the point where I must pause and review what we have discovered about metaphor as a cognitive process before proceeding to interpret this cognitive process in the wider context of metaphor as a knowledge process involving the interaction between the mind and culture. Recall that within the distinction of levels of explanation employed in this book, I have described metaphor as a cognitive process at the third level of depth, the first being surface language and the second being semantics.

Metaphor is the creative cognitive process of activating widely separated areas of the long-term memory and of combining normally unassociated concepts. These concepts are juxtaposed in a meaningful manner because at least some of the semantic features of each concept are similar to one another. The metaphoric conceptual process produces new hypotheses and new expressions of experience and suggests new possibilities for perceiving the world. Often the motivation for this process arises from deeply felt emotions; desiring to express a passionate feeling about life, the poet consciously or unconsciously invents new language. The scientist struggling to understand a strange phenomenon finds the normal theories unable to account for it and so creates a new metaphoric concept by taking the categories of one theory and applying them to another. No single rule seems to be able to govern the creative process of metaphor formation. One does find several descriptions of metaphor formation, such as the ones that I have explored in this chapter, that seem to possess a family of resemblances. These include the observations that conceptual metaphoric activity requires a nonrigid hierarchical organization of concepts, that metaphor production requires simultaneous activation of different parts of the memory, and that features of the referents of a metaphor can be both similar and dissimilar. Ultimately, how the metaphoric process occurs remains a mystery as does a necessary and sufficient account of why some people so easily and readily create metaphors, whereas others rarely produce metaphors. Linguistic and personal experience load the long-term memory (both episodic and semantic) with concepts that can be combined in unusual ways to produce new insights, but not everyone draws creatively on this material to generate metaphors. One wonders whether there exist educational methods for training individuals to learn to conceive of one thing in terms of another. Could one develop an educational program that teaches humans to create stimulating metaphors? One can envision a simple procedure of making lists of concepts, randomly combining normally unassociated concepts, and then examining the novel juxtapositions to see if they produce suggestive hypotheses about standing problems. Imagination would be required to match the novel random juxtapositions with significant intellectual problems. Metaphor is not just the juxtaposition of referents; it involves the cognitive process of combining those referents that illuminate a problem in a novel fashion. Creativity lies in the selection of the proper referents producing enough similarity for recognition and enough dissimilarity, and the right kind of dissimilarity, to generate a hypothetical possibility. The creator of a metaphor selects just those referents whose juxtaposition suggests the new possibility he or she wishes to propose. When William Blake wrote, "Folly is an endless maze," he wanted us to conceive of "folly" as something that when engaged in will never end.[37] One can hardly think of a maze without imagining one. But in a real maze, a way out exists; in Blake's metaphor, no exit exists.

Although many metaphors depend on images for their comprehension, the suggestion of an image is not a necessary condition for the generation of a metaphor. In my conceptual account of metaphor, images pose the problem of whether the sketch of the structure of long-term memory and the retrieval process for semantics presented can also accommodate the creation of images. I found that, although images cannot be fully reduced to propositions in long-term memory, images do possess sufficient propositional content to allow me to retain the structure of semantic long-term memory that I have outlined.

I conclude that metaphor creation and comprehension exist as legitimate cognitive processes compatible with contemporary accounts of memory, creativity, and imaging. Metaphors, however, do not arise from mental activity alone; they depend on a knowledge process involving the interaction of the mind with the culture in which the individual lives. To that larger knowledge process I now turn.

Metaphor as an Evolutionary Knowledge Process

All forms of language mediate between (or interrelate) biological evolution and cultural evolution in the sense that language is an instrument for human survival; those brains that have survived depended in part on language to adapt to the environment. Language has shaped the development of culture; many societal artifacts and institutions, such as storytelling, papyrus scrolls, books, libraries, newspapers, data banks, and television, exist in part to store, manipulate, and transmit language. Our very language ability depends on the capacity of the brain to recognize and generate language, and the symbols used in this transmission are shaped by culture. By itself, the utterance of ordinary, literal language does little to change the interaction between the mind and culture, for in ordinary discourse we merely recreate well-worn neuronal paths in the brain and produce well-accepted cultural forms. Literal language can be used as an instrument to change the environment, thereby affecting human evolution. In the creation of new metaphors, however, new associations somehow are formed in a neuronal process, generating expressions that disturb the status quo of ordinary language. Metaphors bring about changes in the ways in which we perceive the world, and these conceptual changes often bring about changes in the ways in which we act in the world. Some of the most dramatic changes in our environment have resulted from changes in our scientific understanding based on changes in basic metaphors. The shift from Newtonian theory to relativity follows from a conceptual shift in basic metaphors from "The world is a mechanism" to "The world is mathematical." The use of nuclear power has dramatically changed our culture, and it may well affect our biological evolution through the effects of radiation and probably through nuclear war, should that horrible event occur.

My examination of the interaction of the brain and culture in an evolutionary context presumes that the metaphoric operations of the brain are described by the cognitive activity, which I described earlier in this chapter. This interaction between the embodied mind (brain and central nervous system) and culture describes an interaction between biological and cultural evolution that I call evolutionary epistemology.[38] Biological and cultural evolution cannot be described by the same theory, for the former involves variation (mutation), selection (survival of the fittest), and retention (inheritance), whereas the latter involves the interaction of humans and institutions through such devices as families, societies, nations, laboratories, decisions, wars, etc. We would like to believe that cultural evolution proceeds according to a plan achieved through rational decision making, but from historical accounts we know that accidents intervene and that many decisions seem irrational in retrospect. Some scholars attempt to find an analogy between biological and cultural evolution, but such a likeness is held only in a loose sense.[39] Sociobiologists have attempted to reduce culture to genetics, but such a reduction depends on the projection of human traits onto animal behavior; this projection cannot be fully justified.[40] I am content to accept biological and cultural evolution as two types of evolution based on different mechanisms that parallel one another and interact. I agree with Donald T. Campbell that this interaction between biological and cultural evolution forms a knowledge process.

> An evolutionary epistemology would be at minimum an episte-
> mology taking cognizance of and compatible with man's status as
> a product of biological and social evolution. In the present essay
> it is also argued that evolution—even in its biological aspects—is
> a knowledge process, and that the natural-selection paradigm for
> such knowledge increments can be generalized to other epistemic
> activities, such as learning, thought, and science.[41]

Campbell, while finding parallel elements in both forms of evolution, agrees emphatically that the two cannot be fully combined because they operate according to different principles.[42] As an expression of the cognitive activity of the brain, metaphor interacts with culture not only because it depends on society's stock of language acquired by the individual and stored in long-term memory but also because new metaphors change the language. New metaphors change the stock of language used by society, which in turn becomes stored in long-term memory, thereby changing human conceptual activity. Changes in culture can change the environment, thereby affecting the biological adaptability of the human organism. Thus, through conceptual metaphoric changes in language, biological evolution may be influenced. I first look at the possible location of the metaphoric cognitive activity in the brain. Then I consider how a particular metaphor, that of interpreting the mind as a mirror of nature, can affect cultural evolution. Since biological changes occur over such relatively long periods, the possible influence of this metaphor on biological evolution is presumed; it cannot be shown directly.

How the brain produces imaginative new associations of referents remains extremely murky. At best, the two accounts I cite are highly speculative and not completely clear in their distinctions. Eugene G. d'Aquili and Charles D. Laughlin speculated on the location of the mythmaking area of the brain. Since myths usually use metaphors in extended stories, metaphor must be partially involved in this area of the brain also.

> The capacity to mythologize involves at least three critical higher cortical functions: conceptualization, abstract causal thinking, and antinomous thinking. First, all myths are couched in terms of named categories of objects that we call concepts or ideas. Second, all myths, like all other rational thoughts, involve causal sequences. Third, myths involve the orientation of the universe into multiple dyads of polar opposites.

> At the risk of appearing overly simplistic, we note that all three of these higher cortical functions involve, in one way or another, a specific area of the brain. This area of man is composed of the supramarginal and angular gyri, as well as of certain adjacent areas. It can best be visualized as the area of overlap between the somesthetic, visual and auditory association areas. It is, so to speak, an association area of association areas. It allows for direct transfer across sensory modalities without involvement of the limbic or affective system. It is as if three complete systems, one for each of the three major sensory modalies mentioned, were hooked into each other and the information from each became available to all. Such a system allows classes of objects to be set up that are vastly more inclusive than any classifying system within each individual sensory modality.[43]

Myths contain many nonmetaphorical statements, so that even if d'Aquili and Laughlin were correct in their identification, we would have found only that area of the brain where some basic metaphors function.

Recently, Brenda Beck presented a different account of metaphors as devices that mediate between the analogies produced by sensory association and verbal categories. She identified a preverbal form of reasoning in which sensory inputs mix with emotions and motor functions in a manner that remains unclear but generates analogies not usually perceived or comprehended. Her paradigm for this activity is synaesthesia. This preverbal reasoning produces metaphors that mediate between the analogies derived from sensory associations and semantic categories. Her notion of semantics extends beyond mere words because some metaphors result in metaphoric gestures and rituals. About verbal metaphors she says:

> A verbal metaphor can now be understood as a device whose function is to inject the results of analogic reasoning processes into the semantic domain. As J. W. Fernandez has said, a metaphor bridges gaps. We can now understand this as a process whereby images and experiential associations that develop at a level where a network of sensory associations prevails are transferred to a level where thoughts are ordered according to a logic or verbal categories. Metaphors cross over such categorical divides as animate/inanimate, cosmic/biological, human/animal by recourse to associative and sensory logic.[44]

What Beck calls a preverbal sensory process, I prefer to describe as the brain's activity in producing novel juxtapositions of referents that may not all be sensory, for such a process could easily put together a sensory referent with an abstract one.

Neither account tells us precisely where in the brain metaphor formation takes place, nor do they tell us how it occurs, except that both agree that some special process of association takes place. In addition, a critic may argue that how such a process takes place is irrelevant to the significance of metaphor and that in citing accounts of novel associations in the brain, we are confusing the discovery of the origin of a process with an explanatory account that justifies it. My reply is twofold: First, given the widely acknowledged theory-ladenness of observations, a separation of discovery from justificatory accounts cannot itself be justified; second, it is important to look at such accounts to test whether one can reduce metaphoric activity to biological activity in the brain, thereby confirming the metaphor "Humans are animals" as literal. My objection to this reduction does not rest on just the unfinished status of probes into the brain. More importantly it rests on the fundamental role that language as a part of culture plays in the formation of metaphors, even though in a trivial sense there would be no concepts of language without a brain.

The operations of the brain mirror the culture in which we live. The language we speak is learned in a cultural context: communication itself depends on shared assumptions about the meaning of language and the nature of the world. Thus the generation of a new metaphor, such as "The telephone is my umbilical cord to the world," results not just from the firing of neurons; it also reflects the cultural language we have learned and the institutions, like the telephone, and events, like birth, that we share. Not that every metaphor like "The telephone is my umbilical cord to the world" directly changes the brain or culture. Gradually, semantic change affects the way in which we comprehend the world, and the decisions we make in society in terms of our language may affect the ways in which the brain continues to evolve.

The interaction of a metaphor between the brain and culture can be seen in the attempts of philosophers to explain how the mind represents reality. Richard Rorty recently claimed in his highly suggestive book, *Philosophy and the Mirror of Nature*, that Western philosophers have been misled by the metaphor of the mind as a mirror of nature into thinking that philosophy possesses the purpose of constructing secure philosophical foundations for knowledge.[45]

> I hope that what I have been saying has made clear why I chose "Philosophy and the Mirror of Nature" as a title. It is pictures rather than propositions, metaphors rather than statements, which determine most of our philosophical convictions. The picture which holds traditional philosophy captive is that of the mind as a great mirror, containing various representations—some accurate, some not—and capable of being studied by pure, nonempirical methods. Without the notion of the mind as mirror, the notion of knowledge as accuracy of representation would not have suggested itself. Without this latter notion, the strategy common to Descartes and Kant—getting more accurate representations by inspecting, re-pairing, and polishing the mirror, so to speak—would not have made sense. Without this strategy in mind, recent claims that philosophy could consist of "conceptual analysis" or "phenomeno-logical analysis" or "explication of meanings" or examination of "the logic of our language" or of "the structure of the constituting activity of consciousness" would not have made sense.[46]

Rorty argues that the Greek ocular metaphor of the eye of the mind which separates humans from beasts was adopted by Descartes and his followers to reconstruct an account of knowledge. Ironically, the use of the word idea by Descartes broke with the Greek tradition in which it was impossible to describe events in the inner mind or conscious states apart from events in the external world. Descartes adopted only part of the Greek account of knowledge, that of the mind as an eye, but left out the other part of the tradition, that of integral relation of that mind to external events in the world. Rorty notes the difference between Aristotle and Descartes:

> But in Aristotle's conception intellect is not a mirror inspected by an inner eye. It is both mirror and eye in one. The retinal image

is *itself* the model for the "intellect which becomes all things," whereas in the Cartesian model, the intellect *inspects* entities modeled on retinal images. The substantial forms of frogness and starness get right into the Aristotelian intellect, and are there in just the same way they are in the frogs and stars—*not* in the way in which frogs and stars are reflected in mirrors. In Descartes's conception—the one which became the basis for "modern" epistemology—it is *representations* which are in the "mind." The Inner Eye surveys these representations hoping to find some mark which will testify to their fidelity.[47]

Descartes separated the notion of "idea" from that which it signified because he was searching for certainty in clearness and distinctness. Mathematics became the ideal form of knowledge, certain in and of itself. Descartes substituted the notion of the mind as inner arena for the Greek and scholastic notion of the mind as reason. Descartes sought to understand how the ideas in the mind, reflected in the mirror and read by the eye of the mind, could represent objects and events in the world accurately. Where the Greeks sought wisdom, Descartes sought certainty. Descartes made the problem of epistemological certainty the central problem of philosophy, moving to the periphery questions of how to act and how to organize societies. Successors of Descartes adopted the metaphor of the mind as a mirror and even extended and elaborated it as in the case of Kant, who "helped philosophy-as-epistemology to become self-conscious and self-confident."[48] In the twentieth century, however, through the analyses of philosophers such as Sellars and Quine, the possibility of constructing adequate foundations of knowledge based on the mind as mirror metaphor was undermined.[49] Rorty proposed to replace the philosophical quest for secure foundations of knowledge with philosophy as a conversation taking place in culture and stressing hermeneutics.

> Once conversation replaces confrontation, the notion of the mind as Mirror of Nature can be discarded. Then the notion of philosophy as the discipline which looks for privileged representations among those constituting the Mirror becomes unintelligible. A thoroughgoing holism has no place for the notion of philosophy as "conceptual," as "apodictic," as picking out the "foundations" of the rest of knowledge, as explaining which representations are "purely given" or "purely conceptual," as presenting a "canonical notation" rather than an empirical discovery, or as isolating "trans-framework heuristic categories." If we see knowledge as a matter of conversation and of social practice, rather than as an attempt to mirror

nature, we will not be likely to envisage a metapractice which will be the critique of all possible forms of social practice.[50]

Rorty advocates the programs of Wittgenstein, Heidegger, and Dewey as better twentieth-century models for the proper pursuit of philosophy. They exemplify, Rorty believes, philosophers who have sought wisdom through conversations (even though widely different in their approaches) instead of seeking certainty in foundations of knowledge.

Rorty accurately describes the dominant metaphoric model for much of modern philosophy—that of a mind mirroring nature—leaving to the philosopher the task of demonstrating how the mind can represent nature accurately and with certainty. This metaphor has changed culture; philosophy departments have been organized partly on the basis on this metaphor, with courses in the philosophy of mind occupying the center of the academic philosophical stage. Generations of students who have passed through introductory philosophy courses in colleges and universities have come to believe in the division between the mind and nature. The rise of cognitive psychology in opposition to behaviorism, which denied the existence of the mind, finds comfort in the philosophical efforts to build a foundation for knowledge. The account that I have presented of metaphor as a cognitive process presumes the existence of the mind existing as a deeper level of explanation than that of semantics and surface language. The computational metaphor that employs the model of the computer to explain cognitive activities assumes a distinction between the natural world and the mind embodied in the brain. Leaving aside the question of artificial intelligence and because there are no disembodied minds among humans, I argue that through the mind, the brain (and the central nervous system) affects the development of cultural evolution. In the metaphor of the mind as the mirror of nature, which I have chosen to examine, the interaction of the brain through the mind with culture directly affects a knowledge process, the teaching of philosophy and the conceptualization of the mind itself. This seems like a reflexive process; the mind develops a theory about itself based on a basic metaphor.

Demonstrating the effects of these cultural changes resulting from the mind or mirror metaphor on the biological evolution of humans remains extremely difficult. One cannot see directly just how changes in the teaching of philosophy and in the general popular belief about the nature of the mind will change the environment in tangible ways that will affect who survives and with what genetic traits. One might speculate on the kinds of beliefs about human actions that such a mirror theory of mind engenders and on how these beliefs affect individual and institutional behavior. If philosophers present their theories of the foundation of knowledge in causal accounts and these become widely accepted, popular belief in humans as robots might develop, exemplifying a form of hard or strict determinism that determines the ways in which we make institutional accommodations for human actions. Because we know from the theory of biological evolution that selection of genes occurs through adaptation to the environment, I remain confident that changes in culture will affect changes in biological evolution even if I cannot show now exactly how these changes relate to changes in human evolution. If I had chosen to examine a scientific metaphor, such as "The world is mathematical," which has resulted in theories such as relativity and quantum mechanics, I might easily point to the effects that nuclear energy may have on biological evolution through genetic mutations and through the possibility of nuclear war. I chose instead the metaphor of the mind as a mirror not only because it shows the effect of a metaphor on an explicit cultural knowledge process but also because it seems a remote factor in biological evolution, and I want to make the claim that all forms of metaphor as interactive knowledge processes probably affect biological as well as cultural evolution. By altering beliefs about actions and thus by altering actions, the metaphor of the mind as a mirror changes culture, which in turn changes the environment in which the human species evolves through evolutionary selection.

Rorty believes that his unmasking of the metaphor of the mind as a mirror of nature requires its replacement by a conception of philosophy as a hermeneutical conversation. He does not, however, consider the fact that by doing so he is replacing the basic metaphor of philosophy with another basic metaphor—"Philosophy is a conversation" or, expressed at the level of mind, "Mind is a collective social process." Rorty seems to believe that his candidate of the conversation for philosophy is not a metaphor because there are so many different kinds of conversations as to prohibit presenting one definitive account of how to do philosophy properly. Rorty seems to have forgotten that there exist many different philosophical edifices purporting to build foundations for knowledge under the mind as mirror metaphor which he criticizes. I have already discussed extensively the paradoxical problem of the fact that theories rest on basic metaphors and that a theory seeking to explain metaphor will itself presume a basic metaphor. Similarly, a theory of mind utilizes the mind to produce such a theory resting on a basic metaphor, and a theory of philosophy as conversation presumes conversations (arguments) as the guarantors of the legitimacy of the enterprise. The hermeneutics that Rorty wants to use to explore knowledge is also used to justify the claim that philosophy is better described as a conversation seeking wisdom than as a search for certain epistemological foundations. As I have suggested in my discussion of Pepper's root metaphors in chapter 2, which I extended to the concept of a basic metaphor, the choice of which metaphor to employ as the basis for the construction of a theory depends on both the depth of explanation and the comprehension offered by the particular metaphor. Rorty's metaphor of philosophy as conversation seems much more comprehensive than that of philosophy as the construction of apodictic foundations. But in the expression of these metaphors—mind as mirror and mind as social process—the former, especially in the light of extensive experimental work done by cognitive psychologists, seems to offer a much deeper and more useful theoretical explanation. Rorty will have to suggest specific categories that find confirmation before his metaphor of mind as social process can become widely used.

Rorty, however, has provided us with an analysis of the mind as mirror, which exemplifies how a metaphor serves as part of an interactive knowledge process relating the brain to culture and culture to the brain. Even though all language mediates between culture and the brain through the mind, metaphor plays a special role as a device for cognitive and cultural change. The creative novelty of metaphor alters not only thinking and language but also institutions, and changes in institutions may bring about changes in biological evolution.

By placing the cognitive process of metaphor in the context of a knowledge process, I have returned from the cognitive level of explanation to the first level of surface language. Metaphor is primarily a cognitive process originating in the creative process of juxtaposing referents found in the long-term memory and presenting them in linguistic forms. This linguistic presentation, however, changes culture by changing the ways in which we think about such things as scientific problems, human experience, and the educational process. Conceiving of the cognitive metaphoric process as an evolutionary knowledge process places metaphor in a wider biological–cultural context. I have acknowledged that the processes of biological and cultural evolution proceed according to different broad rules but that they do interact. Genetic information is transmitted differently from the ways in which cultural information is transmitted. By calling the two interacting processes a single knowledge process, I do not want to imply anything more than perhaps several similarities between the two evolutions and a mediation between the two. To leave metaphor solely as a cognitive process, however, ignores its wider contextual role in culture; hence I have made the speculative claims that as a creative cognitive device metaphor may play a special role in an evolutionary epistemology.

6
Metaphor as a Speech Act

A Sketch of Metaphor as a Speech Act

An analysis of metaphor would not be complete without a treatment of how metaphors perform speech acts. J. L. Austin first called attention to "performative utterances," sentences that are neither true nor false but that perform actions, such as the "I do" of the marriage ceremony or the act of bequeathing as in a will.[1] Performatives can be adjudged as felicitous or infelicitous according to whether the words used are appropriate to the act performed rather than to whether they are true or false. Austin classified the various aspects of language as (1) locutionary—the declarative force of language or the conveyance of information, (2) illocutionary—the force of what the language does, its performative action, and (3) perlocutionary—the effect of language on the hearer. In chapter 4, I was concerned with showing how the juxtaposition of semantic referents that seem to generate semantic anomaly in metaphors in actuality produced legitimate new semantic meanings. In this chapter I am concerned with showing how metaphors can perform actions that contribute to the understanding of new metaphoric meanings. In the next chapter I will attempt to construct a comprehensive theory of meaning that encompasses the semantics of metaphor, metaphor as a speech act, and the cultural significance of metaphor.

In "Sunday Morning Prophecy," Langston Hughes described "the rumble of death": "Rushes down the drain/Pipe of Eternity."[2] What is the illocutionary force of the metaphors, "Death is a rumble" and "Eternity is a drainpipe," and what is the combinatory function of the verse that locates the "rumble" in the "drainpipe"? These metaphors are acts that cause wonder and puzzlement; they are instruments that, through their generation of semantic anomaly, produce emotional responses in us. On the intuitive level, all successful metaphors possess to some degree an illocutionary force of stirring the emotions—they prick our emotions. Metaphors also are bewildering or perplexing actions—they are acts that intend to destroy complacency in the use of language. We must, however, be careful to distinguish between the illocutionary force—what the metaphor does—and the perlocutionary force—how the audience reacts. Proponents of the tension theory of metaphor—that explanatory account of metaphor that seizes on "emotional tension" as the distinguishing feature of metaphor—concentrate on the emotional effect—the perlocutionary force. As the followers of Austin have discovered, differentiating between illocutionary and perlocutionary force presents a formidable task because the two often seem to fuse into a single feature of language.[3] Formulators of metaphor, such as poets and scientists, intentionally employ language to suggest new possibilities for meaning, and the illocutionary force of their metaphors produces wonder and puzzlement.

Metaphors are instruments for the stimulation of emotions; they at least perform this with illocutionary force. The kind of emotion that they produce—their perlocutionary force—may vary from individual to individual according to the context in which each individual receives the metaphor. "Death rumbling in a drain pipe of eternity" may generate the emotion of fear in a person in a state of depression; so might the pleasant sound of water rushing down a downspout during a gentle summer rain or the ominous sound of thunder echoing in the heavens. Both the type of emotion and the image, if one occurs to us, vary from person to person, whereas the illocutionary force of evoking various forms of emotion from the hearer remains relatively constant. Hughes heightens emotions and perplexes us further when he adds that "hell breaks" into "a thousand smiles." Why should hell smile at the sound of death rumbling in the drain pipe of eternity? Because the drain pipe represents the entire universe and mankind cannot escape from death? Or because drain pipes lead only down, and hell traditionally exists beneath the world; hence mankind can go nowhere but down to hell, and life becomes a cruel joke.

Metaphors force us not only to respond with our emotions but also to wonder; we are perplexed by semantic anomaly. We wonder how what the poet suggests can be real. How do all paths lead down an eternal drain pipe to hell? Is there no escape, no salvation? The specific questions, like the individual emotions stimulated, are the perlocutions of the metaphor. The function of producing a questioning attitude—imaginative speculation—describes another illocutionary force of metaphor. When confronted by a metaphor, we cannot resist attempting to understand it. Semantic anomaly not only stimulates our emotions, it also stimulates us to wonder about how to comprehend the conflict among the semantic referents of the metaphor. From my intuitive description of the illocutionary and perlocutionary forces, one might be tempted to conclude that although the former might demonstrate a universal performative feature of metaphor, the latter can find accurate description only in the relativism of individual responses. Metaphors might well universally jar the emotions and force perplexity, but the effects on individuals vary so widely as to destroy any universality in the perlocutionary force. The semantic content of the metaphor does seem to place certain limits on both the emotions stimulated and the questions posed by a specific metaphor. When considering how death can rush down a drainpipe of eternity to hell, one usually thinks of water rather than of sand flowing through the pipe. Yet if one has read Hughes's "Long Trip," water is identified with sand as "waves" become a "desert."[4] One could, through knowledge of what the poet wrote rather than through the normal associations of words, think of sand flowing down that drainpipe and causing a rumbling sound. In addition to the illocutionary forces of stimulating emotion and producing perplexity, metaphor also has the force of producing intimacy. The inventor of the metaphor, when he or she coins it, and the hearer, when he or she achieves comprehension of it, are united in an intimate bond of insight. Both share the intimacy of a new suggestive possibility and perhaps an emotional feeling that is not normally shared in the ordinary use of language.[5]

Consider the metaphor, "Ambulance attendants rush victims through the doors of bankruptcy." Speaker and hearer both share the ironic possibility that hospitals designed to save people's bodies paradoxically destroy their financial health. Anger or despair at this irony may also be shared. The illocutionary force of sharing may constrain the variety of perlocutions that occur. Although in some suggestive diaphors, the bond of intimacy may be stretched by the difference between the speaker's intention and the hearer's understanding of the metaphor, in many epiphors, such as those identifying hospitals with bankruptcy, cultural experience provides the context in which intimacy occurs. Even in highly speculative diaphors, intimacy may occur with the hearer believing that he or she has comprehended what the author of the metaphor had in mind when in fact the hearer's notion of what the metaphor means diverges greatly from the author's original possibility. Unaware of this delusion, the hearer believes communication has taken place.

My account of metaphor as a speech act bolsters my description of metaphor as a linguistic device that mediates between the world of ordinary language (surface language) and cognition. Metaphor exists at its deepest level of explanation as a knowledge process that through a linguistic expression manifests itself in culture. Although I am primarily concerned in this chapter with the illocutionary forces of metaphor, metaphor as a semantic device and as a speech act finds its origin in a mediating knowledge process; we must not forget that, without the ability to recognize similarities and dissimilarities and without the possibility of developing new forms of cognition, metaphor could not exist, and I would be describing the speech act of an impossibility.

Having suggested three intuitive illocutionary forces of metaphor, those of stimulating emotion, producing perplexity, and creating a sense of intimacy in shared language, I now proceed to develop an outline of a speech act theory adequate to generate metaphors. Among the various candidates for such a theory, I use that of Bach and Harnish as a plausible speech act theory for ordinary usage as well as for metaphor.[6] Before proceeding to an outline of that theory and an adaptation of it to metaphor, I offer a few simple reasons for my rejection of at least one major alternative, that of John Searle in *Speech Acts*.[7]

Constitutive Rules

Searle believed that it was possible "to state a set of necessary and sufficient conditions for the performance of particular kinds of speech acts" and then "to extract" from these conditions "constitutive rules" (semantic rules) governing the operation of these linguistic devices.[8] Constitutive rules create new forms of behavior and can be used to explain how we perform most illocutionary acts, such as promising, asserting, requesting, questioning, and warning. Instead of talking about the locutionary force of utterances as Austin did, Searle prefers to speak of propositional acts, the acts of referring and predicating. He contrasts these with utterance acts, the act of uttering words, and illocutionary acts, the act of performing an action. All propositional acts are illocutionary acts, but not all illocutionary acts are also propositional acts, as in the exclamation "Hurrah!"

Searle analyzes the singly necessary and jointly sufficient conditions for promising as:

1. Normal input and output conditions obtain.

2. S expresses the proposition that p in the utterance of T.

3. In expressing that p, S predicates a future act A of S.

4. H would prefer S's doing A to his not doing A, and S believes H would prefer his doing A to his not doing A.

5. It is not obvious to both S and H that S will do A in the normal course of events.

6. S intends to do A.

7. S intends that the utterance of T will place him under an obligation to do A.

8. S intends (i-I) to produce in H the knowledge (K) that the utterance of T is to count as placing S under an obligation to do A. S intends

to produce K by means of the recognition of i-I, and he intends i-I to be recognized in virtue of (by means of) H's knowledge of the meaning of T.

9. The semantical rules of the dialect spoken by S and H are such that T is correctly and sincerely uttered if and only if conditions 1–8 obtain.[9]

From these conditions, Searle derives his constitutive rules for promising. But a review of these conditions seems to prohibit nonliteral acts of promising. If, by analogy, a condition like 9 above is required as necessary for other illocutionary acts, then all nonliteral illocutionary acts are preempted. In their criticism of Searle, Bach and Harnish summarize this difficulty:

> The fundamental problem for Searle's account of illocutionary acts in terms of constitutive rules, apart from the question of the existence of these rules (those tied specifically to illocutionary acts), is how to specify the rules in such a way as to allow for nonliteral or indirect performances of illocutionary acts. The reason for this is that the rules for a given type of illocutionary act are presented as rules for using the associated illocutionary force indicating device. Thus, for example, the rules for promising are presented as rules for using Pr [promising]. Obviously, Pr does not need to occur in a nonliteral or indirect promise, and thus the constitutive rules for promising cannot be invoked to explain promises made nonliterally or indirectly.[10]

The manner in which Searle develops constitutive rules seems to eliminate the possibility of metaphor and yet his principle of expressibility that "whatever can be meant can be said" seems in a contradictory way to invite metaphor.[11] Searle argues that if an existing language constrains the expression of an intended meaning, then one can enrich it by creating new meanings. Such extensions of the language do not guarantee that "whatever can be said will be understood by others." After allowing flexibility in language to support the principle of expressibility, Searle returns to the rigid demands of literal language in preparing to elaborate the constitutive rules for promising.

> But for the present purposes it [the principle of expressibility] enables us to equate rules for performing speech acts with rules for uttering certain linguistic elements, since for a possible speech act there is a possible linguistic element the meaning of which (given the context of the utterance) is sufficient to determine that its literal utterance is a performance of precisely that speech act. To study the speech acts of promising or apologizing we need only study

sentences whose literal and correct utterance would constitute making a promise or issuing an apology.[12]

In a paper explicitly dealing with metaphor, Searle employs the principle of expressibility to argue that in a trite sense every metaphor can be paraphrased exactly in a literal expression.[13] This does not mean that in every language we can find a literal paraphrase for every metaphor; the language may be too limited in its stock of words and expressions for that. But Searle seems to ignore the paradox of how one could *actually* and not just in principle present a literal paraphrase of a metaphor without *metaphorically* stretching the contraints of ordinary language. In order to find a literal paraphrase for every metaphor, one would be forced to extend metaphorically the bounds of existing language.

In attempting to explain metaphor, Searle presumes that one can recognize a metaphor intuitively by discerning the difference between utterance meaning and sentence meaning. In a metaphor recognized as a metaphor, the hearer observes that what the speaker says ("*S* is *P*") is not what the speaker means ("*S* is *R*"). To comprehend a metaphor, Searle suggests the following preconditions:

Where the utterance is defective if taken literally, look for an utterance meaning that differs from sentence meaning.

When you hear "*S* is *P*," to find possible values of *R* look for ways in which *S* might be like *P*, and to fill in the respect in which *S* might be like *P*, look for salient, well known, and distinctive features of things.

Go back to the *S* term and see which of the many candidates for the values of *R* are likely or even possible properties of *S*.[14]

Searle then outlines in a series of principles the kinds of relations that might relate *R* to *S*. Admitting the legitimacy of metaphor without invoking constitutive rules as the basis for their illocutionary force seems either to deny that metaphors possess any illocutionary force or to deny that constitutive rules apply to metaphors. Neither horn of this dilemma will please Searle or his followers. Because metaphors may not only suggest new meanings but also as epiphors express hidden meanings, they are in Searle's terms propositional acts. Epiphors as propositional acts therefore express an illocutionary force. Denying the applicability of constitutive rules to metaphors seems desirable because the necessary and sufficient conditions that describe speech acts from which constitutive rules are drawn seem to demand that all such legitimate speech acts express language literally. To allow for metaphorical expressions, one must lift the requirement that speech acts employ only literal language.

An Alternative Speech Act Schema

Bach and Harnish reject constitutive rules as a basis for speech acts and develop instead a schema for speech acts that represents "the pattern of inference hearers actually make in identifying speakers' intentions."[15] Involved in every speech act are content, context, and communicative intention. Hearers can comprehend the intentions of speakers because all users of the language make universal presumptions and because both speakers and hearers hold mutual contextual beliefs. Bach and Harnish invoke the following universal presumptions:

> *Linguistic Presumption* (LP): The mutual belief in the linguistic community C^L that
> (i) the members of C^L share L, and
> (ii) that whenever any member S utters any e in L to any other member H, H can identify what S is saying, given that H knows the meaning(s) of e in L and is aware of the appropriate background information.

> *Communicative Presumption* (CP): The mutual belief in C^L that whenever a member S says something in L to another member H, he is doing so with some recognizable illocutionary intent.[16]

The linguistic presumption ensures that an utterance can be understood and the communicative presumption allows the hearer to infer illocutionary force. The latter presumption becomes especially important in the case of metaphor where, unless we presume that the speaker has some purpose in mind in juxtaposing referents that produce semantic anomaly, we might dismiss the utterance as nonsense rather than as a metaphor that suggests a new possibility.

The *mutual contextual beliefs* (MCBs) allow the speaker and hearer to fix on the same meaning for an utterance in a given context. Bach and Harnish offer the example of the sentence, "I love you like my brother." When a woman says this to a male friend, she is indicating that she wishes their relationship to remain one of platonic friendship rather than to become an amorous one. If a man says this sentence to another man, he is indicating a deep and close personal relationship. Linguistic and communicative presumptions and MCBs all operate when a hearer confronts a metaphor. Consider the metaphor, "Bureaucratic fictions dance merrily on the head of a computer disk." LP guarantees that the hearer at least understands the units of the utterance if not the entire sentence since each of the words possesses a standard series of semantic meanings in ordinary language. When these words are combined into a sentence, CP allows us to infer that the speaker has a communicative intention in mind when forming the sentence. Because the sentence employs language figuratively, we suspect that the author has at least the illocutionary intent of surprising us and making us wonder what the language means. From the mutual beliefs of both the speaker and the hearer about the nature of bureaucracy and of computers, we form an image of billions of units of information, perhaps like little elves, dancing on a computer disk. From the choice of the adverb merrily to modify the verb dance, we infer that the author intended to suggest a pleasant image tinged with a happy emotion.

Bach and Harnish develop their speech act schema (SAS) as a rational reconstruction of the psychology of how hearers infer the illocutionary force of language. They do not believe that the hearer consciously runs through the steps of the SAS in order to comprehend the illocutionary force of the expression. Rather, the hearer understands naturally the illocutionary force, and the SAS is developed as a theoretical explanation of *how* such inferences can be made. Bach and Harnish exempt "conventional" illocutionary acts from the SAS and argue that only illocutionary acts with an "R-intentionality" (a reflexive intentionality in which the author is aware of his or her intentionality and the hearer is aware that the author *has* an intentionality) are described by the schema. Bach and Harnish distinguish conventions from rules on the grounds that the latter involve social expectations, whereas the former do not.

> On our conception conventions are not what people expect one another to do in specified situations. Rather, they are actions that, if performed in certain situations, count as doing something else. . . .
>
> Rules, on the other hand, are socially expected forms of behavior.[17]

All illocutionary acts are conventional only in the trivial sense that they also express a locutionary force (presupposed under the principle of LP). Illocutionary acts that are not conventional express a speaker's intentionality that need not be comprehended exactly for communication to occur. The hearer may legitimately misunderstand the illocutionary force of the author; what the hearer cannot do is deny that the author intended to produce an illocutionary force. Even when the hearer does not understand perfectly the illocutionary force of the speaker, he or she may infer a different force, thereby forming an unintended meaning. In a conventional illocutionary speech act, the hearer *must* understand the illocutionary force of the utterance according to the convention established by an institution or a game. If the police officer says, "I arrest you," then by understanding a convention rather than by inferring the illocutionary force of a reflexive intention, you are arrested. The laws of society rather than a social expectation produce the result. Certainly the validity of the laws depends on our mutual beliefs that they are legitimate and that they should be enforced, but our acceptance of the illocutionary force of legal utterances follows strictly from convention rather than from our inference of speaker intention.

That metaphors are unconventional illocutionary acts comes as no surprise, but Bach and Harnish's insistence that most literal language expresses an unconventional illocutionary force, the meaning of which is derived from an inference about the speaker's intentions, does challenge the misapprehension that metaphors result from misuse of grammar. For Bach and Harnish, both literal language and metaphorical language are unconventional in the sense of being speech acts in which the hearer makes inferences about both the locutionary and the illocutionary forces intended by the speaker. "Conventional" in Bach and Harnish's sense means institutionally fixed; they see a continuum between ordinary nonconventional illocutionary acts and metaphorical illocutionary acts. For Bach and Harnish conventional illocutionary acts are quite ordinary, so the conventionality of an utterance does not determine whether it is literal or figurative. What is ordinary includes both conventional and nonconventional; Bach and Harnish disagree with theorists who distinguish between the literal as ordinary and the metaphorical as an intentional misuse of language.

The SAS of Bach and Harnish presents an account of nonconventional languages (those not governed by fixed institutional procedures) that allows for literal and nonliteral expressions as well as direct and indirect language. Let us consider the elaborated SAS and apply it to several actual metaphors.

The Elaborated Speech Act Schema[18]

		Basis
L1.	*S* is uttering *e*.	hearing *S* utter *e*
L2.	*S* means . . . by *e*.	L1, LP, MCBs
L3.	*S* is saying that *(. . . p . . .)*.	L2, LP, MCBs
L4.	*S*, if speaking literally, is *F**-ing that *p*.	L3, CP, MCBs

Either (*direct literal*),

L5.	*S* could be *F**-ing that *p*.	L4, MCBs
L6.	*S* is *F**-ing that *p*.	L5, PL

And possibly (*literally based indirect*),

L7'.   S could not be merely F*-ing than p.   L6, MCBs
L8.   There is some F-ing that p connected in a
       way identifiable under the circumstances to
       F*-ing that p, such that in F*-ing that p, S
       could also be F-ing that P.   L7', CP
L9.   S is F*-ing that p and thereby F-ing that P. L8, MCBs

Or (direct nonliteral),

L5'.   S could not (under the circumstances) be F*-
       ing that p.   L4, MCBs
L6'.   Under the circumstances there is a certain
       recognizable relation R between saying that
       p and some F-ing that P, such that S could
       be F-ing that P.   13, 15', CP
L7.   S is F-ing that P.   L6', MCBs

And possibly (nonliterally based indirect),

L8'.   S could not merely be F-ing that P.   L7, MCBs
L9'.   There is some F'-ing that Q connected in a
       way identifiable under the circumstances to
       F-ing that P, such that in F-ing that P, S
       could also be F'-ing that Q.   L8', CP
L10.   S is F-ing that P and thereby F'-ing that Q. L9', MCBs

Before demonstrating how metaphors fit into this schema, I must explain some of the symbols used. In the notation *(...p...) the asterisk indicates a sentence type, p represents a proposition, and the ellipses indicate a lacuna of uninterpreted form. Hence the meaning of *(...p...) is a function of the intended meaning of the expression e. F represents the illocutionary force, and the expression F*(...p...) indicates the literal expression of a proposition p with illocutionary force F. The expression F(...p...) portrays a nonliteral expression of a proposition p. The term PL represents the presumption of literalness, which is similar in function to the principles of LP and CP. MCB is defined as before. From L1, the inference of L2, L3, and L4 explains the locutionary force, L4 produces either a literal or nonliteral expression (L5 or L5').

Metaphor and the Speech Act Schema

Let us follow the routes of several metaphors through Bach and Harnish's SAS. Consider first Langston Hughes's identification of death with a drum: "That death is a drum/Beating forever."[19]

L1. Hughes is uttering "Death is a drum/Beating forever."

L2. Hughes means that death will come to every man and woman.

L3. Hughes is saying that death is a drum that calls us all to the grave.

L4. Hughes, if speaking literally, is *asserting* that death is a drum that calls us all to the grave.

L5'. Hughes could not (speaking literally) be *asserting* that death is a drum that calls us all to the grave.

L6'. Hughes is *suggesting* that "Death is a drum" in the sense that although men and women may not hear the sound of an invisible and silent drum, all life hears figuratively the beat of the drum of death. The relations $R_1, R_2, \ldots, R_n$ between death and the sound of a drum include the unceasing activity of both, the rhythmic activity of both, the monotony of both, etc. Hughes could be suggesting that "Death is unceasing," "Death is rhythmic," "Death is monotonous."

L7. Hughes is suggesting that "Death is unceasing," "Death is rhythmic," "Death is monotonous."

We could use a similar analysis to demonstrate that Hughes might also be presenting the following illocutionary forces:

Hughes is *conveying* the emotion of despair.

Hughes is *perplexing* the hearer as to how death can have a sound like a drum.

Hughes is *forming* an intimate bond with the hearer in the *sharing* of the knowledge that death is inevitable and in the discovery that death can be like a silent drum beating always and calling mankind.

Note that steps L1 through L4, which convey the locutionary force of the utterance, express in another terminology the semantic identification of the referents "death" and "drum." In my earlier analysis, the juxtaposition of these referents produced semantic anomaly because, although humans may cry out at the time of death, the incessant beating of a drum seems more like the rhythmic heartbeat than like the final cessation of life in death. In becoming a sound, death extends to all humans and probably to all life, especially as Hughes later in the poem has the worms that corrupt the body after death respond to the same drumbeat. The same semantic problem exists here of how a physical event, death, can be identified with another physical event not normally associated with it, that of the constant beating of a drum. The locutionary analysis (L1–L4) merely notes the identification and does not attempt to explain how the referents can be identified successfully. My explanation locates the semantic markers of the referents in fuzzy sets and then allows the identification of seemingly anomalous markers by means of a four-valued logic (true, epiphor, diaphor, false) that avoids outright contradictions.

Hughes intended by his identification of "death" with a "drum" to *perplex* the reader into wondering how death could be like and unlike a drum; he intended to convey an emotional mood, and he intended to build an intimate relationship with every reader of these lines. When one feels the inevitability of death and identifies death itself with the incessant beat of a drum, one feels despair. Hughes heightens this feeling by having the worms that infest a dead body respond to the drum. Hughes may also be suggesting not only that death is continuous but also that life itself arises from death, as the worms depend on death for their life. If hope inhabits these lines, it is a subtle seed living in a pile of putrefaction.

The elaborated SAS presents a rational reconstruction of how the hearer of a metaphor infers the illocutionary intentions of the speaker. In the case of the "drum," we infer that Hughes intended to make a suggestion, to make us feel the emotions of death, to wonder at the combination of "death" and "drum," and to form an intimate bond with us in letting us perceive something that Hughes himself had perceived. The locutionary force of *asserting* that "Death is a drum" becomes an illocutionary force of *suggesting* that "Death is a drum" only on the basis of recognizing that Hughes is not speaking literally. Bach and Harnish offer only the CP and the MCBs as justification for this differentiation. Somehow in a given situation, people can recognize when language is used metaphorically and when it is not. Under CP we assume that poets invent metaphors and do so with "some recognizable illocutionary intent." My earlier contention that metaphors can be recognized as metaphors largely on the basis of their meaningful semantic anomaly does not contradict Bach and Harnish's reliance on CP and MCBs. The MCBs include information about how language is normally used; hence when the language seems strange and we believe that the author of this anomalous language had a communicative intention in putting the words together, we infer the use of nonliteral language.

The act of suggesting a new meaning is both a semantic act and an illocutionary speech act. I claim that suggesting possesses both locutionary and illocutionary force. In the elaborated SAS it looks as if the move from *asserting* to *suggesting* also represents a move from locutionary to illocutionary, but I resist this exclusive division because it seems to imply that *suggesting* lacks a semantic component. My whole development of the semantics of metaphor rests on the foundation of a semantics that can both assert and suggest. I have claimed that all metaphors suggest new possible meanings as well as assert analogies. Recall that epiphors are metaphors that largely assert analogies, whereas diaphors are those that largely suggest. Bach and Harnish recognize the illocutionary force of both assertives (speech acts that assert) and suggestives (speech acts that suggest) by listing them together under the category of constatives (speech acts that state).[20] The line between locutionary and illocutionary forces in metaphors seems to be a fuzzy one with much overlap between *asserting* and *suggesting*. Only by perceiving that an assertion produces semantic anomaly can one go on to the discovery that a suggestion is also being made. The illocutionary forces of producing an emotion, perplexing the hearer, and forming a bond of intimacy do seem separate from semantics. Before proceeding to a discussion of these illocutionary forces of metaphor, let us consider the elaborated SAS as it pertains to a metaphor that can be described as a nonliteral, indirect speech act.

Consider the metaphor, "Nuclear power plants leech the wounds of a sick economy." Under the elaborated SAS I offer the following analysis:

L1.   *S* is uttering, "Nuclear power plants leech the wounds of a sick economy."

L2.   *S* means that "nuclear power plants suck the blood of a sick economy."

L3.   *S* is saying that "nuclear power plants suck the blood of a sick economy."

L4.   *S*, if speaking literally, is *asserting* that "nuclear power plants suck the blood of a sick economy."

L5′.   *S* could not be *asserting* L4 literally.

L6′.   *S* could be *suggesting* that nuclear power plants drain the lifeblood of a sick economy.

L7.   *S* is *suggesting* that nuclear power plants drain the lifeblood of a sick economy.

L8'. *S* is not merely *suggesting* that nuclear power plants drain the lifeblood of a sick economy.

L9'. *S* could be *suggesting* further that the lifeblood of a sick economy is money.

L10. *S* is *suggesting* that nuclear power plants suck the lifeblood of a sick economy and *S* is suggesting that "lifeblood" is money.

This analysis can be extended to three other suggestions that the economy is like a sick person. Again, in this speech act reconstruction, the act of suggesting is both locutionary in its semantic aspects and illocutionary in its act of distinguishing nonliteral from literal. We also receive the emotional force of the metaphor. By the choice of words, the author of this metaphor intends to affect our feelings about nuclear power plants and the economy. Leeches were prescribed by physicians "to cure" patients, although ironically they "debilitated" them. Similarly, the emotional illocutionary force produces the perlocutionary effect in the reader of making nuclear power plants seem like phony panaceas for a diseased economy. The perplexity that we experience in relation to this metaphor depends in large part on our attitude toward nuclear power. If we advocate nuclear power for the production of electricity we may wonder how the author could possibly make such a wrongheaded association. If we consider nuclear power plants as a clear and present danger to our society, we may not be as perplexed by the juxtaposition of them with leeches. Interestingly, the author of this metaphor creates an intimacy with those who share his or her view of the way things in the world are perceived. Those startled by the metaphor and hostile to it eschew the author's illocutionary intention to establish intimacy. Although the illocutionary intention might have been to form a close bond through a similarity of perspective, the perlocutionary effect of the metaphor creates offense among some hearers.

Like the line between locutionary and illocutionary, that between perlocutionary and illocutionary cannot be limned precisely. We saw above that a metaphor like "Nuclear power plants leech the wounds of a sick economy" not only reveals something of the author's illocutionary intention but also has differing perlocutionary effects on the hearer depending on his or her beliefs about the value of nuclear power. The author wants to warn of the danger of employing nuclear power as a therapy for a diseased economy, believing that instead of curing the wounds, nuclear power plants suck the blood and thus worsen the patient's condition. Although the author may want the hearer to feel outraged by the continuing construction of nuclear power plants, the hearer of this metaphor may be outraged because the author has attacked nuclear power itself.

Although not intended for application to speech act theory, Monroe Beardsley developed a pertinent classification of *import*—the capacity of literature to affect the hearer. Beardsley distinguishes between "cognitive import" (the "capacity to affect the hearer's beliefs (i.e., to convey information)"), which he calls *purport*, and *emotive import* (the "capacity to affect the hearer's feelings"). Cognitive import (purport) affects the hearer's beliefs in three possible ways: (1) cognitive purport (the "capacity to convey information about the speaker's beliefs"), (2) emotive purport (the "capacity to convey information about the speaker's feelings"), and (3) general purport (the "capacity to convey information about other characteristics of the speaker").[21] If the illocutionary force of a metaphor arises in the author's intention, then when a metaphor acts as a stimulator of emotions, Beardsley's emotive purport stems from the illocutionary intention in the emotive import, which represents the perlocutionary force.

Consider the following phrases from Wallace Stevens's "The Man on the Dump": "Did the nightingale torture the ear,/Pack the heart and scratch the mind?"[22] Stevens's emotive purport reveals the poet sitting on top of a dump searching for life's meaning and finding anguish in the struggle between the decay of humanity's fabrications and nature's harsh cries as exhibited by the sounds of birds. The hearer of these lines recognizes the poet's anguish, but what emotions do we experience when confronting these lines? What is our emotional import? That depends on what associations we have with the words "dump" and "nightingale" and on how we respond to "nightingales" that incongruously "scratch the mind" rather than offer soothing, beautiful sounds. The incongruity or semantic anomaly of juxtaposing "nightingale" with "torture the ear" and "nightingale" with "scratch the mind" perplexes us; in this puzzlement Stevens achieves his illocutionary intent of making us wonder. His emotive illocutionary force is also successful in stimulating us to have emotions, but the nature of these emotions may be quite different from those of Stevens; his emotional purport may differ greatly from our emotional import—or to state the matter in terms of speech act theory, Stevens's emotional illocutionary intention may be different from our perlocutionary effect.

The equivocation that I noted between *suggesting* as the result of locutionary intention and *suggesting* as the result of an illocutionary intention can be further subdivided into import and purport. Beardsley assumed that cognitive import was the same thing as purport and contrasted only with emotive import. But suppose that we contrast a new definition of cognitive import as the locutionary effect on the hearer—what the hearer believes the words to mean—with cognitive purport—what the hearer believes the author intended the words to mean (locutionary intent). Recognizing the illocutionary intent of the author would be the illocutionary purport, whereas recognizing the effect of the illocution, which Austin and others called the perlocution of the utterance, would be the illocutionary import. With this revised classification (useful for clarity), we can explore the locutionary import, the locutionary purport, the illocutionary import (perlocution), and the illocutionary purport of *suggesting*. For example, in the description of quarks, the term color has been applied to them to suggest certain highly speculative theoretical possibilities. The locutionary intent of the authors of the metaphors remains vague just as the locutionary import cannot be fully specified. Applying "color" to "quarks" causes the hearer to think in terms of definite entities because "color" possesses the connotation of "definiteness"—those objects that we perceive in the physical world to be discrete, solid, tactile objects. By talking about "colored" quarks, we tend to conceive of them more like definite objects rather than as something like fields or plasmas. The illocutionary intent of the inventor of the scientific metaphor "red quark" may be to suggest with clarity rather than to suggest with perplexity, although both may be involved in the metaphor. Even though the use of colored quarks helps the theorist to understand and classify quarks, many who hear these metaphors may be perplexed. The illocutionary intent, the illocutionary purport of *suggesting*, is to clarify, whereas the illocutionary effect (the perlocution) or illocutionary import is to perplex. Earlier I distinguished between the illocutionary forces of *suggesting* and *perplexing*. Here we see that they overlap and are not necessarily exclusive categories of illocutionary force.

The illocutionary emotional intent may have been to comfort the theorist by invoking a secure, comfortable category of description (colors), yet the effect that the emotional perlocution or emotive import may have is to stimulate discomfort through the bizarre juxtaposition of inherently colorless entities with categories of color.

The language used by scientists to describe quarks extends to terms like "strange" and "charmed" and tends in the direction of poetry and certainly brings the hearers into an intimate circle of believers. Little direct evidence can be presented for the existence of quarks, let alone the confirmation of the existence of their attributes of color, strangeness, and charm.[23] Quark theorists and their followers form a band of scientific believers not unlike early religious gnostics. Both groups exhibit an idiosyncratic language that is intelligible only to believers and difficult to challenge from outside the group. As scientific metaphors, however, colored quarks, charmed quarks, and strange quarks all exhibit the illocutionary forces of *suggesting, stimulating emotions, perplexing,* and *creating an intimacy.*

Metaphorizing

Thus far in the consideration of metaphor as a speech act, I have described the locutionary, illocutionary, and perlocutionary forces of metaphor in terms of the actions of suggesting, producing emotions, creating puzzlement, and forming intimacy. Suppose, however, that the use of metaphor is itself a category of speech act. The verb chosen to represent this speech act is "to metaphorize." The *Oxford English Dictionary* describes the meaning of "to metaphorize" as "to change metaphorically *into.*"[24] Whenever one creates a new metaphor, one is engaging in the speech act of metaphorizing. This action includes all those actions that I have previously associated with metaphors plus the more particular action features of metaphors. Not only do metaphors suggest new hypotheses but they also force the hearer to consider analogies and disanalogies. The puzzlement that metaphors force on the audience through the intentionality of the author arises from the metaphor's semantic anomaly. Hypotheses can suggest and nonsense expressions can puzzle hearers without being metaphors. The actions of suggesting, producing emotion, creating puzzlement, and forming intimacy are all necessary but not sufficient features of metaphor as a speech act. To be a genuine metaphor, an utterance must also generate meaning out of semantic anomaly. *Metaphorizing* as a speech act includes the necessary as well as the sufficient conditions to produce an intelligible meaning. From the diaphoric aspect we generate hypotheses by pondering the disanalogies of the referents of the metaphor, whereas from the epiphoric aspect we produce understanding by recognizing the analogies. *Metaphorizing* forces the hearer to develop meaning out of the combined analogy and disanalogy in the intentional metaphoric act of the speaker. Even when the hearer misses the intended meaning of the author, a metaphor may provide a meaningful insight. Where the author meant one thing, the hearer understands another. As a speech act, however, the metaphor forces the hearer to search for a meaning—to examine analogies and disanalogies—in the belief that the author intended these semantically anomalous words to generate meaning rather than gibberish. Unless a hearer believes an odd juxtaposition of referents to be intentionally meaningful, the semantic anomaly is understood as a mistake in grammar rather than as a metaphor. The background knowledge and the context help the hearer to decide whether odd language should be taken as a mistake or as an intentional metaphor. If one tries hard enough, the imagination can convert almost any combination of words into a meaningful expression. But the hearer must decide whether to engage in the imaginative act of trying to construct suggestive hypotheses out of the unusual juxtaposition of referents. If one reads a poem and comes across odd language, one usually assumes that the poet put it there to convey and/or suggest meaning, so the reader takes it as a metaphorizing speech act. If meaning is not discerned in the language, readers of the poem usually assume that they have not understood the poet and go back and try again to comprehend the poetic metaphor. In reading a newspaper, if we come across a strange combination of words in a story, we may be justified in concluding that a typesetter's error has occurred rather than that a difficult to understand metaphor has been formed. To be recognized as a legitimate speech act, metaphorizing must produce the recognition in the hearer of an intentionality in the author that the language be meaningful.

Consider the metaphor, "Bureaucracy drives a paper clip through man's soul." In the context of a contemporary world where governmental and corporate bureaucracy stifles the imagination by endless routine paperwork, we recognize at once that the author had an intention in creating this metaphor. The locutionary intention offers a particular perspective on the world. Not only does the illocutionary force puzzle us, increase our displeasure with bureaucracy (if we share the sentiment of the metaphor), and form a bond between us and the author, but the full metaphorizing action of this language also makes us come to the conclusion that this is a *metaphor* and not some other form of language. We may unconsciously recognize that the semantic anomaly produces meaning; we know that bureaucracy is not literally a person and that paper clips cannot literally penetrate a soul, and yet the combination of these words seems plausible and comprehensible. The emotions produced by this particular act of metaphorizing may be of two kinds: (1) the implicit grammatical surprise that the image of a paper clip running through a soul engenders and (2) the disgust that we have with "bureaucracy" in agreement with the views of the author. I have classified the former as emotive import and the latter as emotive purport (Beardsley).

Consider now another juxtaposition of words with a less familiar sentiment: "The relentless pursuit of witchcraft inevitably leads to a Nobel prize." Is this also a speech act of *metaphorizing*? It does suggest a speculative hypothesis through semantic anomaly—the juxtaposition of "witchcraft" with "Nobel prize." We are puzzled by the combination and if we can solve the puzzle, then we can form a bond of intimacy with the author. Emotions arise in us both from the semantic anomaly and from emotional purport. If this is an act of *metaphorizing*, then from a comparison of the analogies and disanalogies of the referents, we produce a meaningful insight. We hypothetically test the metaphoric identification of "science" with "witchcraft" and find that the disanalogies far outweigh the analogies. We wonder if this is a highly speculative metaphor or a metaphor that has failed. But perhaps another idea occurs to us: that of irony. Perhaps the author intended for "witchcraft" to mean its opposite, "science." If the context seems to indicate this, then we take the sentence to be irony rather than metaphor. As irony, we have another type of speech act closely related to that of metaphor involving some of the same ingredients of action: producing emotion, puzzling, and forming a bond of intimacy. In the function of suggesting, however, irony and metaphor differ, for where irony arises from the use of an opposite to heighten contrast, metaphor brings about at least the hypothetical identification of the opposed referents. The speech act of *metaphorizing* suggests new possibilities by forcing a comparison of analogous and disanalogous elements leading to the formulation of a meaningful hypothesis.

I noted earlier that the illocutionary act of suggesting in a metaphor cannot be divorced from its locutionary action. In developing the notion of metaphorizing we observe that in a similar fashion the illocutionary force of the metaphor that leads us to generate meaning out of semantic anomaly also depends on locutionary recognition of analogies and disanalogies of the referents.

Like other figurative language, *metaphorizing* produces emotion and wonder and forms intimate bonds between speakers and hearers. The distinctive characteristic of *metaphorizing* remains the generation of a suggestive possible meaning from a juxtaposition of referents that seemed to produce semantic anomaly. This distinctive feature, however, cannot be cut off from the locutionary aspect of metaphor or what I called in chapter 4 the semantics of metaphor. Speech act theorists are correct in calling attention to the fact that language does not just convey meaning; it also performs as various types of human action. Metaphor does not just express previously undiscovered analogies and suggest new possible relationships; metaphor as a speech act performs certain functions; it has illocutionary forces.

Before completing the treatment of metaphor as a speech act, I must discuss the relation of *metaphorizing* to metaphoric meaning. Linguistic meaning arises from not only the semantic comprehension but also the perlocutionary effect of metaphors. What I have described here as the locutionary force of language corresponds to semantic meaning. The locutionary aspect of an utterance presents the declarative meaning of the surface language, whereas the semantic aspect presents a deeper structural explanation of the same meaning. A description of the locutionary aspect and the semantic analysis of a metaphor present different ways of explaining the connotative and denotative meaning of a metaphor. Where the diaphoric quality of a metaphor is great and the meaning perhaps ambiguous, there may exist some difference in meaning between that presented by the surface language (locution) and that presented by a deep structural analysis (semantics). When a contextual interpretation of the metaphor occurs, the hearer combines surface description with deep structural analysis to produce a single meaning.

The perlocutionary aspect of metaphor adds both emotive import and emotive purport to the cognitive aspects of meaning. A metaphor not only conveys a possible comprehension of what the author intended cognitively and what the hearer understood cognitively but also teaches something of what the author may have felt emotionally in constructing the metaphor, and the metaphor may be the occasion for the hearer to experience certain emotions. I seize on the perlocutionary effect of metaphor as the aspect of *metaphorizing* that contributes to meaning rather than on the illocutionary force because the latter describes what the metaphor does rather than what it is taken to mean by the hearer. *Metaphorizing* conveys the author's feelings and occasions emotions in the hearer, but these are *actions* rather than the production of meaning. One does not understand the full *significance* of metaphor without describing the illocutionary force of *metaphorizing*. The significance of metaphor includes acknowledgment of both the meaning and the illocutionary force. Metaphors both possess meaning and carry out actions. A description of the meaning of a metaphor includes attention to its semantics, locutionary aspect, and perlocutionary effect.

Context affects the development of metaphoric meaning in both the semantic and the speech act aspects of a metaphor. The situation in which the metaphor is spoken and the beliefs of the hearer affect the semantic meaning, the surface language meaning, and the perlocutionary effect. If one extends the context beyond the particular occasion of the utterance and beyond the individual hearer to the larger culture, then we discover an additional dimension of meaning—that of cultural meaning. Anthropologists and sociologists are concerned with the cultural significance—the cultural meaning and the cultural actions—of metaphors. A full account of the meaning of metaphor should include treatments of the semantics, the locutionary and perlocutionary aspects, and the cultural meaning of metaphor. Thus far I have presented separate accounts of the semantics of metaphor and of the speech act aspects of metaphor, presenting only two parts of the full description of the meaning of metaphor. Next I present the third aspect of meaning—the cultural meaning of metaphor along with a unified account that combines semantic and speech aspects of meaning with the cultural significance of metaphor. For the present I leave metaphor as a speech act (*metaphorizing*) with the discovery that metaphors not only convey and stimulate meanings but also perform significant actions. Metaphors suggest, convey, and generate emotions; puzzle; and often form an intimate bond between speaker and hearer. When considered as a particular performative category, that of *metaphorizing*, metaphors also stimulate a comparison between similarities and dissimilarities of their juxtaposed referents, and when through this implicit process a suggestive meaning is produced out of apparent semantic anomaly, we know that we have confronted a legitimate metaphor and not just nonsense.

7

The Meaning of Metaphor

Stability and Change in Meaning

The meanings of words both remain the same and change. On the one hand, if the meanings of words and sentences were not stable, communication would be impossible. Even though one can never be absolutely certain that the hearer infers exactly what the speaker means, without some common and fixed stability in the meanings of the utterances one can be certain that what the speaker intended differs greatly from what the hearer understood because each means something entirely different by the same words. On the other hand, if the meanings of words could not change, the formulation of new hypothetical meanings through metaphors would also be impossible. One might be tempted to seize on the function of time as an explanation of the stability and changeability of the meanings of words; at any one time the possible meanings of words remains fixed (synchrony), whereas over time the meanings of words change (diachrony), especially through the use of metaphors. Yet in a metaphor we must be able to understand at the same time both the ordinary stable meanings of the literal sense of the referents and the new possibilities of meanings proposed by the hypothetical aspects of the metaphor.

Sylvia Plath wrote in "All the Dead Dears" the following lines on the occasion of seeing a coffin with skeletons of a woman, a mouse, and a shrew. Plath has us "hear," "Stars grinding, crumb by crumb,/ Our own grist down to its bony face."[1] Through our literal comprehension of the meanings of "hear," "stars," and "grind" we know that this can be only a figurative use of language or nonsense because "stars" cannot be "heard" and "stars" cannot "grind" human beings. This metaphoric juxtaposition of words in the poem suggests new possible meanings; only in the stony silence of the stars do we figuratively hear the passage of time that leads to our death and to our becoming mere skeletons.

In the preceding chapters I have presumed that one can understand both the meaning of literal language and the meanings of suggestive new juxtapositions of referents in metaphors. I have also already touched on meaning in my treatments of emotive meaning, the literal and the metaphorical, the semantics of metaphor, and the metaphor as a speech act. My treatment of the semantics of metaphor attempts to present an account at the second level of explanation of how metaphors can create new meanings through the selection of features of similarity and dissimilarity that combine to present new hypothetical views about experience and the world. My analysis of metaphor as a speech act allows those performative aspects of metaphor necessary for an act of communication to take place between speaker and hearer. In this chapter I attempt to present a comprehensive account of meaning as it pertains to metaphor that not only combines semantics and speech act theory but also incorporates metaphoric meaning as it occurs in culture. Attention to cultural meaning provides an exploration of the *context* as a necessary component for completing a semantic interpretation of the meaning of a metaphor as well as an account of possible meanings in the sense of the *significance* of metaphors. Before proceeding to accounts of metaphor in terms of language meaning and cultural meaning, I must discuss briefly several general aspects of meaning.

The reader should be forewarned that my description of meaning as it pertains to metaphor presents a frankly eclectic account. Distinguishing among communicative, iconic, and cognitive aspects of meaning, I draw largely on the analytic tradition for communicative meaning and on the neo-Kantian tradition of Cassirer and Langer for iconic meaning and speculate on the possibilities of cognitive meaning based on my earlier construction of the semantics of metaphor embedded in a cognitive knowledge process that interacts with culture. Eclectic accounts can undermine theories by containing elements within them that clash and even perhaps contradict one another. I hope that in presenting this eclectic account of the meaning of metaphor as a many-dimensional account, I have avoided outright contradiction and minimized clashes among the various aspects.

Readers may find some tension between the analytic aspects of my description of communicative meaning and my claim that metaphors also present iconic meaning. To those who find the claims of analytic philosophy for meaning opposed to the symbolic forms of Cassirer, recall not only that Carnap acknowledged Cassirer's influence on his early conceptions of space but also that Carnap himself later acknowledged the diversity of language and its meaning.[2] Even in the construction of logical languages, Carnap pleaded for a "principle of tolerance" that would allow the construction of different adequate formal structures. Later readers of Carnap sometimes forget that he acknowledged the differences between logical and natural languages as arising from different purposes and allowed the two to achieve their meanings in different ways.

General Considerations of Meaning

I begin the general consideration of meaning by agreeing with L. Jonathan Cohen (*The Diversity of Meaning*) that no single account of meaning can suffice.[3] No one account of meaning can account for how a variety of linguistic expressions, including metaphor, can be understood. An adequate theory of meaning includes semantical aspects, emotive aspects, speech act aspects, contextual aspects, and cultural aspects. Single-aspect theories of meaning are more coherent, but they fail by ignoring too many other aspects of communication, thereby eliminating many expressions ordinarily found to be meaningful.

To dramatize the effects of a limited theory of meaning on the meaningfulness of metaphor, consider one single-aspect theory. By following the tradition of attempting to define meaning by a single aspect, such as reference or denotation, some philosophers and linguists have attempted to define meaning in terms of the truth conditions of an expression.[4] These theorists often relegate aspects of the beliefs of the speaker and the context of the hearer to pragmatics, which they consider to be outside the realm of semantics where meaning arises. Ruth Kempson admits, however, that basing a theory of meaning on a truth-conditional semantics pushes style and metaphor into the area of pragmatics not concerned with meaning. She assumes "that there are principled reasons . . . why a semantic theory should not itself contain an analysis of the problems presented by either metaphorical or stylistic interpretations."[5] By defining meanings in terms of sentences, one limits meaningful language largely to declarative sentences.

One might be tempted to expand the scope of a theory of meaning beyond the declarative sentence by following Frege's distinction between sense and reference. In the sense of a sentence one can find its meaning, whereas in its reference one can establish its truth conditions. For Cohen, however, even Frege's admission of a difference between the sense and the reference of an expression ignores the cultural aspects of words.

It is no use objecting that Frege was right here to ignore culture-words because language-words are more basic. In what respect are they more basic? Perhaps the use of 'word' in the former sense was developed earlier in human history and is still acquired earlier by each individual in his own lifetime. But temporal priorities of this kind are an unreliable guide to intellectual importance. Perhaps the notion of a culture-word is reducible by definition, since it might be defined as a family of inter-translatable language-words. But a language-word might equally well be defined as a uniform example of a culture-word. Perhaps the concept of a culture-word is an even more abstract one than the concept of a language-word. But the level of abstraction at which a science operates is at least one criterion of fundamentality, rather than the reverse. Moreover, from any point of view from which the meaning of a culture-word is a temporal continuant, one must in consistency regard the meanings of the language-words that pertain to it as temporal phenomena. So far as Frege was wrong in omitting to take account of culture-words, he was also wrong in thinking the meanings of language-words to be out of time.[6]

Cohen advocates an account of meaning that avoids an absolute commitment to either timeless semantics or a semantics of change that depends on the passage of time. He conceives of a theory of meaning dependent on both the fixity of meaning of words and the change of meaning that one finds through the passage of time and in metaphors in which the literal reading depends on the fixed semantic reading and the suggestive reading involves a change of standard semantic features. Cohen proceeds to differentiate between de jure and de facto theories of meanings, with the former based on the timelessness of rules and the latter on the temporal features of events in the world. I resist this clean distinction because the semantic meaning of a word depends not only on theoretical relations like those in my description of semantic associations as a hierarchy of relations with the nodes represented by fuzzy sets but also on the context of utterance. The disambiguation of semantic markers associated with the referents of a metaphor depends in part on the context of utterance. One decides how to interpret the meaning of "The locomotive is in bed" partially by identifying the speaker and the context. As I noted, if a railway engineer says to his wife on arriving home, "The locomotive is in bed" we envision a railway engine resting quietly in a roundhouse. But if someone says of a superdynamic salesman, "The locomotive is in bed" we know that the word "locomotive" refers to an individual. Which semantic associations to make depends on de facto events in the world of time. But Cohen is entirely correct in making meaning dependent on both the rules of language and the events of culture.

My theory of meaning as it applies to metaphor can best be envisioned as a matrix of four interrelated elements: semantics, speech acts, context, and culture. The semantic aspects of the meaning of a metaphor arise from the association of the semantic features of the referents of a metaphor. One cannot understand a metaphor unless one knows both the usual semantic associations of the referents and the suggested new associations composed of both similar and dissimilar features. The illocutionary force of a metaphor as a speech act presumes both a linguistic presumption—that the words mean something—and a series of mutual contextual beliefs that the speaker and hearer share. Metaphor as a speech act also conveys the emotive feelings of the speaker and may provoke additional and sometimes different emotive feelings in the hearer. Context offers a pragmatic interpretation of which possible meaning of a metaphor to accept. Context suggests which novel juxtapositions of similarities and dissimilarities among semantic features to accept for this particular metaphor. Culture offers not only a larger context with which to embed the metaphor, thereby affecting its meaning, but also a place where metaphors can have meaning in the sense of significance, rather than being just instruments of communication. The first two aspects of this matrix of meaning fit well the notion of language-words employed by Cohen. The second two aspects of context and culture exemplify Cohen's notion of culture-words. I distinguish between context and culture to emphasize that, even though all contexts occur in a wider culture, there may be a second kind of meaning, that of significance, as differentiated from communicative meaning, that occurs in culture.

The idea of a matrix of aspects of meaning allows for these aspects to conflict with each other in terms of their degree of importance for a particular metaphor. In Plath's metaphor of hearing the stars grind "Our own grist down to its bony face" the semantical meanings of the referents "hear," "stars," "grind," and "bony face" combine to suggest time leading to death, but just how we "hear" this process in time through observations of the stars puzzles us. As a speech act, Plath's metaphor not only jars us semantically but also conveys her own ruminations about death and stimulates in us an awareness of our own mortality. The title of the poem, "All the Dead Dears," provides a larger context in which to view this metaphor, namely, that those whom we love must die. Our own experience of both historical and contemporary culture enlarges the meaning of the poem through our possible identification of Plath's suggestion of mortality with traditional themes of death in other literary works and perhaps even with the role of death in the possible nuclear holocaust faced by contemporary society. The meaning that a hearer gives to Plath's metaphor depends on a combination of all these aspects—the semantics of the referents, its role as a speech act, its context, and its place in culture. The metaphor itself may play a further role in culture by providing a form of cultural significance; this is the second aspect of meaning (with which I deal later in this chapter).

To see the interrelationships among these aspects of meaning, consider the ways in which each might affect the emotive meaning conveyed by Plath's metaphor. The individual words, their combination, and their semantic features all have emotive associations. Although we may have pleasant associations with the process of grinding—our memories of an old mill on a gentle stream grinding wheat into flour—when we think of ourselves, our flesh, as "crumbs" being ground down to our skeleton, the happy memories that we may have had of a gristmill soon turn to horror in this metaphoric transformation. Plath may have intended to convey her sense of horror of mortality and a hearer may understand this, but the hearer may also become angry, an emotion perhaps unintended by Plath. This is the perlocutionary force of the metaphor. Its illocutionary force forms a bond between the speaker, Plath, and the hearer; the illocutionary force also jars the hearer into puzzling about how one can "hear" stars and how "stars" can "grind" us as if we were grain. The context, the title of the poem, and the subtitle set the stage, the last by describing a fourth century A.D. stone coffin in a Cambridge museum. The coffin contains the skeletons of a woman, a mouse, and a shrew. One imagines that the woman died and that the mouse entered the coffin and began to chew on the corpse; then a shrew entered and killed the mouse only to find itself somehow trapped, thus following the woman and mouse in death. Plath asserts that we would laugh inwardly (wink) at the "gross eating game" if we were not ourselves—"didn't hear/stars grinding, crumb by crumb/ Our own grist down to its bony face." In later lines Plath speculates that, even though the dead woman is not a relation, through the mortality that links all human beings, we are all kin with her. Plath also introduces in the last lines of the poem the notion of death by drowning. No matter where we seek refuge, the ghosts of these "long gone darlings" come back through "wakes, weddings, childbirths, or a family barbecue" and drag us down to lie "deadlocked" with them. In this particular poem, the author presents the context explicitly in the subtitle and one cannot escape the physical image she presents. Often, however, one must imagine and invent a context for the poem. Whatever the context is, it affects how we feel about not only the poem but also the experience suggested by the metaphor. Emotive meaning arises from the metaphoric transformation of the meanings of referents, the illocutionary force of the metaphor (what it does to the hearer through its performance), the particular context of this metaphor, and, finally, the cultural context of how the metaphor relates to the wider context of human experience.

Throughout this work I have described metaphor on three levels of explanations: (1) surface language, (2) linguistic descriptions, and (3) a cognitive account of metaphor. I have noted that these three levels are neither discrete nor exclusive, as, for example, when the context of level 1 determines which semantic reading to make on level 2 or when the semantic information of level 2 stored in the long-term memory affects the cognitive process of juxtaposition in level 3. Similarly, metaphoric meaning finds its roots in all three levels. The cultural context exists at level 1, whereas the semantic associations that find transformation exist at level 2. Finally, the cognitive process by which the formulation of the metaphor and its interpretation exist is at level 3.

Gilbert Harman also described meaning as having three levels: how an expression functions in a conceptual scheme, how an expression communicates, and how an expression functions as a speech act.[7] Harman believes that each theory by itself cannot provide an adequate account of meaning but that if they are arranged in levels with each higher level presupposing those below it, one can achieve a better explanation of meaning.

> I shall refer to theories of meaning of level 1, of level 2 and of level 3, respectively. I believe that there is a sense in which later levels presuppose earlier ones. Thus a theory of level 2, i.e., a theory of communication (of thoughts), presupposes a theory of level 1 that would say what various thoughts are. Similarly, a theory of level 3 (e.g., an account of promising) must almost always presuppose a theory of level 2 (since in promising one must communicate what it is one has promised to do).[8]

Harman's level numbers are the reverse of mine. His level 3, where speech acts operate, is my level 1 (surface language). The reason for the inversion arises from the point of view: where Harman outlines presuppositions of meanings, I have concentrated on depth of explanation. I agree with Harman that speech acts do presume both linguistic and cognitive knowledge. From my perspective, however, the "meaning" of a metaphor originates in a cognitive process underlying a linguistic operation that results in the utterance of surface language.

In this chapter I continue to presume these same three levels of explanation and divide this section into three subsections: the communicative meaning of metaphor, the significance of metaphor, and the cognitive meaning of metaphor. The first two subsections find their origins in the function of metaphor with communicative meaning alternating between levels 1 and 2 (surface language and linguistics). Most of my treatment of the significance of metaphor occurs at level 1, but I occasionally resort to concepts derived from level 2. In treating the cognitive meaning of metaphor, I speculate on how the cognitive process that generates metaphors affects their meaning. Some analysts might be tempted to argue that I do not need this speculation because metaphors as linguistic forms should be treated in relation to meaning, also a linguistic phenomenon, only at levels 1 and 2. Such a challenge forgets that many linguistic metaphors originate from nonlinguistic cognitive processes, such as visual imagery. One might also reply that visual metaphors exist in paintings and architectural edifices. I believe that there are such metaphors, but I have not investigated them in this book because I have confined this study to linguistic metaphors. I have already noted, however, that linguistic metaphors also arise from the possession of emotional feelings and that such feelings are not necessarily antithetical to cognitive processes but rather often motivate the unusual juxtapositions found in the combination of metaphoric referents. Let me make two further introductory remarks, the first dealing with the circularity of any explanation of meaning and the second sketching the scope of the units of meaning.

Just as explanations of metaphor are themselves metaphoric and presume a basic metaphor on which to construct a theory, so do all explanations of meaning presume basic understandings of meaning. Among philosophers of language and linguists, it is widely recognized that presenting explanations or definitions of meaning without some circularity remains difficult if not impossible. Resorting to levels of meaning does not avoid circularity fully, but such a hierarchy does clarify that not everything is presumed at once and that one can begin with fewer assumptions of the meanings of terms (concepts) and then construct higher expressions on the presumptions of these lower ones. My attempt to ground metaphoric meaning in a cognitive process is not unlike attempts to ground linguistic meaning in physical actions of stimulus and response. But even within a behavioristic context or in a cognitive process explanatory of metaphor, one must first identify the metaphor as a metaphor—one has to know which referents are juxtaposed—and this presumes acts of recognition that occur apart from the nonlinguistic explanatory account. Even with these meta-linguistic moves, one cannot escape circularity altogether.

Throughout this work I have assumed the basic unit of meaning to be the sentence rather than the word even though I have devoted much semantic analysis to the juxtaposition of the features of the referents of a metaphor. By claiming the sentence as the basic unit of meaning I recognize that syntax affects the meaning of semantics and that context also alters the meaning of the referents of a metaphor. Earlier in this book I noted the danger of forgetting that metaphors do not come only in the form "*A* is *B*." Metaphors also exist as powerful verbal metaphors—we *hear* stars *grind* the grist of ourselves into bony faces. If one limits metaphors to the form "*A* is *B*," then one might be tempted to look only at word meanings. But even this effort fails because through interaction both *A* and *B* are transformed and this transformation involves relations (both contextual and semantic ones) beyond the meanings of the individual words.

Communicative Meaning of Metaphor

Metaphors propose new meanings through their semantic juxtaposition of referents, their illocutionary force, and their interrelation with culture in a particular context. Even though all three of these aspects of meaning combine to produce a holistic meaning, I separate them for purposes of discussion into (1) language meaning composed of semantic and speech act aspects of meaning and (2) cultural meaning in the sense of a context.

Throughout this work, I have advocated an underlying cognitive process as forming the basis of the metaphoric linguistic process of juxtaposing usually unassociated referents. On the semantic level of explanation, new meanings arise from the association of features of similarity and dissimilarity of the metaphor's referents. By locating the semantic features of the referents of a metaphor in fuzzy sets, I allow for degrees of membership in categories defining semantic components. Concurrent with this move, I have also defined four truth values (F, D, E, T) for ranges of membership. This conflicts with the definition of presuppositions of communication in terms of a two-valued logic.

> In (1972) Strawson defines the presupposition relation by saying that a statement S presupposes a statement S' if and only if the truth of S' is a precondition of the truth or falsity of S (p. 175). In other words, to say that a statement object type S presupposes another statement object type S' is to say that the truth of S' is a necessary condition for the truth or falsity of S.[9]

Other semanticists separate the notion of presupposition from that of semantics, relegating the former to pragmatics and defining the latter in terms of truth conditions.[10] I have argued that semantics finds a better explanation in a cognitive theory of how the memory is organized and how a creative process of metaphoric formation occurs rather than in the conditions necessary for ascertaining the truth or falsity of a statement. Many metaphors, especially diaphors, cannot be fully reduced to statements easily discerned as true or false; yet, these suggestive metaphors may be quite meaningful. A semantics that demands that the presuppositions of a metaphor be those necessary linguistic features that determine the truth or falsity of a metaphor would prohibit the possibility of numerous metaphors from being comprehended as meaningful. In Plath's metaphor of "hearing the stars grind us to bony faces," if we rely strictly on the semantic presuppositions of the words that determine either the truth or falsity of the statement, we end up with the semantic anomaly that either we cannot "hear" stars or stars do not "grind," thereby making this utterance meaningless because we cannot determine its truth conditions or because we judge it to be a false statement since it is not true that we can hear stars and that stars can grind. We recall that in the controversion theory of metaphor the latter interpretation is chosen. This interpretation holds that the literal reading of metaphors produces contradictions; I rejected this premise on the grounds that metaphors convey new hypotheses that can be confirmed in experience and events and that inventors of metaphors do not intentionally set forth contradictions; instead they seek to convey and suggest new insights. I agree that metaphors produce semantic anomaly, but I have claimed that it is just this strange use of grammar that forces us to test various hypotheses of how these referents combine to produce a new meaning. In a poem or a scientific treatise, convinced of the sincere intentions of the author, we seek to understand what is suggested by the metaphor. We do not reject Plath's vibrant metaphor as nonsense, nor do we reject it as a contradiction. Instead we search for a new insight; we want to know how we can "hear" the "stars grind us to bony faces." Our discovery of the new meaning rests partly on our presupposition of the usual semantic meanings of these words; our comprehension depends partly on a cognitive process of acceptance and rejection of the similarities and dissimilarities among the semantic features of the metaphoric referents and partly on the context of the poem. Plath's description in the subtitle of the poem of the skeletons of the woman, the mouse, and the shrew reinforces our thinking about mortality, past, present, and future.

Presuppositions of the meanings of the referents of a metaphor are neither solely logical in the sense of searching for truth conditions nor solely pragmatic in the sense of searching for the context in which we can make determinations of truth or falsity.[11] Presuppositions do not depend primarily on searching for semantic or contextual truth conditions but rather involve a combination of semantic and contextual meaning. One can understand the meaning proposed by a metaphor without knowing whether the metaphor is true or false or to what degree the metaphor expresses a truth.

In a similar fashion, the emotive meaning of a metaphor depends on both the semantic associations of the referents and the context in which it occurs. Consider the following striking metaphor by Wordsworth: "Alas! the very murmur of the streams/Breathes o'er the failing soul voluptuous dreams."[12] The "murmur of streams" usually conveys a pleasant association, and "breathes" personifies the streams. From "failing soul" we derive the emotive associations of weariness, depression, sadness, and even perhaps declining toward death. But then we receive both a semantic and an emotive shock, how can the "murmur of streams breathe voluptuous dreams"? "Dreams" are imagined or thought about, not breathed in spoken words or sighs. Emotively, the "murmur of streams" does not sound like something "voluptuous." Is Wordsworth suggesting the return of sexual potency to an aging person through the symbol of water? The combination of words suggests various emotive feelings that depend on not only the traditional associations of emotions with words but also the present state of the hearer. If the hearer is a youth filled with passion, the "murmur of streams" may express his or her voluptuous feelings and he or she may experience exuberance. If the hearer is an an old man or woman, then this metaphor may bring with it the experience of sadness and nostalgia.

Both semantic non–truth-conditional presuppositions and pragmatic presuppositions combine in a single interpretation to produce metaphoric meaning. A common universal meaning may underlie the particular contexts of each hearer. All men and women comprehend the mortality suggested by Plath's metaphoric "stars" and the need for rebirth suggested by Wordsworth's metaphoric "streams." In both cases, the particular experience of an individual hearer and the universal experience of all hearers and the semantic emotive associations of the referents and the emotive aspects of each context unite to generate a single meaning in the mind of the hearer.

As a speech act, the metaphor also affects the meaning of the metaphor through the author's intention to produce a metaphor that convinces the hearer of the value of searching for meaning when confronted with semantic anomaly. The metaphor also performs the locutionary function of conveying the common semantic associations that both speaker and hearer presume and the perlocutionary function of affecting the feelings and beliefs of the hearer. The hearer of Wordsworth's metaphor may grasp a new insight, that hearing streams may stimulate greater life and vitality. Or the hearer in a depressed state may consider the metaphor and plunge further into despair as he or she can imagine no "voluptuous dreams" when considering streams. Or the hearer may be depressed and find rejuvenation of spirits when considering the "voluptuous dreams" suggested by "murmuring streams." In Plath's metaphor, one finds it difficult to experience rejuvenation or joy; the sense of mortality suggested by "stars" that "grind" us "crumb by crumb" into skeletons may arouse feelings of inevitability but not those of optimism.

The communicative meaning produced by metaphors arises from several aspects: the semantic associations of both cognitive and emotive referents, the function performed by the metaphor as a speech act, and the pragmatic context in which the metaphor is heard. We differentiate between semantic cognitive meaning and semantic emotive meaning only because it is traditional to do so. Throughout this work, I have found a close identification between emotion and cognition. In the account of semantic memory I found the motivation for the activation of widely disparate storage areas in emotive feelings. Emotions thus form an integral part of the cognitive process, but explaining exactly how emotions and concepts interrelate remains unclear, hence my retention of the traditional division.

Communicative meaning in metaphors operates largely at levels 1 and 2 of explanation; semantic associations occur at level 2, whereas speech acts and pragmatics occur at level 1. Neither, however, could occur without the underlying cognitive process that produces mechanisms by which new semantic meanings are created. Through the operation of syntactic and semantic rules these new cognitive combinations are presented in surface language. One cannot explain the operation of communicative meaning in metaphors without attention to the semantics of metaphor, the aspects of metaphor as a speech act, the context in which the metaphor occurs, and its wider cultural context. The concept "meaning" when applied to metaphor serves as a collection of the interrelationships of various types of meaning, all combining to produce comprehension in the hearer. The communicative meaning achieved exists independently of whether the metaphor can be said to convey truth. The degree to which a metaphor can be described as true depends on how well it expresses experience or confirms a hypothetical event. The meaning of a metaphor does not depend on whether one can set forth the exact truth conditions for that figurative expression. Theories of meaning based on truth conditions usually exclude metaphors as legitimate linguistic entities because they cannot find full specification in a procedure that would determine the truth or falsity of the metaphor. My treatment of the communicative meaning of metaphor has been necessarily brief since so much of this topic was covered in chapters 4 and 6. Now let us turn to an aspect of the meaning of metaphor that I have not yet covered, namely, the significance of metaphor.

Significance of Metaphor
Metaphors not only communicate suggestive and expressive meanings but they also become iconic objects through their fusion of sense with

sound. Paul Ricoeur suggests that this iconic function of metaphors forms a second type of reference.[13] Metaphors refer, often indirectly, to objects and experiences in the physical world—this is the first type of reference, called denotation by many philosophers. In the second type of reference (reference without denotation), metaphors refer to themselves as signs, their iconic function. Ricoeur observed that the first type of reference arises from a semantic analysis of metaphor and the second from treating metaphor as a type of semiotic reference.

If one confines the analysis of metaphor to the semantic function of communication, then the cultural significance of metaphor is a particular meaning derived from the aspects of semantics, metaphor as a speech act, and the context of this particular metaphor. But if one attends to the second type of reference, then the cultural significance of metaphor may be determined more generally by how metaphors function as icons. All words have an iconic function as signs; they also function as symbols representing other things. Metaphors, however, are an unusual type of icon and symbol in that they juxtapose normally unassociated referents and suggest new hypotheses about the physical world in their communicative function as well as the nature of the fictional world presupposed often in their literary functions as icons. Ricoeur believes that by investigating the iconic level of reference, one can discover a metaphorical meaning beyond that of communicative meaning found in semantic acts of denotation and in speech acts.

> It may be indeed, that the metaphorical statement is precisely the one that points out most clearly this relationship between suspended reference and displayed reference. Just as the metaphorical statement captures its sense as metaphorical midst the ruins of the literal sense, it also achieves its reference upon the ruins of what might be called (in symmetrical fashion) its literal reference. If it is true that literal sense and metaphorical sense are distinguished and articulated within an interpretation, so too it is within an interpretation that a second-level reference, which is properly the metaphorical reference, is set free by means of the suspension of the first-level reference.[14]

Ricoeur suggests that through their iconic function metaphors may create a meaning of their own that is not dependent on the relation of the referents of a metaphor to the physical world. From Ricoeur's proposal one might claim that metaphors "present" meaning in addition to "representing" meanings that might be found in the external world. A metaphor not only may suggest a new hypothesis about the world but also may present a new hypothesis about itself as a form of language.

In a manner similar to my claim that metaphors are linguistic expressions of cognitive processes, Ricoeur builds his theory of metaphor as an icon on a cognitive notion, namely, that of "seeing as," which was proposed by Wittgenstein and explicitly applied to metaphor by Marcus Hester in his *The Meaning of Poetic Metaphor*.[15]

> Thus, the 'seeing as' activated in reading ensures the joining of verbal meaning with imagistic fullness. And this conjunction is no longer something outside language, since it can be reflected as a relationship. 'Seeing as' contains a ground, a foundation, that is, precisely, resemblance—no longer the resemblance between two ideas, but that very resemblance the 'seeing as' establishes. Hester claims emphatically that similarity is what results from the experience-act of 'seeing as.' *'Seeing as'* defines the resemblance, and not the reverse. This priority of 'seeing as' over the resemblance relationship is proper to the language-game in which meaning functions in an iconic manner. That is why the 'seeing as' can succeed or fail. It can fail as in forced metaphor, because they are inconsistent or fortuitous, or on the contrary, as in banal and commonplace metaphors; and succeed as in those that fashion the surprise of discovery.[16]

The resemblance that the "seeing as" establishes when metaphor functions as an icon need not be found in the physical world; that resemblance can be a fictional construction. The structure of a literary world can be constructed largely without reference to the world of ordinary experience. Carried to an extreme, the literary world of the poem creates its own meaning through the iconic function of its metaphors. Ricoeur, however, seems to stop short of this extreme when he observes that hermeneutics relates the structure of a literary work to the physical world.

Northrop Frye, however, does seem to confine the meaning of poetic metaphors to the literary context in which they occur. Frye conceives of literature as a self-contained language that can apply to the empirical world only through conscious interpretation. In making this assertion, he drew an analogy with mathematics: "Both literature and mathematics proceed from postulates, not facts; both can be applied to external reality and yet exist also in a 'pure' or self-contained form."[17] Frye went on to argue that the study of archetypes warrants the concept of an entire sphere of literature isolated from the ordinary material world: "The study of archetypes is the study of literary symbols as parts of a whole. If there are such things as archetypes at all, then we have to take yet another step and conceive the possibility of a self-contained literary universe."[18] But how then can literature deal with the very stuff of life with which we are familiar? If the literary universe is completely removed, then literature would seem to be totally irrelevant to humanity. Frye sensed this problem and attempted to solve it by allowing the context of literature to be derived from experience while reserving its forms to this "self-contained literary universe."

> Literature may have life, reality, experience, nature, imaginative truth, social conditions, or what you will for its *content*; but literature itself is not made out of these things. Poetry can only be made out of other poems; novels out of other novels. Literature shapes itself, and is not shaped externally; the *forms* of literature can no more exist outside literature than the forms of sonata and fugue and rondo can exist outside music.[19]

And one of those forms is a metaphor. What happens to a metaphor when it is confined to a self-contained universe? If that universe is literature, then metaphors can express only literary meanings, and if we confine ourselves to the mythic mode, then the metaphor unites only one literary meaning with another.

> Archetypically, where the symbol is an associative cluster, the metaphor unites two individual images, each of which is a specific representative of a class or genus. The rose in Dante's *Paradiso* and the rose in Yeats' early lyrics are identified *with* different things, but both stand for all roses—all poetic roses, of course, not all botanical ones. Archetypal metaphor thus involves the use of what has been called the concrete universal, the individual identified with its class, Wordsworth's 'tree of many one.' Of course, there are no *real* universals in poetry, only poetic ones.[20]

If a poetic rose is not associated with a botanical rose, do the words found in literature have meanings that are esoteric and confined solely to their literary usage? When readers see the word "rose" in a poem, how can they fail to associate it with its normal meanings and perhaps also with their own personal remembrances of beautiful roses they have encountered? Even if the poetic rose operates as a symbol or metaphor suggesting something other than the usual meanings of the term, readers retain their normal associations with that word. If readers were to follow Frye's exclusive division of roses into poetic and botanical, the poetic rose would be unintelligible. What could be the meaning of a poetic rose if it did not stand also for a botanical rose? Confining the meaning of a poetic rose to literature would force us into the impossible position of attempting to forget our normal associations for that word and then to learn new ones determined by the literary context in which the word appears. Carried to a logical extreme, it would prevent us from understanding any literary terms; we cannot allow them to convey the normal meanings they have from everyday experience, and in order to learn their literary meanings we would have to understand literature, a thing we cannot do until we know the meanings of the literary terms. This dilemma of circularity arises only when one demands that the meanings of literary terms be determined by only the literary context in which they occur. Better to identify the poetic rose with the botanical rose and then to suggest by the metaphoric use of that poetic rose how the two are different.

The application of Northrop Frye's theory of literary criticism to metaphor demonstrates the impossibility of separating completely the iconic meaning of a metaphor from its semantic meaning. From the point of view of metaphor as a cognitive process, one gains another perspective on the impossibility of separating literature from life; in the long-term semantic memory, the various semantic meanings of "rose" exist in a hierarchical network with the nodes of that network (fuzzy sets) defining associations of words with semantic features. To ensure the divorce of the literary meaning of a word from its ordinary meaning, one would have to erase the information stored in long-term semantic memory, a virtual impossibility. Within the semantic memory, the figurative uses of a word are added to its ordinary associations. After learning the poetic meaning of the "rose" in Dante's *Paradiso* one cannot also forget or unlearn the botanical meaning of "rose" acquired much earlier during one's own language acquisition.

The discovery that the iconic meaning of a metaphor cannot be separated fully from its semantic meaning does not prevent a metaphor from having an aesthetic cultural meaning in addition to its communicative meaning. The aesthetic meaning of a metaphor may be an integral part or at least an accompaniment of the communicative meaning. Wordsworth's "murmur of the streams/Breathes o'er the failing soul voluptuous dreams" may suggest not only the communicative meaning of a feature of nature, flowing water, reviving a tired and/or old person but also the aesthetic meaning of the archetypal, literary association of water with rebirth. Hearers unacquainted with the symbolic meaning of "water" in literature may still understand the metaphor, but they may not understand the full possibility of its cultural meaning without knowing the tradition in which the poem stands.

Susanne K. Langer also applied an aesthetic theory of meaning to metaphor by considering the nondiscursive aspect of poetry.[21] She describes art as "the creation of forms symbolic of human feeling."[22] By "feeling" Langer means much more than just emotion; she describes it as a much larger category of experience.

Feeling, in the broad sense of whatever is felt in any way, as sensory stimulus or inward tension, pain, emotion or intent, is the mark of mentality. In its most primitive forms it is the forerunner of the phenomena that constitute the subject matter of psychology. Organic activity is not "physiological" unless it terminates, however remotely or indirectly, in something felt. Physiology is different from psychology, not because it deals with different events—the overlapping of the two fields is patent—but because it is not oriented toward the aspects of sensibility, awareness, excitement, gratification or suffering which belong to those events.[23]

Langer does not believe that language in its iconic, nondiscursive aspect expresses feeling, but rather that language as an aesthetic symbol conveys ideas of feeling to the hearer. These ideas of feeling express the feelings of the author of the poem and may also suggest feelings not intended. Works of art, including poetry, convey knowledge that cannot be expressed discursively without loss of content.

Non-discursive form in art has a different office, namely to articulate knowledge that cannot be rendered discursively because it concerns experiences that are not *formally* amenable to the discursive projection. Such experiences are the rhythms of life, organic, emotional and mental (the rhythm of attention is an interesting link among them all), which are not simply periodic, but endlessly complex, and sensitive to every sort of influence. All together they compose the dynamic pattern of feeling. It is this pattern that only non-discursive symbolic forms can present, and that is the point and purpose of artistic construction.[24]

Like Frye, Langer argues that art creates a virtual world, but not one that we live in; rather, we look at this virtual world and use objects from the actual world—like the words of a poem—to create the art object that expresses symbolic feeling. Langer, however, does stress that the laws of imagination of the poet are *not* the laws of discursive language.[25] In treating the virtual world created by the perception of an art object and its relation to the actual world, Langer ambivalently moves from one to the other. The virtual world exists apart from the actual world and its laws are those of its own genre, but the virtual world employs materials from the actual world and these materials are, in the case of words, their ordinary meanings. When Wordsworth takes the word "murmur" and juxtaposes it with "breathe" and then further juxtaposes "breathe" with "dream," the virtual world of that poetry retains the discursive meaning along with the aesthetic meaning suggested by the metaphorical transformation of meaning. Frye's closed literary world seems to eliminate the ambiguity of having two or more types of meaning in poetry, the communicative meaning and the iconic meaning.

Langer also indicates the ambivalence of the meaning of an art object by attempting to subsume both aesthetics and cognition under the same category of feeling. She argues that the creation of a poem as a symbolic form is no less a mental act than the formation of language intended to communicate practical or scientific ideas. In comparing a work of art with a metaphor, however, Langer implies that these two types of meaning, communicative and what she calls the nondiscursive, operate with two different forms of understanding.

> The creative processes which build up an artist's image of subjective acts are numberless, because they can work in combination by many projective techniques at once, mingling several principles of presentation. A work of art is like a metaphor, to be understood without translation or comparison of ideas; it exhibits its form, and the import is immediately perceived in it. So far, I have always called its characteristc symbolic mode simply "non-discursive"; but there are other non-discursive symbols, such as maps and plans, which have not the organic structure or the implicit signif- icance of art. One might well call a work of art a metaphorical symbol.[26]

I believe that even in the apprehension of the iconic or aesthetic meaning of a metaphor, one must compare the semantic features of the referents if one is to understand the language as a metaphor and not as literal. The same cognitive process, albeit perhaps implicit, underlies both the discursive and the nondiscursive recognition of a combination of words as metaphorical. If Langer's contention were correct, then the recognition of an art object as a metaphoric symbol would occur as an immediate intuition. I agree that artistic recognition may be immediate, but under- lying that immediacy must be a cognitive process involving memory, retrieval, and the formation of an idea or image. I do not deny that the long-term memory may be filled with nondiscursive elements, for example, images. I do deny, however, that nondiscursive recognition can occur without some form of cognitive processing enabling one to discern similarities and dissimilarities.

If the same cognitive process underlies both the recognition of the communicative meaning and the aesthetic cultural meaning, then what is the difference between the two? I have already noted that the two are not completely separate because the virtual world of the poetic metaphor draws on elements from the actual world, and these elements come with their ordinary meanings that cannot be forgotten. One can have communicative meaning without aesthetic meaning, but one cannot derive aesthetic meaning from language without also deriving communicative meaning because words always retain their ordinary meanings in our memory. Frye's "literary rose" always retains its biological aspects; when one talks about a rose, however, even metaphorically, one need not necessarily derive aesthetic symbolic meanings. Suppose a father speaks of his daughter as "the rose of his life"; he need not necessarily invoke the literary or archetypal associations of "rose," although he could do that if those associations occurred. Or suppose a woman speaks of her personal computer as "the rose of her life"; one would have to ponder for a while what the speaker meant by this metaphor.

My claim that the same cognitive process underlies the comprehension of both communicative and iconic meanings may not be incompatible with Langer's contention that "a work of art is like a metaphor, to be understood without translation or comparison of ideas . . ." if she is describing the ways in which we operate at level 1, that of surface language. People do indeed perceive immediately the meanings of works of art in their iconic as well as communicative aspects. I have been arguing that beneath the function of both communicative and artistic recognition of meaning one finds a cognitive process necessary for both. If Langer intended to describe artistic metaphoric recognition as an intuitive act not dependent on an underlying cognitive process, then I must respectfully disagree.

The cultural meaning of metaphor depends on its relations to other iconic or symbolic literary meanings and to the context of the world in which the metaphor exists. The virtual world of the aesthetic meaning of a metaphor about which Langer speaks cannot generate a meaning without retaining its relationship to communicative meaning, especially semantics. Even the most poetic metaphor does not fully divorce itself from both the literal meaning of its referents and the communicative metaphoric meaning of its referents. At the level of surface language, Ricoeur may be correct in his claim that metaphors have two types of reference, the denotative and the nondenotative of the metaphor as an icon. But these references never occur without presuming the semantic associations of the referents at a deeper level of explanation.

Some metaphors may, as Langer claims, convey nondiscursive meanings through discursive language; but other metaphors may also represent *new* discursive meanings through new juxtapositions of ordinary language. And still other metaphors may perform both functions, expressing both verbal and nonverbal meanings. Langer's category of feeling allows intuitions of all sorts, perceptions, emotions, and reasons.

Since metaphors as iconic art objects present a symbolic expression of feeling, they can express verbal *and* nonverbal meanings.

Cognitive Meaning

Just as communicative and cultural meaning at level 1 presume semantic meaning at level 2, all three types of meaning presume a cognitive process at level 3. The reader may wonder why I even bother to speak of cognitive meanings when "meaning" by definition depends on some form of expression in entities such as words or paintings or sounds. What is cognitive meaning? Can something such as emotive meaning (the conveyance of the author's emotions or the evocation of the hearer's emotions) about which I spoke earlier suggest that cognitive meaning conveys the author's knowledge or evokes knowledge in the hearer? The cognitive meaning of a metaphor can be the ability of the metaphor to suggest new hypothetical knowledge. But these suggestions might also in a reflexive sense affect the cognitive process by which metaphors are produced. This would put the generator of metaphors in the position of reflexively modifying the cognitive process from which metaphors arise. That such a process operates is the contention of this section. The production of metaphors changes the ways in which we understand the world, thereby affecting the cognitive process by which we produce metaphors. I have already noted this reflexive and quasi-circular process in the treatment of metaphors as participants in a knowledge process that mediates between biological and cultural evolution (chapter 5).

Hayden White investigated the ways in which figurative language, especially metaphor, has influenced the manner in which we understand the nature of history.[27] White begins with the assumption that all discourse describes not only subject matter but also itself. He follows a line similar to my notion that cognitive meaning might be self-reflective: "Discourse, in a word, is quintessentially a *mediative* enterprise. As such, it is both interpretive and preinterpretive; it is always as much *about* the nature of interpretation itself as it is *about* the subject matter which is the manifest occasion of its own elaboration."[28] In White's theory, language reveals not only the meaning of events in the sense of both communicative and cultural meaning but also a type of cognitive meaning. The latter finds expression in the tropes of metaphor, metonymy, synecdoche, and irony.

> As thus envisaged, a discourse is itself a kind of model of the processes of consciousness by which a given area of experience, originally apprehended as simply a field of phenomena demanding understanding, is assimilated by analogy to those areas of experience felt to be *already* understood as to *their* essential natures.

Understanding is a process of rendering the unfamiliar, or the "uncanny" in Freud's sense of that term, familiar; of removing it from the domain of things felt to be "exotic" and unclassified into one or another domain of experience encoded adequately enough to be felt to be humanly useful, nonthreatening, or simply known by association. This process of understanding can only be tropological in nature, for what is involved in the rendering of the unfamiliar into the familiar is a troping that is generally figurative. It follows, I think, that this process of understanding proceeds by the exploitation of the principal modalities of figuration, identified in post-Renaissance rhetorical theory as the "master tropes" (Kenneth Burke's phrase) of metaphor, metonymy, synecdoche, and irony.[29]

White grounds these tropes in a "metaphorical consciousness," which might be "a primitive form of knowing in the ontogenesis of human consciousness in its passage from infancy to maturity."[30] The choice of a trope by a historian not only forms an organization of "the facts" but also serves as a cognitive process of selection of what constitutes the facts for an explanation.

> For we should recognize that what constitutes the facts themselves is the problem that the historian, like the artist, has tried to solve in the choice of the metaphor by which he orders his world, past, present, and future. We should ask only that the historian show some tact in the use of his governing metaphors: that he neither overburden them with data or fail to use them to their limit; that he respect the logic implicit in the mode of discourse he has decided upon; and that, when his metaphor begins to show itself unable to accommodate certain kinds of data, he abandon that metaphor and seek another, richer, and more inclusive metaphor than that with which he began—in the same way that a scientist abandons a hypothesis when its use is exhausted.[31]

White believes that the reflection on the choice of metaphors prevents the historian or scientist from falling into a mistaken quest for objectivity or into a radical relativism. The choice of a particular trope does not reconstruct *all* the facts, but awareness of these *choices* also does not imply that any explanation is as good as any other since the researcher has to justify the selection of a particular metaphor.

Jeremy Rifkin described disagreements about explanation in biology in terms similar to those White used in analyzing historical explanations.

> The battle over competing biological paradigms is as much a struggle over competing languages and metaphors as anything else.

The neo-Darwinists continue to use the language and metaphors of the industrial age, while a new generation of scientists are using the language and metaphors of the age of biotechnology. It's a battle between those who continue to think in terms of the best-built machines versus those who think in terms of the best-designed programs.[32]

Both White and Rifkin suggest that the meanings we attribute to theories arise not only from the semantics of metaphor but also from a cognitive process underlying the linguistic associations of the referents of a metaphor. The production of new metaphors creates new semantic concepts expressed in both communicative and cultural meanings. Reflection on the process of producing metaphors, however, also modifies how that process occurs. In choosing a metaphor to both define and organize the facts in an explanation, we limit the ways in which we think about a problem, thus channeling the production of future metaphors. These channels of cognition can be broken either intentionally or accidentally when the ordinary way of thinking about a problem is challenged by a new theoretical possibility. I have already noted in chapter 5 that one cannot provide rules for the formation of metaphors because their creation seems to defy any regular pattern.

The notion of cognitive meaning employed thus far indicates a self-conscious understanding of the cognitive process by which metaphors are generated. And the choice of which metaphor is produced influences the process of future choices of other explanatory metaphors. But if there were a "language of thought," one might more properly talk about cognitive meaning differently. One could then talk about cognitive meaning with respect to an awareness of the process of metaphor formation and specify the contents of that process by comprehending the linguistic units of the language of thought. In the earlier effort to show that my theory of semantic change can be embedded in a cognitive theory, I noted that many psychologists conjecture that units of information are stored as propositions in long-term memory. If the organization of the memory is propositional, then in what language are those propositions written? A natural language? An abstract deep structure of linguistics? An internal language similar to machine language of a computer? If one follows the computational metaphor for cognition, then shouldn't one also postulate the existence of a mental machine language into which the propositions stored in memory must be translated?

In a series of highly controversial arguments, Jerry Fodor proposed the existence of a language of thought.[33]

It seems to me that all these considerations point towards a fundamental and pervasive feature of higher cognitive processes: *the intelligent management of internal representations.* Serious psychology begins with the recognition that it matters how the organism specifies imagining stimuli and response options. It thus presupposes an internal language rich enough to represent whatever inputs can affect behavior and whatever outputs the organism can deploy.[34]

I cannot within the scope of this work adjudicate the question of the existence of an internal language of thought; but I can suggest that if one does exist, then there is a cognitive meaning at the third level of explanation. Whether one could reductively translate the meanings of a machine language process that ultimately produced a metaphor to either or both the communicative and cultural meaning of the metaphor produced would pose an interesting problem. One might also speculatively consider whether machine language metaphors different from ordinary language metaphors can be produced. One would also be left with the question of whether a machine language metaphor possesses any significance beyond the realm of machine language. These are extremely complicated questions and are only posed as possibilities.

Metaphorical Meaning

Meaning comes in a variety of types, and the meaning of metaphor can be described in a variety of ways. In this chapter I have described three overlapping types of meaning: communicative meaning, cultural meaning, and cognitive meaning. Within communicative meaning I included semantic meaning (the meaning that arises from the association of the semantic features of the referents of a metaphor), the meaning derived from metaphor considered as a speech act, including its illocutionary and perlocutionary forces, and the meaning of a metaphor determined by the context in which it is uttered. Under the rubric cultural meaning I concentrated on the iconic and symbolic meaning of a metaphor—the metaphor's own reference to itself as an art object that produces a symbolic expression of feeling in Langer's wider notion of feeling. In a less restricted sense, cultural meaning also includes the particular context of a metaphor so that communicative meaning depends in part on culture. Under cognitive meaning I described the ways in which a metaphor may change the entire structure of what we consider to be knowledge and facts. By determining the nature of knowledge, the production of a metaphor can alter, through self-awareness on the part of the creator of a metaphor, the cognitive process underlying metaphor production. I also suggested that, if there exists an internal language of thought, then the notion of cognitive meaning might itself have an additional meaning, namely, that of designating the meaning of the cognitive process by which surface language metaphors are generated.

The division of the types of meaning is not necessarily the only way to talk about how a metaphor conveys information and acts as a symbol. I could have described the meaning of a metaphor in the more traditional fashion of its cognitive and emotive meanings. This division, however, artificially divides the role of emotions in the cognitive process—I have argued that emotions often provide the motivation for the process of retrieval in memory, resulting in the unusual juxtaposition of referents. Even the referents themselves possess emotive associations such that the emotive information conveyed by a metaphor cannot be separated from the metaphor's expression of information traditionally labeled "cognitive." By separating the meaning of a metaphor from assessments of its truth, I opened the door to this more complex understanding of meaning by combining various linguistic and nonlinguistic elements from various levels of explanation. Before proceeding to the treatment of the relation of metaphor to truth (chapter 8), consider an example taken from Newton's physics of how a scientific metaphor achieves the various types of meaning I have described. I have chosen Newton's metaphors because I believe them to be a harder case for my theory than poetic metaphors, for many may wonder if metaphors other than literary ones can possess an iconic meaning.

Ernan McMullin described in careful detail Newton's struggle to formulate concepts of matter, gravity, and activity and his efforts to interrelate these entities.[35] In the *Principia* Newton was concerned with the mathematical analysis of laws of force and with the *physics* of the operations of these laws within nature. Outside the *Principia* and for the rest of his life, Newton was concerned as a natural philosopher with discovering the philosophical causes of these forces. McMullin shows how Newton resorted to the formulation of a series of metaphorical explanations to resolve the conflict between his newly formulated mathematical physics and the intuitions of common sense. In attempting to answer the question of how matter is moved, Newton vacillated between the Cartesian tradition, which demands that motion requires contact, and the neo-Platonic and alchemical traditions, which involve a variety of "active principles" to explain motion. Newton's metaphors, conjectured to resolve this tension, ranged from that of absolute space, viewed as extensionally identical with God, to "aetheral spirits," which are responsible for the *initiation* of motion in refraction, electrical attraction, gravitation, muscular action, and other such phenomena in which new motion clearly appears.[36] Newton speculated on the possibility that the activity of bodies might be caused by the nature of light. Newton considered the possibility that an "electric spirit" "could bring about the emission of light, besides causing small objects to move."[37] Newton also proposed aether as an active principle causing motion but ran into difficulties when his mechanical metaphors describing the action of aether implied that aether was composed of finite material particles. Adamant that matter itself could not be a source of motion, attributing an active principle of motion to material, Newton found that particles of aether seemed to contradict this conceptual postulate. McMullin notes that "there can be little doubt that the metaphors of spirit and active principle, with their overtone of a mode of presence in space other than that of material occupation, helped to dissolve the doubts he [Newton] had expressed about action at a distance."[38]

Let us examine two of Newton's metaphors, "God is space" and "An electric spirit moves small objects," to see how they achieve various types of meaning. As expressions of communicative meaning, both metaphors depend on the juxtaposition of the semantic features of Animate with Inanimate. The usual association with "God" is that of a living, transcendent being, whereas "space" remains Inanimate and part of the physical world. Similarly, "electricity" is Inanimate, and "spirit" by definition is "living" or Animate. The interactions of these features produces a semantic meaning. As speech acts, they shock the hearer emotionally and have the force of suggesting as a metaphorical act that these combinations are indeed worthy of communicative consideration. The hearer must think about how an electric spirit could move an object or how a transcendent God could be imminent in the spatial dimensions of the world. Newton's context for coining these metaphors arises from both his mathematical laws of motion and his secular and theological intuitions about experience and the transcendent nature of the world.

The cultural meaning of both metaphors arises from the images that they suggest. Following Hester and Ricoeur we may try to imagine how God represented by a human figure can be extended in space; does God's face appear in the sky or clouds? We may imagine the "electric spirit" to be like a wood nymph. The iconic values of these metaphors depend on our seeing them as imagined figures, an act of imagination just as possible for scientific metaphors as for poetic metaphors.

The cognitive meanings of "God is space" and "An electric spirit moves small objects" arise from the ways in which these metaphors affect our perceptions of the world. If we were to adopt either metaphor as useful for determining the nature of the world, determining what data we consider to be significant as factual, then in the future when we construct other metaphors to express hypotheses, the cognitive process of formulation will be affected by this view of the world.

These three overlapping types of meaning, communicative, cultural, and cognitive, all combine to produce in the audience a metaphorical meaning. No single meaning need be given any particular metaphor because the context can vary, the semantic associations of the hearer can vary, and the significance can vary from culture to culture. Metaphors create new meanings of various types; without them, neither knowledge nor language can grow. Without cognitively based linguistic devices to juxtapose the old in unfamiliar ways, new ways of thinking and new expressions for those thoughts cannot emerge.

8
Metaphor and Truth

The Problem of Metaphor and Truth

Can metaphors make "true" assertions? I have already noted (chapter 2) that advocates of the controversion theory believe that every proper metaphor when taken literally asserts a false statement. Hence they claim metaphors can be described as false statements that generate new insights. A commitment to the controversion theory puts the creator of a metaphor in the position of intentionally formulating a false statement in order to convey a new idea. Why should the originator of a metaphor want to say something false in order to convey a new idea? And the more epiphoric the metaphor, the greater the similarity among the metaphor's referents, which strains the contention that the juxtaposition of the referents produces a false statement. Constable's assertion that "Painting is a science . . . of which pictures are but experiments" seems to produce an insight that the hearer on first encounter takes to be a true assertion in some sense.[1] The artist's studio does have similarities to the scientist's laboratory; the painter attempts to express new ideas through new techniques, whereas the scientist attempts to evaluate new theoretical hypotheses through experiments with newly designed tests and apparatus. Paul Olscamp disagreed with the contention that metaphors necessarily express false statements.

> I think that metaphors are *either* true or false, that their truth or falsity, depending upon the context, may or may not be one of the criteria for judging whether or not they are apt and fitting, and that the question of their truth or falsity has little or nothing to do with their special meanings. I shall try to defend these claims in what follows. But first I want to *exclude* one class of metaphors from my discussion: I shall not examine, nor do I wish to say my remarks are true of, that kind of metaphor which Wheelwright calls "diaphoric" metaphor.[2]

I agree with Olscamp as far as he has gone, and I extend the applicability of truth to metaphors by claiming that diaphor can also be included if

one changes the notion of truth itself from an absolute either/or concept
to one involving degrees of truth. Earlier in this book I described the
semantics of metaphor as embodied in a hierarchical network of linguistic associations with the nodes of the network defined by fuzzy
sets in which words find membership to varying degrees. I assigned
to words four possible truth values (F, D, E, T) in the interval 0 to 1
within a fuzzy set defining a semantic marker. In this chapter I consider
further the nature of this system of truth values as it applies to metaphor
and in relation to more usual philosophical notions of truth.

I assert that all metaphors are true to a degree; that is, through their
novel juxtaposition of referents they express insights that are proper
assertions. Because these assertions are hypothetical, the degree of truth
expressed in a metaphor derives its value largely from the epiphoric
analogy of similarities of referents rather than from the diaphoric value
resulting from the disanalogies. Olscamp's intuition was correct, but
he did not extend it far enough to cover diaphors. Even the most
speculative diaphor must have some analogy in order to be understood
as a metaphor, and it is this modicum of similarity that guarantees an
expression of truth in the metaphor.

To defend my thesis, I have to consider the objections to and the
consequences of changing the normal notion of truth as a two-valued
function. As a prelude to this consideration, I reconsider the controversion theory, attempt to relate my theory to traditional correspondence
and coherence theories of truth, consider the problem of truth and
relativity of metaphor as formulated by Nelson Goodman, and speculate
on how a many-valued notion of truth applies to presuppositions in
semantics. After I have explored the notion of a four-valued system of
truth in more detail, I will also consider the relation of knowledge
construed as a cognitively based evolutionary epistemology to my notion
of truth.

The Controversion Theory Reconsidered

Monroe Beardsley formulated the controversion theory in his *Aesthetics*,
asserting that ". . . a metaphor is a significant attribution that is either
indirectly self-contradictory or obviously false in its context, and in
which the modifier connotes characteristics that can be attributed, truly
or falsely, to the subject."[3] Beardsley drew on the obvious observation
that many metaphors do indeed seem to be false or self-contradictory
when they are taken literally. "Painting" is *not* literally a "science,"
and "pictures" are *not* "experiments," but Constable never really intended to put forth these denials as assertions. Instead he wanted to
call attention in a novel way to the similarities between "painting" and

"science" and between "pictures" and "experiments." Beardsley would agree that Constable's intention was to say something of significance; his means, however, consisted of uttering an intentionally false statement that the hearer recognized as intentionally false and therefore of conveying a significant meaning different from the false assertion. In "The metaphorical twist," Beardsley not only renamed the controversion theory as the verbal-opposition theory but also elaborated a mechanism by which one shifts from literal falsity to metaphorical meaning.[4] He asserted that metaphors can be analyzed on two different levels: (1) the logical opposition of the literal referents and (2) the semantic meaning derived from the referents taken metaphorically rather than literally. He suggested that the movement from (1) to (2) occurs as a cognitive process involving a shift from concerns about extension (denotation) to concerns about intension (connotation).

I agree with Beardsley that the strangeness of metaphors arises from their semantical anomaly, but I deny that metaphors necessarily produce false assertions. Only occasionally do we first encounter a metaphor that seems literally to be a false assertion; usually our first encounter with a metaphor occurs as an immediate recognition that the language is metaphorical. Our cognitive process allows us to find semantical meaning in seeming semantic anomaly by discovering sufficient similarity among the semantic markers of the referents of the metaphor. Beardsley may be correct in judging that *if* we took a metaphor to be literal, it would produce contradiction or falsehood, but I contend that normally we do *not* consider the juxtaposition of terms to be literal.

At this point, the disagreement between Beardsley and me may seem to be a quibble about a hypothetical question of whether hearers of metaphors do actually cognitively process metaphors first as literally false and second as having semantic, metaphorical meaning. But the debate takes on significance when one connects the controversion theory with Beardsley's desire to ground literature in empiricism.[5] As the arbiter of truth and falsity, literal language also offers a haven in which literature and poetry can find assertions as true or false if the literary metaphors can be reduced to literal language. Beardsley followed this direction.

> But even if we can seldom, in practice, paraphrase *all* of a given poem, we can nevertheless paraphrase *any* of it that we wish to paraphrase. And the number of meanings is, after all, not infinite, so there is not necessarily something that in principle eludes us.[6]

In a metaphor such as "He is a fox" one does not, according to Beardsley, determine the truth or falsity of the *metaphorical* meaning by testing the literal terms but rather by paraphrasing this metaphor as "He is cunning, cruel, sly, dangerous." Beardsley admitted that, although in practice it may be difficult to paraphrase all of a poem, in principle there exists no argument against this possibility.

By contrast, my road to the actual empirical world follows the fit of prototypical categories to experience rather than the correspondence of words to things by means of assertions that are true or false. Hence I have not been concerned with the need to paraphrase metaphors, reducing them to literal language. In the association of "painting" with "science" we are concerned with the cognitive process by which the semantic markers of the referents find both similarity and dissimilarity. The greater the degree of similarity, the more epiphoric and less suggestive the metaphor. The greater the degree of dissimilarity, the more suggestive and less expressive. Even the most suggestive metaphor, if recognized as a legitimate metaphor, can have a degree of truth through the membership of the attributes of its referents in fuzzy sets defining semantic markers. The truth of a metaphor, therefore, does not rest solely on its paraphrase in literal language. Nor does the recognition of a metaphor depend on a requirement that metaphors when taken literally produce self-contradiction or falsity.

Timothy Binkley produced an argument with counterexamples against the controversion theory's claim that the characteristic mark of a metaphor is the generation of self-contradiction or falsity by taking it literally.[7] Consider the statement "Anchorage is a cold city" uttered as both a literal statement about the climate of the city and as a metaphorical statement about the hospitality of its citizens. Here is a metaphor that does not produce literal absurdity. Binkley also argued that it makes sense to argue about the truth and falsity of metaphorical statements.

> Consider the following exchange between two persons discussing, say, a lawyer:
> A. That Richard is a fox, isn't he? Did you notice how he slyly equivocated on the defendant's statement?
> B. Oh, I don't think he's a fox. It was probably just a lucky blunder. You should have seen him last week and you'd find it hard to believe he's a fox too.[8]

Admitting that Binkley had cast doubts on the comprehensiveness of the controversion theory, Beardsley still contended that a "huge number of metaphors, old, new, and yet unborn" usually produce an "implicit contradiction."[9]

Earlier in this work I contended that the controversion theory rested on a strange assumption that poets, scientists, and others who formulate metaphors do so with two intentions in mind: to state something literally that is false and to state something significant. I do not deny that

Beardsley has captured the sense of anomaly and strangeness that metaphors produce, but I contend that he has needlessly complicated metaphor by arguing that it *intentionally* performs two functions at once. If one takes metaphor to be literal, it *may* produce a false statement, but few people take them in that fashion; rather we comprehend the analogy expressed in the metaphor and puzzle about the disanalogy.

Correspondence and/or Coherence

The controversion theory, with its identification of the falsity of most metaphors taken literally and its desire to assert true statements through paraphrase, illustrates the problem of understanding the phenomenon of metaphor in relation to coherence and correspondence theories of truth. Beardsley's renaming the controversion theory a verbal-opposition theory exemplifies that operation of a coherence theory. One judges truth or falsity by how the linguistic parts of the metaphor fit together; the literal reading of the referents of most metaphors produces a contradiction or falsity. One does not compare the referents of the metaphor with objects in the world. But in the paraphrase of a metaphor, one does compare the words of the paraphrase with objects or events in the empirical world to decide whether the paraphrase expresses a true or false statement. Tests about the truth or falsity of the paraphrase, therefore, indicate the operation of a correspondence theory of truth. We saw a similar implicit adoption of these two types of theories of truth in Lakoff and Johnson's claims that all language is metaphorical. Their descriptions of the conceptual interrelationships among various types of metaphor, literal metaphors and figurative metaphors, represent the operation of a coherence theory. Their efforts to demonstrate how concepts emerge without linguistic mediation from direct experience of things, like space, indicate the implicit assumption of a correspondence theory of truth. Lakoff and Johnson were concerned with demonstrating how one could relate direct experiences (self-evident) to beliefs expressed in linguistic concepts (metaphors).

I use the notions of a correspondence theory of truth and a coherence theory of truth loosely. These concepts cover various families of theories about truth with the former usually describing theories that attempt to relate objects and events in the physical world to propositions or statements through some perceptual or experiential account. The proposition under consideration is determined to be true or false independently of the proposition itself. Tarski offered perhaps the starkest expression of this theory when he claimed that the proposition "Snow is white" is true if and only if in fact snow is white. Coherence theories describe efforts to relate one proposition to another proposition without necessarily resorting to testing procedures related to the physical world. In a coherence theory one can test the truth or falsity of one proposition by assessing its relationship to the other proposition already known to be true or false.

I use the correspondence theory of truth to refer to the process of judging the fit between events and objects in the world and the prototypical categories I have posited as some of the fuzzy-set nodes in our semantic network. These prototypical categories *correspond* to events and objects in the world by their accurate categorical description of them. I use coherence theory to describe the assessment of the relationship among semantical markers (words) not necessarily related to the physical world through prototypical categories. Words *cohere* successfully when they are synonyms or close to synonyms. Instead of employing the words correspondence and coherence, I might have chosen material truth and lexical truth, with the former describing the relationship of successful prototypical categories to the world and the latter describing successful synonymous relationship between words. I have retained the traditional usages because I believe that the truth-functional relationships I am describing belong within the loosely construed families of theories of truth.

I also employ the notions of analytical truth and synthetic truth. These terms have their usual meanings; the former refers to propositions or statements that are true by definition, whereas the latter involves a testing procedure by which the assertion can be inferred to be true or false. Both analytic and synthetic truths can be found in what I call the correspondence theory of truth and the coherence theory of truth. The material nature of my correspondence theory and the lexical nature of my coherence theory describe most of the analytic truths in the coherence theory as synonymy and most of the synthetic truths in the correspondence theory as descriptions of the fit between categories and objects and events in the world.

My semantic account of metaphor also presumes the operation of both a coherence and a correspondence theory of truth. My contention that the attributes of the referents of metaphors find partial membership in semantic markers defined by fuzzy sets illustrates my assumption of a coherence theory of truth. The degrees to which words can be associated (arranged in a hierarchy) indicates the degrees to which linguistic meanings cohere. Later I will explore more fully the consequences of assigning the four truth values (F, D, E, T) to degrees of membership in fuzzy sets. The presumption of this linguistic network combines with the presumption of an evaluation of the parts of metaphors as legitimately associated to form a coherence theory of truth. The associations among words determine the truth value of a metaphor.

I also presume, however, a correspondence theory of truth when I claim that many of the fuzzy sets that define semantic markers are fuzzy prototypical categories descriptive of the way the world is. The fuzzy categories of many of the nodes of the semantic hierarchical network build a bridge to the objects and events of the physical world. Without this correspondence, the semantic network might not bear any resemblance to the world that we actually experience through our senses.

Consider the following metaphor as the starting point for a discussion of how the cognitive theory of metaphor assumes both a coherence and correspondence theory of truth: "Nature prescribes snow as an occasional antidote to the gasoline habit." This metaphor identifies "Nature" as a physician, "snow" as a drug that brings temporary relief, and "driving cars" as an addictive drug. The personification of Nature associates the semantic marker Human with that of Inhuman probably to a high degree of membership because Nature has been personified so often in poetry and prose. But the identification of "snow" with a medicinal chemical that alleviates addiction to another drug probably indicates a lower degree of membership in the fuzzy sets defining the attributes of "snow" and "drugs." The similarities between drug addiction and driving as a habit reveal a high degree of membership among the attributes of these referents. The given metaphor probably combines three supporting metaphors—"Nature is a physician," "Snow is a beneficial drug," and "Driving is drug addiction"—into a single, complex metaphor. How the semantic markers of the various attributes of the referents of this single metaphor fit together—the values of the degrees of membership in fuzzy sets—expresses the coherence theory of truth of this metaphor.

The relationship of the categories of fuzzy sets to the physical world expresses the correspondence theory of this metaphor. "Nature," "snow," "physicians," "drugs," "addictions," and "driving gasoline-powered automobiles" are all found in the physical world of human experience. Similarly, the superordinate and subordinate categories of these objects and events are experienced through our senses.

If Beardsley's controversion theory and my theory of semantic anomaly presume coherence and correspondence theories of truth and employ them in similar ways, then are the differences between the two theories significant? Is it important that, where Beardsley sees contradiction in the literal reading of a metaphor, I find metaphorical meaning arising from a cognitive process that has already changed the normal semantic meanings of the metaphor's referents? Beardsley's claim that the juxtaposition of the referents of a metaphor produces literal contradiction seems to arise from a semantic analysis of surface language; in the explanatory terms of this study Beardsley views level 1 from level 2.

Given the normal semantic meanings of the referents of most metaphors, the literal juxtaposition often produces contradiction or falsity. But if one views metaphors from level 3, an explanatory level that presumes a cognitive process underlying semantic operations, then the juxtaposition of referents seems not only to be meaningful but also to convey certain insights, or put another way, degrees of truth. My description of metaphor as producing semantic anomaly is a partial concession to Beardsley's point of view that metaphors do make us uneasy. From the vantage point of level 2, that of a semantic analysis, metaphors generate tension in the hearer. When one examines the cognitive process involving creativity and memory, however, metaphors do not produce contradiction or falsity; from level 3 we cannot claim that metaphors produce contradictions. The recognition of a metaphor as meaningful forces us to comprehend the epiphoric analogies among the referents, and the claim that a cognitive device that produces meaning simultaneously produces contradiction seems unwarranted.

Maintaining the difference from the controversion theory seems important also because the formulation of metaphors arises from desires to express and suggest truths and possible truths rather than from a desire to express contradictions and falsehoods. My intuition about the motives for creating metaphors arises as follows: a person who wishes to express a deeply felt experience or a person who wishes to formulate a new hypothesis stretches language metaphorically in order to produce insight and meaning; he or she does not intentionally formulate falsehoods. The cognitive process underlying metaphoric production and metaphoric comprehension transforms the referents into meaningful combinations before they can be described as contradictions.

The discovery that both the coherence and correspondence theories of truth operate in metaphoric understanding suggests the existence of the two traditional types of truth in metaphor: (1) analytical truth, which operates in the coherence theory of degrees of truth among features of referents, and (2) synthetic truth, in which prototypical categories relate fuzzy sets defining semantic markers to objects and events in the physical world. How these two types of truth are related remains one of the perennial philosophical questions. Attempts to construct all analytical truths from empirical observations fail to account for the cognitive, creative formation of metaphors. Efforts to absorb all synthetic truths into a semantic network of coherent associations eliminates the ontological ground that language finds in its relation to the world of events and objects. This latter move, if taken, would produce relativistic worlds of language, casting grave doubts on my contention that the recognition of a metaphor as a metaphor rests on a discrimination between literal and metaphorical language. If one cannot speak literally about common everyday experiences, one may not be able to know when figurative language is being employed and when the speaker is not talking about the ordinary. The ontological ground of language in the everyday world producing synthetic truths usually expressed in literal language provides a linguistic Archimedian point of reference from which one can discern language that is figurative. The final reconciliation of these two types of truth remains beyond the scope of this study.

The anchoring of my semantic theory in the world through prototypical categories that sometimes appear as fuzzy sets in hierarchical semantic network that produces synthetic truths (by means of correspondence) does not rule out the use of metaphors in fiction. One can just as readily state, "Odysseus is a fox" rather than "Smith is a fox," using "Smith" to refer to an actual person in the present or past. Metaphors in fiction derive their truth from the contextual associations in which their referents occur. From his role in the *Odyssey*, we can determine whether certain character traits of Odysseus warrant calling him a fox, and the literary context justifies calling the metaphor an epiphor. Suppose, however, that one coined the metaphor "Odysseus is a microcomputer." One would have to think about Odysseus's behavior to see just how rational he was in the deductive sense, how rapidly his powers of reasoning occurred, etc. The facts that the semantic attributes of Odysseus find their meaning in fiction and that the semantic features of microcomputers are defined in the physical world do not matter because the juxtaposition of these referents finds justification in how well the similarities cohere in the semantic network. Relating semantic markers to the real world anchors the entire network but does not require that each and every fuzzy set defining a semantic marker be so anchored. "Odysseus is a microcomputer" can be analytically true or false along a range of degrees (F, D, E, T) found in the semantic network, and it can be synthetically true or false in the physical world. The fact that "Odysseus is a microcomputer" is synthetically false seems trivial because no one expects the metaphors of fiction to be assertions of degrees of truth in the physical world. Most metaphors assert degrees of truth by means of the coherence theory of how many similarities of features occur among the attributes of their referents. I am interested in how metaphors can provide true insights into the nature of either fiction or actuality. The grounding of semantic markers in prototypical categories (correspondence theory) generates synthetic truths that guarantee an empirical ontological basis not only for metaphor but for literal language as well. Without this ground metaphoric language as well as all language would be relative to the conceptual framework invoked, and to this problem of relativism I now turn.

Relativism and Metaphor

The contention by advocates of the controversion theory that metaphors can be adjudged as false on the basis of their literal meaning and as significant on the basis of their metaphorical meaning suggests that metaphoric truth may be relativistic. To Beardsley, a metaphor could be false when interpreted literally, and its paraphrase could be true when tested by perception. If one eliminates the requirement of paraphrase, then under this theory a metaphor could be false when taken literally and true when taken figuratively. Hence the truth or falsity of the metaphor is relative to its context of interpretation.

Relativistic theories of truth are by no means new to metaphor. Earlier in this work we encountered them in Turbayne's *The Myth of Metaphor* and in Pepper's *World Hypotheses*. To avoid the dangers of myth, Turbayne urged scholars to uncover metaphors expressed by theories and to replace them with alternative metaphors. Such a procedure, he thought, would prevent one from committing oneself to a metaphorical theory and forgetting that such an explanation is always tentative and hypothetical. Exposing theoretical metaphors may avoid belief in myths, but the price for such safeguards is an assumption that truth is relativistic. Pepper more explicitly acknowledged that truth is relativistic by advocating four world hypotheses based on four different root metaphors. Not one of these hypotheses is adequate by itself, and none should be dismissed by criticisms leveled from the perspective of any of the others.

Douglas Berggren claimed legitimacy for metaphorical truth on the grounds that metaphors were essential for both poets and scientists and that understanding a metaphor involved possession of a stereoscopic vision enabling one to recognize simultaneously both the principal and subsidiary subjects.[10] Metaphors understood stereoscopically generate dialectical truths. Although not a relativistic system of truth, Berggren's contention for metaphorical truth acknowledges different contextual areas of truth and then combines them through metaphors.

> While it is possible to develop a literal or univocal language for spatial reality, and while an equally univocal language for non-spatial reality is also at least theoretically conceivable, their philosophically necessary interconnections or correlations can be formulated only in terms of vital metaphors. In other words, just as the coordinative definitions and theoretical entities of mathematical physics must be irresolvably tensional, so any conceivable substitute for Descartes' pineal gland, Platonic participation, Christ, Sancho Panza, or Cinderella's glass slipper must preserve an equally tensional status. The only possible solution to the dilemma of monism

versus dualism, that is to say, is man's intellectual ability to play two diverse language games stereoscopically. While construing one mode of reality in terms of the other, the autonomy of each must be preserved even while they are being simultaneously assimilated or integrated.[11]

Nelson Goodman went far beyond Berggren in presenting a relativistic view of truth in which metaphor plays a major role.[12] Although Goodman spoke of the difference between the literal and the metaphorical, the literal did not become the standard by which metaphors are judged to be true or false. Instead, Goodman described both the literal and the metaphorical as interrelated in symbolic language out of which relativistic worlds are created.

> Insofar as a version is verbal and consists of statements, truth may be relevant. But truth cannot be defined or tested by agreement with 'the world'; for not only do truths differ for different worlds but the nature of agreement between a version and a world apart from it is notoriously nebulous. Rather—speaking loosely and without trying to answer either Pilate's question or Tarski's—a version is taken to be true when it offends no unyielding beliefs and none of its own precepts. . . .

> Truth, moreover, pertains solely to what is said, and literal truth solely to what is said literally. We have seen, though, that worlds are made not only by what is said literally but also by what is said metaphorically and not only by what is said either literally or metaphorically but also by what is exemplified and expressed— by what is shown as well as by what is said.[13]

Unlike Pepper, Goodman did not assume that worlds or world views must rest solely on root metaphors. For Goodman, worlds were created out of both verbal and nonverbal processes, including representation, exemplification, expression, and metaphor.[14]

The question of relativism in truth and its relation to metaphor arises when theorists assert that metaphors define by their suggestions the context in which truth claims can be made. Only because a metaphor expresses a world hypothesis that competes with other world hypotheses established by other root metaphors or because a metaphor defines the parameters of a conceptual world does the issue of relativism arise. Throughout this study I have contended that metaphor exists as a cognitively based knowledge process in which the creator of a metaphor expresses a meaningful hypothesis about the world or experience and which conveys a degree of truth. If we view the truth of metaphor solely in terms of a coherence theory, then we too might join the ranks of the relativists because truth would be solely a matter of relating words to other words (to degrees) within contexts defined by linguistic meaning alone. My contention, however, that the nodes of our semantic hierarchy consist of some prototypical fuzzy categories prevents my theory from being completely relativistic. Some metaphors may indeed be defined to be true in the analytical sense of expressing juxtapositions that exist only in the world of fiction. But those metaphors that express not only analytical truths but also synthetic truths through the relationship of their referents to prototypical categories find their truth values grounded in universal, intersubjective, testable experience. Without this grounding, metaphors would be in the position of establishing by their meaning the very contextual world in which their truth or falsity could be decided. And because they define different linguistic contexts of meaning, truth would become relativistic. Such a situation would make it difficult for metaphors to convey universal meaning or to express universal expressions of truth. I do not claim that all metaphors convey universal meaning or universal truths; I do, however, assert that some metaphors can legitimately perform these functions.

Metaphor and Degrees of Semantic Truth

In my development of a hierarchical semantical network, the nodes of the network are represented by fuzzy sets that define semantic markers. The association of the semantic feature of the referent of a metaphor with a semantic marker is measured by the degree to which that feature finds membership in the fuzzy set representing the semantic marker. We saw that a "locomotive" understood as a person indicates that the semantic feature Inanimate finds membership to a degree in the fuzzy set of the semantic marker Animate. I described four values of possible membership of Inanimate (locomotive) in Animate (human): F, D, E, and T. The value F indicates a degree of membership so low that one would have to say of the juxtaposition that it is false in the ordinary sense of the literal combination of "locomotive" and "person" as being absurd and impossible. The D value represents a low degree of membership but not so low that the hypothesis is not possible—that there are not enough similarities between a "locomotive" and a "person" to warrant considering one to be the other. But under D the dissimilarities outweigh the similarities so that the metaphor remains a highly speculative possibility rather than a probability. The value of E represents a higher degree of participation, with the similarities between "locomotive" and "person" outweighing the dissimilarities between the two. Finally, T indicates the ordinary sense of true, where "locomotive" and "person" almost become synonyms and we find a high degree of membership of the semantic features of each in the fuzzy sets representing their semantic markers.

This range of possible membership in fuzzy sets defining semantic markers indicates a measure of the degrees of similarity and dissimilarity found in the metaphor. In terms of a coherence theory of truth, F, D, E, and T measure the degree to which an association of semantic markers can legitimately be associated, and the degrees of association of the semantic markers are a reflection of the degrees of association of the referents of the metaphor under consideration. From the perspective of a coherence theory of semantics, F, D, E, and T are measures of the truth of the metaphor.

A troublesome problem arises when one considers a possible F value for a metaphor. If some metaphors take the value F, then my contention against the controversion theory, which viewed all metaphors as producing literal falsity or contradiction on level 1 of explanation, may indeed be undermined. My reply that most metaphors fall into the D and E range does not suffice either; if metaphors that are described as false do exist (because there is so much dissimilarity between the referents that we label the metaphor an F), either we have denied that the metaphor is genuine or we have presented a case that fits the claims of the controversion theorists that metaphors are false. By allowing the designation F for metaphors, I intend neither to admit an instance of the controversion theory nor to deny that the juxtaposition of referents *is* a metaphor.

A metaphor that expresses a degree of coherent truth, D, could through exploration lapse into F when the association of the semantic markers of the referents is found to have little or no similarity. Take the labeling of quarks as "colored," "strange," "charmed," and more recently "beautiful" and "true."[15] Some debate has taken place as to whether these descriptions of quarks are metaphoric or arbitrary.[16] Those who claim that they are metaphoric point to the speculation supporting the choice of these labels and find some justification of the choice of "color," for example, in the development of a "chromodynamic" theory of quark development.[17] Opponents who see these labels as merely arbitrary claim that prime numbers or any other designation could have been employed. For them, "color," "charm," "strange," "beauty," and "truth" all serve a mnemonic function of enabling the scientist to remember and talk about these particles. Suppose, however, that at least "color" finds justification as a highly speculative and suggestive metaphor in its initial formulation, but that later as the theory of quarks develops, the similarities between the discovered properties of quarks and the properties of color diminish to the point that a "colored" quark finds justification only as a historical linguistic usage. People may still talk of "colored quarks," but the significance of the combination has become arbitrary rather than the insightful production of a metaphor. Now we can say that the metaphor has moved from D to F on the scale without committing ourselves to the position that at least some metaphors must be recognized as false, as claimed by the controversion theory, before they can be recognized as metaphors.

Consider the metaphor "The Mona Lisa is a wart." Could this be a metaphor that is false because it expresses an untrue statement? One might be tempted to argue that we can understand the statement only because it *is* a metaphor, and that when we do so comprehend it, we determine it to be false because the Mona Lisa cannot be called ugly by anyone except the demented. Certainly, when we confront the utterance "The Mona Lisa is a wart," we immediately understand it as a metaphor. As we consider the possibility that the Mona Lisa might be ugly, we reject the metaphor as improperly juxtaposing the referents "Mona Lisa" and "wart." Only in the sense of saying that "The Mona Lisa is a wart" was once considered a possible metaphor can we say that it was a metaphor and false.

Now consider the similar process that occurs in the other direction of truth value, i.e., when a metaphor becomes part of ordinary language and therefore becomes true; such a metaphor, when true, is no longer a metaphor. The reason for including T on the coherence scale of truth for metaphors finds easier justification in the fact that many metaphors do move from highly expressive metaphors, E, into ordinary language, T, as the similarities between the referents become widely recognized and accepted. Such metaphors die and become new entries in dictionaries.

The fact that most metaphors fall into the D and E ranges of coherent truth raises still another difficult issue—that of understanding the notion of contradiction under an interpretation of fuzziness. Metaphors can be true and false at the same time: true to the degree that their referents have similar properties and false to the degree that their referents have dissimilar properties. Newton's identification of God with space produces a highly speculative metaphor in which the identification of the attributes of God as similar with the attributes of space produces a degree of coherent truth and the dissimilarities between the attributes of the two produces a degree of coherent falsity. "The basic insight is that of space as 'a disposition of being *qua* being,' an absolute within which bodies move (unlike the relative space of Descartes), extensionally identical with God."[18] The absolute character of Newton's understanding of space and the absolute nature of a traditional theological notion of God forms the bond of similarity enabling the metaphorical identification of God with space. The traditional theological contention that

God stands apart from the physical world, his creation, as a transcendent being produces the basis of dissimilarity between the two and the degree of falsity of the metaphor.

Within the tradition of the development of many-valued logics, although the law of noncontradiction holds in many, it does not apply to all.[19] Nicholas Rescher's survey of many-valued logics indicates that only the following version of the law of contradiction can be construed as a "strictly necessary feature of many-valued logics in general."[20]

> ... the "exclusion principle" that p and $\neg p$ cannot both be true together, i.e., at most one can be true. We cannot have both $/p/ = T$ and $/\neg p/ = T$, that is $(/p/ \neq T)$ -or- $(/\neg p/ \neq F)$.[21]

I have attempted to preserve this principle by reserving the labels T and F for the metaphors that have died and become ordinary language (T) and the metaphors that have been discarded as diaphoric hypotheses (F). This move prevents any metaphor from being labeled T and F at the same time. I have spoken of metaphors labeled D and E as true to a degree and false to a degree, and by that I mean expressions of the value of degrees of membership of one word, the attribute of a semantic feature of the referent of a metaphor, in a fuzzy set defining a semantic marker. The labels D and E are measures of coherent truth; they are peculiar in the ways in which they cannot be both fully T and fully F, but they can express degrees of similarity and dissimilarity and do express partial truths in the normal sense.

When I introduced fuzzy-set theory into the semantics of metaphor, the reader may have wondered why I insisted on a range of four values (F, D, E, T) to express coherence among associations of words instead of relying on the usual two values, T and F. Had I followed the latter course I would have violated the exclusion principle cited by Rescher as it applies to all many-valued logics, and I would have diminished the sense that metaphor may be a dynamic cognitive process in which epiphors may become ordinary language (with the value T) or diaphors may become nonsense (with the value F). The values D and E indicate coherence truth values between F and T that are consistent with fuzzy-set theory and do not violate the rules of many-valued logic and that fit my intuition that metaphors need not be strictly false (F) in order to express an insight (a rejection of the controversion theory).

The Relation of Metaphoric Knowledge to Truth

I have identified two theories of truth, coherence and correspondence, as applicable to metaphoric insight. The coherence theory applies to the semantics of metaphor, whereas the correspondence theory relates the semantics of metaphor to the physical world. But what is the relationship between these two theories? Do we encounter two different types of truth (already identified as analytic truth and synthetic truth), and if so, does this entail relativism?

Context does play a legitimate role in the determination of both the meaning and the truth of a metaphor. When a metaphor juxtaposes referents applicable to the physical world, the coherence theory of truth applicable to the semantics of metaphor becomes integrally related to the correspondence theory with the fuzzy sets defining the attributes of the semantic features from prototypical categories of actual objects or events. In deciding the degree to which the features of the attributes of the referents are similar and dissimilar, we depend on an integral relationship to the physical world through the fit of some of the features' fuzzy-set categories to real objects and events.

When a metaphor juxtaposes referents that are fictional or speculative, then the truth of the metaphor depends entirely on the degrees of similarity between the attributes of the referents. Here, the coherence theory dominates the question of truth. If one asks whether such a metaphor with fictional referents is true, one can reply that it conveys metaphorical truth to the degree that the cognitive process underlying the semantic process has allowed identification among some of the semantic features. This kind of metaphor is true relative to the fictional or speculative context in which it occurs. If one asks if such a metaphor conveys truth about the real world, the answer of course is no, just as one might deny that a fictional character like Don Quixote refers to a real person.

Some metaphors combine a fictional referent with a real referent, and here the correspondence theory takes precedence over the coherence theory because we want to know not only the degrees of similarity between the attributes of the referents but also the applicability of the fuzzy category relating the real category to the world. Among metaphors this combination of concrete with speculative often produces diaphors that suggest new ways of perceiving and conceiving of the world.

Let us consider two metaphors that I have already cited and a new one to illustrate these relationships between the coherence and correspondence theories of truth: (1) "A locomotive is a person,"(2) "Quarks are colored," and (3) "Odysseus is a dragon." For the first metaphor, analysis of the attributes of "locomotives" and "persons" depends on the fuzzy sets representing their semantic markers, and these fuzzy sets are determined by the prototypical categories of perceived objects in the physical world. We cannot make judgments about how an Animate person would be an Inanimate engine without knowing about the status of these entities in the perceptual world. The degrees of truth (F, D, E, T) expressed by the degrees of membership in the fuzzy sets of semantic markers—the truth of coherence—depend on the judgments we make about the attributes of these objects (locomotives and persons) in the real world. Expressions of the coherent truth of this metaphor depend on the adequacy of correspondence. The metaphor "The locomotive is in bed" (taken to mean a dynamic person is sleeping) presents a metaphorical truth in which the coherence and correspondence aspects of metaphor are unified by the cognitive process that generates semantic change of meaning.

Metaphors such as "Odysseus is a dragon" sometimes occur in literature but rarely occur outside a special fixed context. In the *Odyssey*, Odysseus may be represented as a fox or a lion; the juxtaposition of Odysseus with a dragon combines two fictional entities. The truth of the metaphor depends on the coherence of the attributes of Odysseus with those of a dragon. Metaphors that combine two or more fictional referents seem rare: most often metaphors combine a fictional referent with a referent from the real world. In these metaphors the correspondence theory plays a role when one compares the attributes of the real-world referent with those of the fictional referent.

The metaphor "Quarks are colored" combines a hypothetical referent, the quark—which may turn out to be either fictional or real—with a real-world referent, color. In this metaphor the correspondence theory of truth plays a major role because decisions about the similarities between the properties of quarks and color depend not only on theory but also on the perceptual experience of color in the physical world. Quark theorists, however, have denied that quarks have anything to do with "visual color." "Colored quarks" exists as a highly speculative metaphor suggesting an analogy between the observed properties of how colors combine and the indirectly observed properties of how quarks combine. But the metaphoric truth does not just depend on a coherence of semantic properties. The correspondence theory of truth enters into the metaphoric truth of "colored quarks" in two ways: (1) As already noted, analogies are built between the interactions of colors and interactions of quarks, and (2) using colors as labels for properties of quarks contributes to the researchers' tendency to think of quarks as *definite objects*. It remains difficult to conceive of things as colored (even if color is attributed on an analogical basis) without also conceiving of them as finite, definite, and available. The act of calling quarks "colored" even though claimed to be arbitrary rests on an analogy (the interactions of colors) and, as a metaphor attempting to specify real properties for hypothetical entities, affects the way we conceive of quarks. Such a metaphor does not merely express a truth of coherence; it also depends on perceptual and conceptual relations to the physical world and expresses a metaphorical truth implicated in a correspondence theory.

These three metaphors illustrate the operation of the coherence and the correspondence theories of truth in my explanatory account of metaphor expressed in three levels: (1) surface language, (2) semantics, and (3) cognitive process. Both theories of truth depend on cognitive processes; the coherence theory involves a cognitive process that finds similarities and dissimilarities among the semantic attributes of the referents at level 2. The correspondence theory involves a cognitive process that identifies some of the fuzzy sets defining words at level 2 with prototypical categories of objects and events existing in the world. Metaphors could not exist without either theory of truth operating, for without the operation of a coherence theory we could not juxtapose seemingly semantically anomalous referents and produce both meaning and truth, and without the correspondence theory we could not judge metaphors to be metaphors by comparing them with literal language in the physical world. One consequence of adopting the correspondence theory is metaphors become grounded in the empirical world. Even those metaphors that juxtapose fictional referents are linked through our hierarchical semantic network to other words that are grounded in prototypical categories that form the basis of literal language.

Metaphorical truth established by coherence and correspondence theories can also be understood as part of my earlier description of metaphor as a knowledge process. Metaphors that juxtapose referents derived from the physical world or those that juxtapose one referent from the world with a hypothetical or fictional one require the operation of a correspondence theory that moves from a node in the semantic network to observations. This movement from semantics to the world and then back to semantics, in which the coherence theory changes coherent truth values, forms part of the knowledge process of cultural evolution. The ordinary language we speak and sometimes the ways in which we perceive and conceive of our experiences are transformed by changes in semantic meaning resulting from the formation of metaphorical truth in the selection of features of similarity by a cognitive process and then by the relation of this truth to the real world through the fit of these same prototypical fuzzy categories to objects and events. Metaphorical truth alters culture by changing language, theories, and even perceptions.

Metaphorical truth could be viewed as completely relative if it were not for its participation in this evolutionary process in which the stability of the ordinary, banal perceptions and expressions of the world in literal language provides an objective base for metaphor. Metaphorical truth and literal truth exist on a continuum; one does not necessarily need to reduce metaphors to literal language in order to assess their truth value. Truth value arises from the new possibilities and new insights that metaphors provide, and metaphoric suggestions presume an integral semantic and cognitive connection with the ordinary world, hence the assertion of a continuum.

Afterword

We have reached the end of our journey through the cognitive world of metaphor, observing along the way that metaphor results from a creative process in which widely disparate referents are drawn from the long-term memory and juxtaposed to produce new possibilities for knowledge. As cognitive processes, metaphors also mediate between culture and the mind, influencing both cultural and biological evolution. Metaphors present insights that express degrees of truth measured by the suggestiveness (diaphoric quality) of the juxtaposition of the referents. Metaphors do not have to be paraphrased in order to convey truth. Nor does one have to interpret metaphors as presenting literal falsehoods in order to recognize their metaphoric quality. The meaning of metaphors results from the semantical aspects of communication, the context in cultural settings, and the creation of new concepts. Like the determination of meaning in ordinary language, metaphorical meaning arises from various dimensions of metaphor—communication, culture, and cognition.

I have shown that an abstract, quasi-mathematical account can be given of metaphor. To understand this deep abstract structure better I divided it into two levels, those of semantics (level 2) and cognition (level 3). These two levels along with level 1, surface language, are interrelated through a knowledge process and are not mutually exclusive. The contention that the hearer can distinguish between literal and metaphorical language is crucial to my theory of metaphor. Without such a distinction one would not be able to recognize metaphor as a special cognitive device that suggests new hypotheses. I also claim that the literal offers an Archimedian point for objectivity in knowledge. The operation of the correspondence theory in metaphor links the abstractions of semantics to the attributes of the referents of metaphors by identifying some of the fuzzy sets (nodes in the hierarchical network) defining words with prototypical categories. Without this kind of linkage, my theory of metaphor would express truth solely by means of a coherence theory. As a theory of language, without some ground in the empirical world, my account of metaphor may have been relativistic.

My study of metaphor, however, has only suggested an ontology. In the future the ontological consequences of employing prototypical categories and their interrelation with a theory of truth derived from a combination of the coherence and correspondence theories must be explored further. Although Stephen Pepper developed his notion of root metaphor to explain how competing world hypotheses arise, I began at the opposite end of the problem with investigations of metaphor. Now I must consider the metaphysical considerations of what I have done. In addition to presenting arguments for the existence of the literal, I must explore what world view these arguments presume and whether my presumption damages my theory. I have already noted that the assumption of a basic metaphor underlying my theory of metaphor does not necessarily entail that every statement either in the theory or in ordinary language must be metaphorical. But I have not investigated the contents of these assumptions. I have presupposed that "A theory of metaphor is metaphorical," that "The metaphorical quality of a theory of metaphor is abstract," and that in the linkage to the physical world "Metaphor is literal." How are these three metaphorical assumptions related? Can they be related by an even more fundamental underlying basic metaphor, and if so, what is that metaphor? What are the ontological consequences of this complex series of metaphorical assumptions about the world. This task of considering the metaphysics of a theory of metaphor awaits future attention.

Throughout this study I became intrigued by the role that the visual imagination plays in the formation of metaphor. I observed that many metaphors depend on an image as the basis of the analogous relationship among the referents. Yet many other legitimate metaphors do not either depend on or express imagery. Metaphors with visual aspects, however, may be related to nonverbal metaphors. Visual metaphors, such as a painting, may express and suggest insights into literature. Painters often seek to express insights into aspects of literature and music through their works. Similarly, musicians have represented paintings in their compositions. Computer scientists employ graphics to represent a variety of algorithms. If one can construct visual metaphors for nonvisual insights, one may enter into a new dimension of hypothesis construction. One may even construct different dimensions of knowing from those that we ordinarily confront. Through the exploration of visual metaphors one may learn to perceive in four or more dimensions rather than in the usual three. The early Cubists were attempting to represent the world in geometrical forms, thereby affecting the manner in which we perceive the world. By suggesting new ways of conceiving, the Cubists hoped that nature would imitate art.

My own interest in pursuing the study of visual metaphor has been furthered by the graphical dimensions of the computer and by reflection on how we think about the problem of metaphor. Throughout this study, the structures generating metaphor were imagined in visual terms. The realization that we generate visual metaphors to explain the abstract features of metaphor suggests that we should pursue this question further. Is this phenomenon limited to the discovery process of particular individuals? Is visual metaphor the process of creative discovery for which we are searching? When I admitted that I could offer little more than the identification of intensity of experience usually expressed in emotion as part of the motivation for the creative juxtaposition of referents in the generation of new metaphors, perhaps I should have considered the possibility that images lie behind those intensities.

I devoted a chapter in *Metaphor and Myth in Science and Religion* to the relationship between metaphor and myth, arguing that all myths arise from metaphors (usually basic metaphors). I claimed that by forgetting that theories presuppose basic metaphors and thereby by taking theories literally, both scientists and theologians create myths. Only by recovering the metaphoric and hypothetical status of the theory could one avoid myth making. But this meant that one must make these judgments from the present and from a literal perspective—a difficult if not impossible task. When I consider the ontological consequences of my present cognitive theory of metaphor, I must also reconsider what I wrote about myth. Is it still necessarily the case that myths can be discovered to be myths only when theories are discovered to be metaphorical? Can myths be recognized as myths and still be said to convey truth? Reviewers of the earlier work severely criticized my notion of myth, saying that it deviated from normal usage and rendered myth useless, because I contended that all theories should be acknowledged as metaphorical and therefore as speculative. The latter contention meant that myths would never occur if the theorist, theologian, or scientist attended properly to the nature of theories. In this work, however, with my view of metaphoric truth including both correspondence and coherence aspects, my view of myth probably will have to change. Perhaps, my notion of myth when revised will allow myth as well as metaphors to express degrees of truth.

Throughout this study, the primary value advocated for metaphor has been that of a creative cognitive device that allows the generator to express and suggest new hypotheses. Included among the new insights are feelings as well as concepts. Metaphor also possesses iconic value as a cultural entity. For cultural and biological evolution, metaphor has value as a mediator between the mind and the world. As one begins to list these values of metaphor, one recognizes them as descriptive values. The question immediately follows of whether one can find a normative theory for metaphor.

Is there an ethics of metaphor specifying how metaphor should be used? Is metaphor so distinctive a cognitive process as to warrant its own normative ethical theory? Are there legitimate and proper normative ways of suggesting new insights? Is metaphor like innuendo? When a poet suggests a possible new conception, we usually know that this metaphor is a speculative possibility and not an actuality because it is poetry. But when a scientist suggests a possibility, do we have the same awareness of the status of the metaphor? Or when politicians create metaphors, do they have the responsibility of using epiphors rather than diaphors? Or if they use diaphors do they have the responsibility of warning their audiences of the tentativeness of what they have suggested? Perhaps an extension of my speech act theory is required to develop a specialized normative theory of metaphor.

With so much attention devoted to metaphor, the time seems right for consideration of a theory of ethics as applicable to metaphor. So engaged have I become in questions about metaphor that I tend not only to see metaphors everywhere but also to view the human condition as metaphoric. As a symbol user, metaphor differentiates humans from animals. Humans not only discover analogies, but in metaphors they also combine analogies with disanalogies to produce creative metaphors extending our knowledge into the unknown.

Notes

Introduction

1. John Donne, *The Complete Poetry of John Donne*, John T. Shawcross, ed. (Garden City, New York: Anchor Books, 1967), 98.
2. Kenneth A. Johnson, "The bag model of quark confinement," *Scientific American* 241 (1979), 112–121.
3. See Andrew Ortony, ed., *Metaphor and Thought* (Cambridge: Cambridge University Press, 1979).
4. Earl R. Mac Cormac, *Metaphor and Myth in Science and Religion* (Durham, North Carolina: Duke University Press, 1976).

Chapter 1

1. Zenon W. Pylyshyn, "Computation and cognition: Issues in the foundation of cognitive science," *The Behavioral and Brain Sciences* 3 (1980), 111.
2. Julien Offray de La Mettrie, *Man a Machine* (LaSalle, Illinois: Open Court, 1912), 89.
3. La Mettrie, *Man a Machine*, 141.
4. La Mettrie, *Man a Machine*, 107.
5. La Mettrie, *Man a Machine*, 107.
6. La Mettrie, *Man a Machine*, 128.
7. La Mettrie, *Man a Machine*, 97–98.
8. La Mettrie, *Man a Machine*, 101.
9. Michael A. Arbib, *The Metaphorical Brain* (New York: Wiley-Interscience, 1972), vii.
10. Pylyshyn, "Computation and cognition," 114.
11. Pylyshyn, "Computation and cognition," 115.
12. Pamela McCorduck, *Machines Who Think* (San Francisco: W. H. Freeman, 1979), 96.
13. John McCarthy, "Ascribing mental qualities to machines," in *Philosophical Perspectives in Artificial Intelligence*, Martin Ringle, ed. (New York: Humanities Press, 1979), 61.
14. Daniel C. Dennett, "Why you can't make a computer that feels pain," in his *Brainstorms* (Montgomery, Vermont: Bradford Books, 1978). Reprinted by The MIT Press. Dennett also believes that "pain" is a confused concept.
15. A. M. Turing, "Computing machinery and intelligence," in *Minds and Machines*, Alan Ross Anderson, ed. (Englewood Cliffs, New Jersey: Prentice-Hall, 1964).
16. Margaret A. Boden, *Artificial Intelligence and Natural Man* (New York: Basic books, 1977), 134ff.
17. Hubert L. Dreyfus, *What Computers Can't Do* (New York: Harper Colophon Book, 1979), chap. 7.

Chapter 2

1. James Joyce, *A Portrait of the Artist as a Young Man* (New York: Penguin Books, 1978), 234.
2. I do not mean to suggest that this exhausts the list of theories about metaphor. Others exist, such as the substitution theory, the comparison theory, and the presentation theory, just to mention a few. I present the three I do as offering possible ways of differentiating between metaphor and analogy.
3. See I. A. Richards, *The Philosophy of Rhetoric* (New York: Oxford University Press, 1936); Max Black, "Metaphor," in his *Models and Metaphors* (Ithaca, New York: Cornell University Press, 1962); and Robert Verbrugge and Nancy McCarrell, "Metaphoric comprehension," *Cognitive Psychology* 9 (1977), 494–533.
4. Tom Robbins, *Another Roadside Attraction* (New York: Ballantine Books, 1977), 206.
5. I. A. Richards, "Science and poetry," in *Criticism: The Foundations of Modern Literary Judgment*, Mark Shorer, et al., eds. (New York: Harcourt, Brace & Co., 1948).
6. I came perilously close to this position in chapter 3 of my book *Metaphor and Myth in Science and Religion*. I now recognize that tension alone is not sufficient to differentiate metaphor from analogy.
7. Monroe C. Beardsley is the foremost exponent of the controversion theory. See the sections on metaphor in his *Aesthetics* (New York: Harcourt, Brace & Co., 1958) and his "The metaphorical twist," *Philosophy and Phenomenological Research* 22 (1962), 293–307.
8. Cited in E. O. Wilson, *On Human Nature* (Cambridge, Mass.: Harvard University Press, 1978), 74–75.
9. Earl R. Mac Cormac, "Metaphors and fuzzy sets," *Fuzzy Sets and Systems* 7 (1982), 243–256.
10. Noam Chomsky, *Aspects of a Theory of Syntax* (Cambridge, Mass.: MIT Press, 1965), 148ff.
11. Noam Chomsky, "Degrees of grammaticalness," in *The Structure of Language*, Jerry A. Fodor and Jerrold J. Katz, eds. (Englewood Cliffs, New Jersey, 1964).
12. Robert J. Matthews, "Concerning a 'linguistic theory' of metaphor," *Foundations of Language* 7 (1971), 424.
13. Matthews, "Concerning a 'linguistic theory,' " 417.
14. I accepted this theory in my *Metaphor and Myth in Science and Religion* but reject it now for the reasons given.
15. This metaphor is taken from Verbrugge and McCarrell, "Metaphoric comprehension."
16. Douglas Berggren, "The use and abuse of metaphor I, II" *The Review of Metaphysics* 16 (1962, 1963), 237–258, 450–472; and "From myth to metaphor," *The Monist* 50 (1966), 530–552.
17. See W. Bedell Stanford, *Greek Metaphor* (New York: Johnson Reprint Corp., 1972), 25–30.
18. John Middleton Murry, "Metaphor," in his *Countries of the Mind*, second series (Freeport, New York: Books for Libraries Press, 1968), 3.
19. Stanford, *Greek Metaphor*, 29–30.
20. Wallace Stevens, "Extracts from Address to the Academy of Fine Ideas," in his *The Palm at the End of the Mind* (New York: Vintage Press, 1972), 180.
21. Carl Hempel, *The Philosophy of Natural Science* (Englewood Cliffs, New Jersey: Prentice-Hall, 1966), 94.
22. Max Black, *Models and Metaphors*, 33.
23. Philip Wheelwright, *Metaphor and Reality* (Bloomington, Indiana: Indiana University Press, 1962), chap. 4.
24. Wheelwright, *Metaphor and Reality*, 73.

25. Verbrugge and McCarrell, "Metaphoric comprehension," 494.
26. Wheelwright, *Metaphor and Reality*, 79.
27. This analysis is taken from Frank W. Bliss and Earl R. Mac Cormac, "Two poles of metaphor: Frye and Beardsley," *The Journal of Aesthetic Education* 11 (1977), 37.
28. Bliss and Mac Cormac, "Two poles of metaphor," 37.
29. Christine Brooke-Rose, *A Grammar of Metaphor* (London: Seeker & Warburg, 1970).
30. Brooke-Rose, *A Grammar of Metaphor*, 3.
31. Brooke-Rose, *A Grammar of Metaphor*, 15–16.
32. Brooke-Rose, *A Grammar of Metaphor*, 24–25.
33. Brooke-Rose, *A Grammar of Metaphor*, 137.
34. Brooke-Rose, *A Grammar of Metaphor*, 211–212.
35. Wallace Stevens, "Sunday morning," in *Palm at the End of the Mind*, 7.
36. Theodosius Dobzhansky, et al., *Evolution* (San Francisco: W. H. Freeman, 1977), 29. The reference in the quotation is F. Jacob and J. Monod, "Genetic regulatory mechanisms in the synthesis of proteins," *Journal of Molecular Biology* 2 (1961), 318–356.
37. Stephen C. Pepper, *World Hypotheses* (Berkeley: University of California Press, 1970).
38. Pepper, *World Hypotheses*, 91.
39. Pepper, *World Hypotheses*, 85.

Chapter 3

1. Colin Murray Turbayne, *The Myth of Metaphor*, revised edition (Columbia, South Carolina: University of South Carolina Press, 1970).
2. Turbayne, *Myth of Metaphor*, 70–71.
3. Turbayne, *Myth of Metaphor*, 64–65.
4. Turbayne, *Myth of Metaphor*, 76.
5. W. V. O. Quine, "Natural kinds," in Naming, Necessity, and Natural Kinds, Stephen P. Schwartz, ed. (Ithaca, New York: Cornell University Press, 1977), 165.
6. George Lakoff and Mark Johnson, *Metaphors We Live By* (Chicago: University of Chicago Press, 1980); and "Conceptual metaphor in everyday language," *The Journal of Philosophy* 77 (1980), 453–486.
7. Lakoff and Johnson, *Metaphors We Live By*, 54; "Conceptual metaphor in everyday language," 472–473.
8. Lakoff and Johnson, *Metaphors We Live By*, 52.
9. Lakoff and Johnson, *Metaphors We Live By*, 53–54.
10. Lakoff and Johnson, *Metaphors We Live By*, 55.
11. Lakoff and Johnson, *Metaphors We Live By*, 5.
12. Philip B. Gove, ed., *Webster's Third New International Dictionary* (Springfield, Mass.: G. & C. Merriam Co., 1971), 2575; Samuel Johnson, *A Dictionary of the English Language* (New York: AMS Press, 1967).
13. Lakoff and Johnson, "Conceptual metaphor in everyday language," 474. Note that Lakoff and Johnson present other arguments against abstraction. I treat only what I consider to be their main argument.
14. Lakoff and Johnson, *Metaphors We Live By*, 110.
15. L. Jonathan Cohen and Avishai Margalit, "The role of inductive reasoning in the interpretation of metaphor," in *Semantics of Natural Language*, D. Davidson and G. Harmon, eds. (Boston: Reidel, 1972), 723.
16. Samuel R. Levin, *The Semantics of Metaphor* (Baltimore: Johns Hopkins University Press, 1977).
17. Lakoff and Johnson, *Metaphors We Live By*, 110.
18. Lakoff and Johnson, *Metaphors We Live By*, 114.

19. Lakoff and Johnson, *Metaphors We Live By*, 209. The quotations are taken from the same page. In a private communication, Lakoff claims that in associating objectivism with intrasubjectivity, I am using the term in a very different fashion from that which he and Johnson intended in *Metaphors We Live By*.

20. For a longer discussion of the "conduit· metaphor" on which Lakoff and Johnson draw, see Michael J. Reddy, "the Conduit Metaphor," in *Metaphor and Thought*, Ortony, ed.

21. Lakoff and Johnson, *Metaphors We Live By*, 215.

22. Lakoff and Johnson, *Metaphors We Live By*, 56.

23. Lakoff and Johnson, *Metaphors We Live By*, 58.

24. Lakoff and Johnson, *Metaphors We Live By*, 58.

25. Lakoff and Johnson, *Metaphors We Live By*, 59.

26. Lakoff and Johnson, *Metaphors We Live By*, 161.

27. Lakoff and Johnson, *Metaphors We Live By*, 75.

28. Eleanor Rosch, "Principles of categorization," in *Cognition and Categorization*, Eleanor Rosch and Barbara B. Lloyd, eds. (Hillsdale, New Jersey: Lawrence Erlbaum Associates, 1978).

29. Lakoff and Johnson, *Metaphors We Live By*, 75.

30. Benjamin Lee Whorf, *Language, Thought, and Reality* (Cambridge, Mass.: MIT Press, 1967); D. G. Mandelbaum, ed., *Selected Writings of Edward Sapir* (Berkeley: University of California Press, 1949); see also Max Black, "Linguistic relativity: The views of Benjamin Lee Whorf," in his *Models and Metaphors*.

31. Brent Berlin and Paul Kay, *Basic Color Terms: Their Universality and Evolution* (Berkeley: University of California Press, 1969), 2–3.

32. Berlin and Kay, *Basic Color Terms*, 104.

33. Eleanor Rosch, "Linguistic relativity," in *Human Communication*, A. Silverstein, ed. (New York: Halsted Press, 1974). See also "Probabilities, sampling, and ethnographic method: The case of Dani color names, *Man* 7 (1972), 448–466; " 'Focal' color areas and the development of color names," *Developmental Psychology* 4 (1971), 447–455; "On the internal structure of perceptual and semantic categories," in *Cognitive Development and the Acquisition of Language*, T. E. Moore, ed. (New York: Academic Press, 1973); Eleanor Rosch (Heider) and D. C. Olivier, "The structure of the color space in naming and memory for two languages," *Cognitive Psychology* 3 (1972), 337–354; "Cognitive reference points," *Cognitive Psychology* 7 (1975), 523–547; "The nature of mental codes for color categories," *Journal of Experimental Psychology: Human Perception and Performance* 1 (1975), 303–322; and "Universals and cultural specifics in human categorization," in *Cross Cultural Perspectives on Learning*, R. Brislin, S. Bochner, and W. Lonner, eds. (New York: Halsted Press, 1975).

34. Rosch, "Linguistic relativity," 116.

35. Rosch, "Linguistic relativity," 117.

36. Earl R. Mac Cormac, "Ostensive instances in language learning," *Foundations of Language* 7 (1971), 199–210.

37. W. B. Yeats, "Mohini Chatterjee," in *The Collected Poems of W. B. Yeats* (New York: Macmillan Co., 1953), 243.

38. See Mary Hesse, "The explanatory function of metaphor," in her *Revolutions and Reconstructions in the Philosophy of Science* (Bloomington, Indiana: Indiana University Press, 1980).

Chapter 4

1. Mac Cormac, "Metaphors and fuzzy sets."

2. See Charles E. Osgood, George J. Suci, and Percy H. Tannenbaum, *The Measurement of Meaning* (Urbana, Illinois: University of Illinois Press, 1957); Charles E. Osgood, William H. May, and Murray S. Miron, *Cross-Cultural Universals of Affective Meaning* (Urbana, Illinois: University of Illinois Press, 1975); Levin, *The Semantics of Metaphor.*

3. Mac Cormac, "Ostensive instances in language learning."

4. I use "semantic feature" and "semantic marker" interchangeably.

5. For more complete accounts of componential analysis, see John Lyons, *Semantics* (Cambridge: Cambridge University Press, 1977), vol. 1, section 9.9; Geoffrey Leech, *Semantics* (New York: Penguin Books, 1974), chapter 6.

6. This example is taken from Leech, *Semantics*, chap. 6.

7. Leech, *Semantics*, 97.

8. Leech, *Semantics*, 122–124.

9. W. V. O. Quine, "Two dogmas of empiricism," in his *From a Logical Point of View* (Cambridge, Mass.: Harvard University Press, 1953).

10. Jess Stein, ed., *The Random House Dictionary* (New York: Random House, 1969), 1316. These entries have been abbreviated.

11. Jerrold J. Katz and Paul M. Postal, *An Integrated Theory of Linguistic Descriptions* (Cambridge, Mass.: MIT Press, 1964).

12. This metaphor was suggested by Levin in his *The Semantics of Metaphor.*

13. L. A. Zadeh, "Fuzzy sets," *Information and Control* 8 (1965), 339.

14. L. A. Zadeh, "Quantitative fuzzy semantics," *Information Sciences* 3 (1971), 159–176.

15. George Lakoff, "Hedges: A study in meaning criteria and the logic of fuzzy concepts," *Proceedings of the Chicago Linguistics Society*, 1972. Lakoff also cites examples, which do not fit the notion of fuzzy concepts.

16. Zadeh, "Fuzzy sets," 342. The reference in the quotation is Stephen C. Kleene, *Introduction to Metamathematics* (New York: Van Nostrand, 1952).

17. The ontological implcations of this scheme of a four-valued logic are developed further in chapter 8.

18. Zadeh, "Quantitative fuzzy semantics."

19. Zadeh, "Quantitative fuzzy semantics," 162–163.

20. Zadeh, "Quantitative fuzzy semantics," 164–165.

21. Zadeh, "Quantitative fuzzy semantics," 167.

22. Zadeh, "Quantitative fuzzy semantics," 166.

23. Black, "Metaphor."

24. Brooke-Rose, *A Grammar of Metaphor*, chap. 9.

25. See Eleanor Rosch, "Principles of categorization;" "Universals and cultural specifics in human categorization;" "Human categorization," in *Advances in Cross-Cultural Psychology*, vol. 1, N. Warren, ed. (London: Academic Press, 1977); "Cognitive reference points;" Eleanor Rosch and Carolyn B. Mervis, "Family resemblances," *Cognitive Psychology* 7 (1975), 573–605; Eleanor Rosch, et al., "Basic objects in natural categories," *Cognitive Psychology* 8 (1976), 382–439.

26. Rosch, "Principles of categorization," 39.

27. Rosch, "Principles of categorization," 31.

28. I explore this question of ontology further in chapter 5.

29. Rosch, "Universals and cultural specifics in human categorization," 180–181. The reference in the quotation is Jerrold A. Katz and Paul M. Postal, *An Integrated Theory of Linguistic Descriptions* (Cambridge, Mass.: MIT Press, 1964).

30. Rosch, "Principles of categorization," 35.

31. Rosch, "Universals and cultural specifics in human categorization," 191. The reference in the quotation is George Lakoff, "Hedges: a study in meaning criteria and the logic of fuzzy concepts."

32. See Leech, *Semantics*, chaps. 6 and 7.

33. Fred Sommers, "The ordinary language tree," *Mind* 68 (1959), 160–185; "Types and ontology," *Philosophical Review* 72 (1963), 327–367; and "Predictability," in *Philosophy in America*, Max Black, ed. (Ithaca, New York: Cornell University Press, 1965). For a review of Sommers's work and many criticisms including the reviewers' suggestion that the "marriage" might not be successful, see Jonathan Bennett, "Review," *The Journal of Symbolic Logic* 36 (1971), 666–670.

34. Sommers, "The ordinary language tree," 161.

35. Sommers, "The ordinary language tree," 172–173.

36. Sommers, "The ordinary language tree," 172–173.

37. Sommers, "The ordinary language tree," 177ff.

38. This is suggested by Ronald B. de Sousa, "The tree of English bears bitter fruit," *The Journal of Philosophy* 63 (1966), 37—46.

39. Sommers, "The ordinary language tree," 179.

40 Sommers, "The ordinary language tree," 181.

41. Dan Passell in "On Sommers' logic of sense and nonsense" (*Mind* 70 (1969), 132–133) demonstrates that Sommers's rules from which $R(U)$ is derived do not necessarily ensure that A will be above B and C in a tree diagram.

42. Sommers, "The ordinary language tree," 164. Jonathan Bennett makes the same observation in his "Review": "If Sommers's theories are interpreted in terms of what could "make sense" literally or *metaphorically*, they will become vacuous, for there will be virtually no failures of predictability or of U-relatedness." (p. 668)

43. A. G. Elgood, "Sommers's rule of sense," *The Philosophical Quarterly*, 20 (1970), 166–169.

44. Osgood, Suci, and Tannenbaum, *The Measurement of Meaning*; see also Marjorie B. Creelman, *The Experimental Investigation of Meaning: A Review of the Literature* (New York: Springer, 1966); James G. Snider and Charles E. Osgood, eds., *Semantic Differential Technique* (Chicago: Aldine Atherton, 1969).

45. Osgood, May, and Miron, *Cross-Cultural Universals of Affective Meaning*.

46. John B. Carroll, "Review of measurement of meaning," and Uriel Weinreich, "Travels through semantic space," both in *Semantic Differential Technique*.

47. Osgood, May, and Miron, *Cross-Cultural Universals in Affective Meaning*.

48. Osgood, May, and Miron, *Cross-Cultural Universals in Affective Meaning*, chap. 2.

49. Levin, *The Semantics of Metaphor*, 48.

50. Levin cited the metaphor "The locomotive is in bed," and I had to modify it to "The locomotive sleeps" to fit his own scheme of relations. Certainly "The locomotive sleeps" generates different interpretations from "The locomotive is in bed." Despite these differences, let us consider the two metaphors similar enough to warrant the analysis I present. Note that I have used δ and λ for α and β in Levin's original relationship. I have done this to avoid confusion with α and β in this paper, which stand for values of degrees of membership in fuzzy sets.

51. Lakoff and Johnson, *Metaphors We Live By*.

52. Lakoff and Johnson, *Metaphors We Live By*, 18.

53. Uriel Weinreich, *Explorations in Semantic Theory* (The Hague: Mouton, 1972).

54. Weinreich, *Explorations in Semantic Theory*, 46–47.

55. These are selected from entries in *The Oxford English Dictionary*.

56. Stevens, "On the manner of addressing clouds," *The Palm at the End of the Mind*, 56.

57. Thomas L. Saaty, *The Analytic Hierarchy Process* (New York: McGraw-Hill, 1980).

58. Thomas L. Saaty, "Exploring the interface between hierarchies, multiple objectives and fuzzy sets," *Fuzzy Sets and Systems* 1 (1978), 57–68; Edward J. Lusk, "Priority assignment: A conditioned sets approach," *Fuzzy Sets and Systems* 7 (1982), 43–55.

59. Lusk, "Priority assignment," 43.
60. Saaty, *The Analytic Hierarchy Process*, x.
61. Robbins, *Another Roadside Attraction*, 206. The entire passage reads, "Stars are merely projections of the human psyche—they are pimples of consciousness—but they are at the same time quite real."

Chapter 5

1. Thomas Hardy, *Tess of the D'Urbervilles*, Scott Elledge, ed. (New York: Norton, 1979), 269.
2. A. Collins and E. F. Loftus, "Spreading activation theory of semantic processing," *Psychological Review* 82 (1975), 407–428.
3. Danny R. Moates and Gary M. Schumacher, *An Introduction to Cognitive Psychology* (Belmont, California: Wadsworth, 1980), 129–131, 200–204.
4. Collins and Loftus, "Spreading activation theory."
5. J. L. Freedman and E. F. Loftus, "Retrieval of words from long-term memory," *Journal of Verbal Learning and Verbal Behavior* 10 (1971), 107–115.
6. T. S. Eliot, "The Waste Land," in *T. S. Eliot: The Complete Poems and Plays* (New York: Harcourt, Brace & Co., 1952), 38.
7. Edward E. Smith, Edward J. Shoben, and Lance J. Rips, "Structure and process in semantic memory: A featural model for semantic decisions," *Psychological Review* 81 (1974), 220.
8. Smith, Shoben, and Rips, "Structure and process," 226–230.
9. James D. Hollan, "Features and semantic memory: Set-theoretic or network model?" *Psychological Review* 82 (1975), 154–155.
10. Hollan, "Features and semantic memory," 154–155.
11. John R. Anderson, *Language, Memory and Thought* (Hillsdale, New Jersey: Lawrence Erlbaum Associates, 1976).
12. Anderson, *Language, Memory and Thought*, 147–148.
13. Wallace Stevens, "Man and bottle," in *The Palm at the End of the Mind*.
14. Arthur Koestler, *The Act of Creation* (New York: Macmillan, 1964).
15. Koestler, *Act of Creation*, 226.
16. William Shakespeare, "Antony and Cleopatra," *Shakespeare's Works*, vol. 15, William J. Rolfe, ed. (New York: Harper and Brothers, 1894), Act III, Scene XIII/67.
17. Moates and Schumacher, *An Introduction to Cognitive Psychology*, 119. The reference in the quotation is F. A. Yates, *The Art of Memory* (Chicago: University of Chicago Press, 1966).
18. William J. Gorden, *Synectics: The Development of Creative Capacity* (New York: Harper, 1961).
19. David Hume, *A Treatise of Human Nature*, L. A. Selby-Bigge, ed. (Oxford: Clarendon Press, 1968).
20. Both Pylyshyn and Kosslyn agree on this. See Zenon W. Pylyshyn, "What the mind's eye tells the mind's brain: A critique of mental imagery," *Psychological Bulletin* 80 (1973), 1–24; Stephen Michael Kosslyn, *Image and Mind* (Cambridge, Mass.: Harvard University Press, 1980).
21. In addition to the papers by Pylyshyn and Kosslyn cited in note 20, see Allan Paivio, *Imagery and Verbal Processes* (New York: Holt, Rinehart and Winston, 1971).
22. Pylyshyn, "What the mind's eye tells."
23. Paivio, *Imagery and Verbal Processes*.
24. Paivio, *Imagery and Verbal Processes*, 8.
25. Kosslyn, *Image and Mind*, 33–34.

26. Kosslyn, *Image and Mind*, 146–147.
27. Verbrugge and McCarrell, "Metaphoric comprehension."
28. Verbrugge and McCarrell, "Metaphoric comprehension," 494.
29. Verbrugge and McCarrell, "Metaphoric comprehension," 530.
30. Amos Tversky, "Features of similarity," *Psychological Review* 84 (1977), 327–352. See also Eva Feder Kittay, "The creation of similarity: A discussion of metaphor in light of Tversky's theory of similarity," in *PSA 1982*, P. D. Asquith and T. Nickles, eds. (East Lansing, Michigan: Philosophy of Science Association, 1982).
31. Tversky, "Features of similarity," 328.
32. Tversky, "Features of similarity," 328.
33. Tversky, "Features of similarity," 343.
34. Tversky, "Features of similarity," 331–332.
35. Tversky, "Features of similarity," 336–337.
36. Carol L. Krumhansl, "Concerning the applicability of geometric models," *Psychological Review* 85 (1978), 445–463.
37. William Blake, quoted in Brooke-Rose, *A Grammar of Metaphor*, 106.
38. Donald T. Campbell, "Evolutionary epistemology," in *The Philosophy of Karl Popper*, Paul A. Schilpp, ed. (LaSalle, Illinois: Open Court, 1974).
39. See Stephen Toulmin, *Human Understanding* (Princeton: Princeton University Press, 1972); for a criticism of Toulmin, see Carla E. Kary, "Can Darwinism be extended from biology to epistemology," in *PSA 1982*.
40. Wilson, *On Human Nature*. For a criticism see my "Religious metaphors: Mediators between biological and cultural evolution that generate transcendent meaning," *Zygon* 18 (1983), 45–65.
41. Campbell, "Evolutionary epistemology," 413.
42. Donald T. Campbell, "On the conflicts between biological and social evolution and between psychological and moral tradition," *American Psychologist* 30 (1975), 1103–1126.
43. E. G. d'Aquili and C. D. Laughlin, Jr., "The Neurobiology of myth and ritual," in *The Spectrum of Ritual: A Biogenetic Structural Analysis*, E. G. d'Aquili, C. D. Laughlin, Jr., and J. McManus, eds. (New York: Columbia University Press, 1979), 162–163.
44. Brenda E. F. Beck, "The metaphor as a mediator between semantic and analogic modes of thought," *Current Anthropology* 19 (1978), 83–97.
45. Richard Rorty, *Philosophy and the Mirror of Nature* (Princeton: Princeton University Press, 1979).
46. Rorty, *Mirror of Nature*, 12.
47. Rorty, *Mirror of Nature*, 45.
48. Rorty, *Mirror of Nature*, 138.
49. Rorty, *Mirror of Nature*, chap. 4.
50. Rorty, *Mirror of Nature*, 170–171.

Chapter 6

1. J. L. Austin, *How to Do Things with Words* (New York: Oxford University Press, 1965).
2. Langston Hughes, *Selected Poems of Langston Hughes* (New York: Vintage, 1974), 21.
3. Ted Cohen, "Illocutions and perlocutions," *Foundations of Language* 9 (1973), 492–503.
4. Hughes, "Long Trip," *Selected Poems of Langston Hughes*, 52.
5. Cohen, "Illocutions and perlocutions."
6. Kent Bach and Robert M. Harnish, *Linguistic Communication and Speech Acts* (Cambridge, Mass.: MIT Press, 1979).
7. John Searle, *Speech Acts* (Cambridge: Cambridge University Press, 1969). One might also have evaluated Jerrold M. Sadock, *Toward a Linguistic Theory of Speech Acts* (New

York: Academic Press, 1974). My purpose is not to evaluate various theories of speech acts to decide on the best explanation but rather to select one that seems reasonable and applicable to illuminating the nature of metaphor.

8. Searle, *Speech Acts*, 22.
9. Searle, *Speech Acts*, 57–61. Searle put these conditions in italics and explained each one. I have omitted his expositions.
10. Bach and Harnish, *Linguistic Communication*, 130–131.
11. Searle, *Speech Acts*, 19–21.
12. Searle, *Speech Acts*, 20–21.
13. John R. Searle, "Metaphor," in *Metaphor and Thought*, Ortony, ed.
14. Searle, "Metaphor," 114–115.
15. Bach and Harnish, *Linguistic Communication*, 84–85.
16. Bach and Harnish, *Linguistic Communication*, 7.
17. Bach and Harnish, *Linguistic Communication*, 121.
18. Bach and Harnish, *Linguistic Communication*, 76–77. Reprinted with permission.
19. Hughes, "Drum," in *Selected Poems of Langston Hughes*, 87.
20. Bach and Harnish, *Linguistic Communication*, 41.
21. Beardsley, *Aesthetics*, 116–122.
22. Stevens, "The Man on the Dump," *The Palm at the End of the Mind*, 164.
23. K. S. Shrader-Frechette, "High energy models and the ontological status of the quark," *Synthese* 42 (1979), 173–189.
24. *The Compact Edition of the Oxford English Dictionary* (Oxford: Oxford University Press, 1971).

Chapter 7

1. Sylvia Plath, "All the Dead Dears," in *The Collected Poems*, Ted Hughes, ed. (New York: Harper & Row, 1981), 70.
2. Rudolf Carnap, "Intellectual autobiography," in *The Philosophy of Rudolf Carnap*, Paul Arthur Schilpp, ed. (LaSalle, Illinois: Open Court, 1963), especially 12, 53–67.
3. L. Jonathan Cohen, *The Diversity of Meaning* (London: Methuen, 1966).
4. See Ruth M. Kempson, *Presupposition and the Delimitation of Semantics* (Cambridge: Cambridge University Press, 1975) and *Semantic Theory* (Cambridge: Cambridge University Press, 1977).
5. Kempson, *Semantic Theory*, 74.
6. Jonathan Cohen, *The Diversity of Meaning*, 22.
7. Gilbert H. Harman, "Three levels of meaning," in *Semantics: An Interdisciplinary Reader in Philosophy, Linguistics and Psychology*, Danny D. Steinberg and Leon A. Jakobovits, eds. (Cambridge: Cambridge University Press, 1974).
8. Harman, "Three levels," 68.
9. Richard Garner, "Presupposition in philosophy and linguistics," in *Studies in Linguistic Semantics*, Charles J. Fillmore and D. Terrence Langendoen, eds. (New York: Holt, Rinehart and Winston, 1971), 29. The reference to Strawson is Peter Strawson, *Introduction to Logical Theory* (London: Methuen, 1952).
10. See Deidre Wilson, *Presupposition and Non-Truth Conditional Semantics* (London: Academic Press, 1975) and Kempson, *Presupposition and the Delimitation of Semantics*.
11. Edward L. Keenan, "Two kinds of presupposition in natural language," in *Studies in Linguistic Semantics*, Fillmore and Langendoen, eds. Keenan described "logical" and "pragmatic" notions of presupposition but did not attempt to relate the two.
12. William Wordsworth, "Descriptive Sketches," in *Selected Poetry*, Mark Van Doren, ed. (New York: Modern Library, 1950), 17.

13. Paul Ricoeur, *The Rule of Metaphor* (Toronto: University of Toronto Press, 1975), especially study 6 and study 7.
14. Ricoeur, *Rule of Metaphor*, 221.
15. Marcus Hester, *The Meaning of Poetic Metaphor* (The Hague: Mouton, 1967).
16. Ricoeur, *Rule of Metaphor*, 213.
17. Northrop Frye, *Anatomy of Criticism: Four Essays* (Princeton: Princeton University Press, 1973), 351. R. Kuhn, "Professor Frye's criticism," *The Journal of Philosophy* 56 (1959), 745–755.
18. Frye, *Anatomy of Criticism*, 118.
19. Frye, *Anatomy of Criticism*, 97.
20. Frye, *Anatomy of Criticism*, 124.
21. Susanne K. Langer, *Feeling and Form: A Theory of Art* (New York: Charles Scribner's Sons, 1973); and *Mind: An Essay on Human Feeling* (Baltimore: Johns Hopkins University Press, 1967), vol. 1.
22. Langer, *Feeling and Form*, 40.
23. Langer, *Mind*, 4.
24. Langer, *Feeling and Form*, 240–241.
25. Langer, *Feeling and Form*, 234.
26. Langer, *Mind*, 104.
27. Hayden White, *Tropics of Discourse: Essays in Cultural Criticism* (Baltimore: Johns Hopkins University Press, 1978).
28. White, *Tropics of Discourse*, 4.
29. White, *Tropics of Discourse*, 5.
30. White, *Tropics of Discourse*, 10.
31. White, *Tropics of Discourse*, 47.
32. Jeremy Rifkin, "The other half of the computer revolution," *Datamation* 29 (1983), 273. Excerpted from Rifkin's book, *Algeny* (New York: Viking Press, 1983).
33. Jerry A. Fodor, *The Language of Thought* (New York: Thomas Y. Crowell, 1975).
34. Fodor, *The Language of Thought*, 164–165.
35. Ernan McMullin, *Newton on Matter and Activity* (Notre Dame, Indiana: University of Notre Dame Press, 1978). See also Earl R. Mac Cormac, "Scientific metaphors as necessary conceptual limitations of science," in *The Limits of Lawfulness*, Nicholas Rescher, ed. (Pittsburgh: University of Pittsburgh Center for the Philosophy of Science, 1983).
36. McMullin, *Newton on Matter*, 77.
37. McMullin, *Newton on Matter*, 94.
38. McMullin, *Newton on Matter*, 103.

Chapter 8

1. From Constable's Fourth Lecture of the Royal Institution in 1836; see C. R. Leslie, *Memoirs of the Life of John Constable*, Jonathan Mayne, ed. (London: Phaidon Press, 1951), 323, as cited in Nelson Goodman, *Languages of Art* (Indianapolis: Hackett Publishing Co., 1976), 33.
2. Paul J. Olscamp, "How some metaphors may be true or false," *The Journal of Aesthetics and Art Criticism* 29 (1970), 78.
3. Beardsley, *Aesthetics*, 142.
4. Beardsley, "The metaphorical twist."
5. Beardsley, *Aesthetics*, 429ff.
6. Beardsley, *Aesthetics*, 436.
7. Timothy Binkley, "On the truth and probity of metaphor," *The Journal of Aesthetics and Art Criticism* 33 (1974), 171–180.

8. Binkley, "Truth and probity," 173–174.

9. Monroe C. Beardsley, "Metaphor and falsity," *The Journal of Aesthetics and Art Criticism* 35 (1976), 218–222.

10. Berggren, "Use and abuse of metaphor."

11. Berggren, "Use and abuse of metaphor," 470–471.

12. Goodman, *Languages of Art*, chap. 2; and his *Ways of Worldmaking* (Indianapolis: Hackett Publishing Co., 1978), chap. 1.

13. Goodman, *Ways of Worldmaking*, 17–18.

14. Goodman, *Languages of Art*, 92ff.

15. Norman B. Misty, Ronald A. Poling, and Edward H. Thorndike, "Particles with naked beauty," *Scientific American* 249 (1983).

16. I encountered these objections to my paper "Scientific metaphors as necessary conceptual limitations of science," presented at the Center for the Philosophy of Science at the University of Pittsburgh.

17. Johnson, "The bag model of quark confinement," 115.

18. McMullin, *Newton on Matter and Activity*, 76.

19. Nicholas Rescher, *Many-valued Logic* (New York: McGraw-Hill, 1969), 143ff.

20. Rescher, *Many-valued Logic*, 146.

21. Rescher, *Many-valued Logic*, 144.

References

Anderson, Alan Ross, ed., 1964. *Minds and Machines*. Englewood Cliffs, New Jersey: Prentice Hall.

Anderson, John R., 1976. *Language, Memory and Thought*. Hillsdale, New Jersey: Lawrence Erlbaum Associates.

d'Aquili, E. G., C. D. Laughlin, Jr., and J. McManus, eds., 1979. *The Spectrum of Ritual: A Biogenetic Structural Analysis*. New York: Columbia University Press.

d'Aquili, E. G., and C. D. Laughlin, Jr., 1979. The neurobiology of myth and ritual. In *The Spectrum of Ritual: A Biogenetic Analysis*, E. G. d'Aquili, C. D. Laughlin, Jr., and J. McManus, eds. New York: Columbia University Press.

Arbib, Michael A., 1972. *The Metaphorical Brain*. New York: Wiley-Interscience.

Asquith, P. D., and T. Nickles, eds., 1982. *PSA 1982*. East Lansing, Michigan: Philosophy of Science Association.

Austin, J. L., 1965. *How to Do Things with Words*. New York: Oxford University Press.

Bach, Kent, and Robert M. Harnish, 1979. *Linguistic Communication and Speech Acts*. Cambridge, Mass.: MIT Press.

Beardsley, Monroe C., 1958. *Aesthetics*. New York: Harcourt, Brace & Co.

Beardsley, Monroe C., 1962. The metaphorical twist. *Philosophy and Phenomenological Research* 22:293–307.

Beardsley, Monroe C., 1976. Metaphor and falsity. *The Journal of Aesthetics and Art Criticism* 35:218–222.

Beck, Brenda E. F., 1978. The metaphor as a mediator between semantic and analogic modes of thought. *Current Anthropology* 19:83–97.

Bennett, Jonathan, 1971. Review of Sommers. *The Journal of Symbolic Logic* 36:666–670.

Berggren, Douglas, 1962,1963. The use and abuse of metaphor, I & II. *The Review of Metaphysics* 16:237–258, 450–472.

Berggren, Douglas, 1966. From myth to metaphor. *The Monist* 50:530–552.

Berlin, Brent, and Paul Kay, 1969. *Basic Color Terms: Their Universality and Evolution*. Berkeley: University of California Press.

Binkley, Timothy, 1974. On the truth and probity of metaphor. *The Journal of Aesthetics and Art Criticism* 33:171–180.

Black, Max, 1962. *Models and Metaphors*. Ithaca, New York: Cornell University Press.

Black, Max, ed., 1965. *Philosophy in America*. Ithaca, New York: Cornell University Press.

Bliss, Frank W., and Earl R. Mac Cormac, 1977. Two poles of metaphor: Frye and Beardsley. *The Journal of Aesthetic Education* 11:33–49.

Boden, Margaret A., 1977. *Artificial Intelligence and Natural Man*. New York: Basic Books.

Brislin, R., S. Bochner, and W. Lonner, eds., 1975. *Cross Cultural Perspectives in Learning*. New York: Halsted Press.

Brooke-Rose, Christine, 1970. *A Grammar of Metaphor*. London: Seeker and Warburg.

Campbell, Donald T., 1974. Evolutionary epistemology. In *The Philosophy of Karl Popper*, Paul A. Schilpp, ed. LaSalle, Illinois: Open Court.

Campbell, Donald T., 1975. On the conflicts between biological and social evolution and between psychological and moral tradition. *American Psychologist* 30:1103–1126.

Carnap, Rudolf, 1963. Intellectual autobiography. In *The Philosophy of Rudolf Carnap*, Paul Arthur Schilpp, ed. LaSalle, Illinois: Open Court.

Carroll, John B., 1969. Review of measurement of meaning. In *Semantic Differential Technique*, James G. Snider and Charles E. Osgood, eds. Chicago: Aldine Atherton.

Chomsky, Noam, 1964. Degrees of grammaticalness. In *The Structure of Language*, Jerry A. Fodor and Jerrold J. Katz, eds. Englewood Cliffs, New Jersey: Prentice-Hall.

Chomsky, Noam, 1965. *Aspects of a Theory of Syntax*. Cambridge, Mass.: MIT Press.

Cohen, L. Jonathan, 1966. *The Diversity of Meaning*. London: Methuen.

Cohen, L. Jonathan, and Avishai Margalit, 1972. The role of inductive reasoning in the interpretation of metaphor. In *Semantics of Natural Language*, D. Davidson and G. Harman, eds. Boston: Reidel.

Cohen, Ted, 1973. Illocutions and perlocutions. *Foundations of Language* 9:492–503.

Collins, A., and E. F. Loftus, 1975. Spreading activation theory of semantic processing. *Psychological Review* 82:407–428.

The Compact Edition of the Oxford English Dictionary, 1971. Oxford: Oxford University Press.

Creelman, Marjorie B., 1966. *The Experimental Investigation of Meaning: A Review of the Literature*. New York: Springer.

Davidson, D., and G. Harman, eds., 1972. *Semantics of Natural Language*. Boston: Reidel.

Dennett, Daniel C., 1978. *Brainstorms*. Montgomery, Vermont: Bradford Books. Reprinted by The MIT Press, Cambridge, Massachusetts.

Dobzhansky, Theodosius, et al., eds., 1977. *Evolution*. San Francisco: W. H. Freeman.

Donne, John, 1967. *The Complete Poetry of John Donne*, John T. Shawcross, ed. Garden City, New York: Anchor Books.

Dreyfus, Hubert L., 1979. *What Computers Can't Do*. New York: Harper Colophon Book.

Elgood, A. G., 1970. Sommers's rules of sense. *The Philosophical Quarterly* 20:166–169.

Eliot, T. S., 1952. *T. S. Eliot: The Complete Poems and Plays*. New York: Harcourt, Brace & Co.

Fillmore, Charles J., and D. Terrei   Langendoen, eds., 1971. *Studies in Linguistic Semantics*. New York: Holt, Rinehart and Winston.

Fodor, Jerry A., 1975. *The Language of Thought*. New York: Thomas Y. Crowell.

Fodor, Jerry, and Jerrold J. Katz, eds., 1964. *The Structure of Language*. Englewood Cliffs, New Jersey: Prentice-Hall.

Freedman, J. L., and E. F. Loftus, 1971. Retrieval of words from long-term memory. *Journal of Verbal Learning and Verbal Behavior* 10:107–115.

Frye, Northrop, 1973. *Anatomy of Criticism: Four Essays*. Princeton: Princeton University Press.

Garner, Richard, 1971. Presupposition in philosophy and linguistics. In *Studies in Linguistic Semantics*, Charles J. Fillmore and D. Terrence Langendoen, eds. New York: Holt, Rinehart and Winston.

Goodman, Nelson, 1976. *Languages of Art*. Indianapolis: Hackett Publishing Co.

Goodman, Nelson, 1978. *Ways of Worldmaking*. Indianapolis: Hackett Publishing Co.

Gorden, William J., 1961. *Synectics: The Development of Creative Capacity*. New York: Harper.

Gove, Philip B., ed., 1971. *Webster's Third New International Dictionary*. Springfield, Mass.: G. & C. Merriam Co.

Hardy, Thomas, 1979. *Tess of the D'Urbervilles*, Scott Elledge, ed. New York: Norton.

Harman, Gilbert H., 1974. Three levels of meaning. In *Semantics: An Interdisciplinary Reader in Philosophy, Linguistics and Psychology*, Danny D. Steinberg and Leon A. Jakobovits, eds. Cambridge: Cambridge University Press.

Hempel, Carl, 1966. *The Philosophy of Natural Science*. Englewood Cliffs, New Jersey: Prentice-Hall.

Hesse, Mary, 1980. *Revolutions and Reconstructions in the Philosophy of Science*. Bloomington, Indiana: Indiana University Press.

Hester, Marcus B., 1967. *The Meaning of Poetic Metaphor*. The Hague: Mouton.

Hollan, James D., 1975. Features and semantic memory: Set-theoretic or network model? *Psychological Review* 82:154–155.

Hughes, Langston, 1974. *Selected Poems of Langston Hughes*. New York: Vintage.

Hume, David, 1968. *A Treatise of Human Nature*, L. A. Selby-Bigge, ed. Oxford: Clarendon Press.

Johnson, Kenneth A., 1979. The bag model of quark confinement. *Scientific American* 241:112–121.

Johnson, Samuel, 1967. *A Dictionary of the English Language*. New York: AMS Press.

Joyce, James, 1978. *A Portrait of the Artist as a Young Man*. New York: Penguin Books.

Kary, Carla E., 1982. Can Darwinism be extended from biology to epistemology. *PSA 1982*, P. D. Asquith and T. Nickles, eds. East Lansing, Michigan: Philosophy of Science Association.

Katz, Jerrold J., and Paul M. Postal, 1964. *An Integrated Theory of Linguistic Descriptions*. Cambridge, Mass.: MIT Press.

Keenan, Edward L., 1971. Two kinds of presupposition in natural language. In *Studies in Linguistic Semantics*, Charles J. Fillmore and D. Terrence Langendoen, eds. New York: Holt, Rinehart and Winston.

Kempson, Ruth M., 1975. *Presupposition and the Delimitation of Semantics*. Cambridge: Cambridge University Press.

Kempson, Ruth M., 1977. *Semantic Theory*. Cambridge: Cambridge University Press.

Kittay, Eva Feder, 1982. The creation of similarity: A discussion of metaphor in the light of Tversky's theory of similarity. *PSA 1982*, P. D. Asquith and T. Nickles, eds. East Lansing, Michigan: Philosophy of Science Association.

Koestler, Arthur, 1964. *The Act of Creation*. New York: Macmillan.

Kosslyn, Stephen Michael, 1980. *Image and Mind*. Cambridge, Mass.: Harvard University Press.

Krumhansl, Carol L., 1978. Concerning the applicability of geometric models. *Psychological Review* 85:445–463.

Kuhn, R., 1959. Professor Frye's criticism. *The Journal of Philosophy* 56:745–755.

Lakoff, George, 1972. Hedges: A study in meaning criteria and the logic of fuzzy concepts. *Proceedings of the Chicago Linguistics Society*.

Lakoff, George, and Mark Johnson, 1980a. Conceptual metaphor in everyday language. *The Journal of Philosophy* 77:453–486.

Lakoff, George, and Mark Johnson, 1980b. *Metaphors We Live By*. Chicago: University of Chicago Press.

de La Mettrie, Julien Offray, 1912. *Man a Machine*. LaSalle, Illinois: Open Court.

Langer, Susanne K., 1967. *Mind: An Essay on Human Feeling*, vol. 1. Baltimore: Johns Hopkins University Press.

Langer, Susanne K., 1973. *Feeling and Form: A Theory of Art*. New York: Charles Scribner's Sons.

Leech, Geoffrey, 1974. *Semantics*. New York: Penguin Books.

Leslie, C. R., 1951. *Memoirs of the Life of John Constable*, Jonathan Mayne, ed. London: Phaidon Press.

Levin, Samuel R., 1977. *The Semantics of Metaphor*. Baltimore: Johns Hopkins University Press.

Lusk, Edward J., 1982. Priority assignment: A conditioned sets approach. *Fuzzy Sets and Systems* 7:43–55.

Lyons, John, 1977. *Semantics*. Cambridge: Cambridge University Press.

Mac Cormac, Earl R., 1971. Ostensive instances in language learning. *Foundations of Language* 7:199–210.

Mac Cormac, Earl R., 1976. *Metaphor and Myth in Science and Religion*. Durham, North Carolina: Duke University Press.

Mac Cormac, Earl R., 1982. Metaphors and fuzzy sets. *Fuzzy Sets and Systems* 7:243–256.

Mac Cormac, Earl R., 1983a. Religious metaphors: Mediators between biological and cultural evolution that generate transcendent meaning. *Zygon* 18:45–65.

Mac Cormac, Earl R., 1983b. Scientific metaphors as necessary conceptual limitations of science. In *The Limits of Lawfulness*, Nicholas Rescher, ed. Pittsburgh: University of Pittsburgh Center for the Philosophy of Science.

Mandelbaum, D. G., ed., 1949. *Selected Writings of Edward Sapir*. Berkeley: University of California Press.

Matthews, Robert J., 1971. Concerning a "linguistic theory" of metaphor. *Foundations of Language* 7:413–425.

McCarthy, John, 1979. Ascribing mental qualities to machines. In *Philosophical Perspectives in Artificial Intelligence*, Martin Ringle, ed. New York: Humanities Press.

McCorduck, Pamela, 1979. *Machines Who Think*. San Francisco: W. H. Freeman.

McMullin, Ernan, 1978. *Newton on Matter and Activity*. Notre Dame: University of Notre Dame Press.

Misty, Norman B., Ronald A. Poling, and Edward H. Thorndike, 1983. Particles with naked beauty. *Scientific American* 249:106–115.

Moates, Danny R., and Gary M. Schumacher, 1980. *An Introduction to Cognitive Psychology*. Belmont, California: Wadsworth.

Moore, T. E., ed., 1973. *Cognitive Development and the Acquisition of Language*. New York: Academic Press.

Murry, John Middleton, 1968. *Countries of the Mind*. Freeport, New York: Books for Libraries Press.

Olscamp, Paul J., 1970. How some metaphors may be true or false. *The Journal of Aesthetics and Art Criticism* 29:77–86.

Ortony, Andrew, ed., 1979. *Metaphor and Thought*. Cambridge: Cambridge University Press.

Osgood, Charles E., William H. May, and Murray S. Miron, 1975. *Cross-Cultural Universals of Affective Meaning*. Urbana, Illinois: University of Illinois Press.

Osgood, Charles E., George J. Suci, and Percy H. Tannenbaum, 1957. *The Measurement of Meaning*. Urbana, Illinois: University of Illinois Press.

Paivio, Allan, 1971. *Imagery and Verbal Processes*. New York: Holt, Rinehart and Winston.

Passell, Dan, 1969. On Sommers' logic of sense and nonsense. *Mind* 70:132–133.

Pepper, Stephen C., 1970. *World Hypotheses*. Berkeley: University of California Press.

Plath, Sylvia, 1981. *The Collected Poems*, Ted Hughes, ed. New York: Harper & Row.

Pylyshyn, Zenon W., 1973. What the mind's eye tells the mind's brain: A critique of mental imagery. *Psychological Bulletin* 80:1–24.

Pylyshyn, Zenon W., 1980. Computation and cognition: Issues in the foundation of cognitive science. *The Behavioral and Brain Sciences* 3:111–132.

Quine, W. V. O., 1953. *From a Logical Point of View*. Cambridge, Mass.: Harvard University Press.

Quine, W. V. O., 1977. Natural kinds. In *Naming, Necessity and Natural Kinds*, Stephen P. Schwartz, ed. Ithaca, New York: Cornell University Press.

Reddy, Michael J., 1979. The conduit metaphor. In *Metaphor and Thought*, Andrew Ortony, ed. Cambridge: Cambridge University Press.

Rescher, Nicholas, 1969. *Many-Valued Logic*. New York: McGraw-Hill.

Rescher, Nicholas, ed., 1983. *The Limits of Lawfulness*. Pittsburgh: University of Pittsburgh Center for the Philosophy of Science.

Richards, I. A., 1936. *The Philosophy of Rhetoric*. New York: Oxford University Press.

Richards, I. A., 1948. Science and poetry. In *Criticism: Foundations of Modern Literary Judgment*, Mark Schorer, et al., eds. New York: Harcourt, Brace & Co.

Ricoeur, Paul, 1975. *The Rule of Metaphor*. Toronto: University of Toronto Press.

Rifkin, Jeremy, 1983. *Algeny*. New York: Viking Press.

Ringle, Martin, ed., 1979. *Philosophical Perspectives in Artificial Intelligence*. New York: Humanities Press.

Robbins, Tom, 1977. *Another Roadside Attraction*. New York: Ballantine Books.

Rorty, Richard, 1979. *Philosophy and the Mirror of Nature*. Princeton: Princeton University Press.

Rosch, Eleanor, 1971. "Focal" color areas and the development of color names. *Developmental Psychology* 4:447–455.

Rosch, Eleanor, 1972. Probabilities, sampling and ethnographic method: The case of Dani color names. *Man* 7:448–466.

Rosch, Eleanor, 1973. On the internal structure of perceptual and semantic categories. In *Cognitive Development and the Acquistion of Language*, T. E. Moore, ed. New York: Academic Press.

Rosch, Eleanor, 1974. Linguistic relativity. In *Human Communication*, A. Silverstein, ed. New York: Halsted Press.

Rosch, Eleanor, 1975a. Cognitive reference points. *Cognitive Psychology* 7:523–547.

Rosch, Eleanor, 1975b. The nature of mental codes for color categories. *Journal of Experimental Psychology: Human Perception and Performance* 1:303–322.

Rosch, Eleanor, 1975c. unversals and cultural specifics in human categorization. In *Cross Cultural Perspectives on Learning*, R. Brislin, S. Bochner, and W. Lonner, eds. New York: Halsted Press.

Rosch, Eleanor, 1977. Human categorization. In *Advances in Cross-Cultural Psychology*, vol. 1, N. Warren, ed. London: Academic Press.

Rosch, Eleanor, 1978. Principles of categorization. In *Cognition and Categorization*, Eleanor Rosch and Barbara B. Lloyd, eds. Hillsdale, New Jersey: Lawrence Erlbaum Associates.

Rosch, Eleanor, C. B. Mervis, et al., 1976. Basic objects in natural categories. *Cognitive Psychology* 8:382–439.

Rosch, Eleanor, and Barbara B. Lloyd, eds., 1978. *Cognition and Categorization*. Hillsdale, New Jersey: Lawrence Erlbaum Associates.

Rosch, Eleanor, and Carolyn B. Mervis, 1975. Family resemblances. *Cognitive Psychology* 7:573–605.

Rosch (Heider), Eleanor, and D. C. Olivier, 1972. The structure of the color space in naming and memory for two languages. *Cognitive Psychology* 3:337–354.

Saaty, Thomas L., 1978. Exploring the interface between hierarchies, multiple objectives and fuzzy sets. *Fuzzy Sets and Systems* 1:57–68.

Saaty, Thomas L., 1980. *The Analytic Hierarchy Process*. New York: McGraw-Hill.

Sadock, Jerrold M., 1974. *Toward a Linguistic Theory of Speech Acts*. New York: Academic Press.

Sapir, Edward, 1949. *Selected Writings of Edward Sapir*, D. G. Mandelbaum, ed. Berkeley: University of California Press.

Schilpp, Paul Arthur, ed., 1963. *The Philosophy of Rudolf Carnap*. LaSalle, Illinois: Open Court.

Schilpp, Paul Arthur, ed., 1974. *The Philosophy of Karl Popper*. LaSalle, Illinois: Open Court.

Schorer, Mark, et al., eds., 1948. *Criticism: Foundations of Modern Literary Judgment*. New York: Harcourt, Brace & Co.

Schwartz, Stephen P., 1977. *Naming, Necessity and Natural Kinds*. Ithaca, New York: Cornell University Press.

Searle, John, 1969. *Speech Acts*. Cambridge: Cambridge University Press.

Searle, John, 1979. Metaphor. In *Metaphor and Thought*, Andrew Ortony, ed. Cambridge: Cambridge University Press.

Shakespeare, William, 1894. *Shakespeare's Works*, William J. Rolfe, ed. New York: Harper and Brothers.

Shrader-Frechette, K. S., 1979. High energy models and the ontological status of the quark. *Synthese* 42:173–189.

Silverstein, A., ed., 1974. *Human Communication*. New York: Halsted Press.

Smith, Edward E., Edward J. Shoben, and Lance J. Rips, 1974. Structure and process in semantic memory: A featural model for semantic decisions. *Psychological Review* 81:214–241.

Snider, James G., and Charles E. Osgood, eds., 1969. *Semantic Differential Technique*. Chicago: Aldine Atherton.

Sommers, Fred, 1959. The ordinary language tree. *Mind* 68:160–185.

Sommers, Fred, 1963. Types and ontology. *Philosophical Review* 72:327–367.

Sommers, Fred, 1965. Predictability. In *Philosophy in America*, Max Black, ed. Ithaca, New York: Cornell University Press.

de Sousa, Ronald B., 1966. The tree of English bears bitter fruit. *The Journal of Philosophy* 63:37–46.

Stanford, W. Bedell, 1972, *Greek Metaphor*. New York: Johnson Reprint Corporation.

Stein, Jess, ed., 1969. *The Random House Dictionary*. New York: Random House.

Steinberg, Danny D., and Leon A. Jakobovits, eds., 1974. *Semantics: An Interdisciplinary Reader in Philosophy, Linguistics and Psychology*. Cambridge: Cambridge University Press.

Stevens, Wallace, 1972. *The Palm at the End of the Mind*. New York: Vintage Press.

Strawson, Peter, 1952. *Introduction to Logical Theory*. London: Methuen.

Toulmin, Stephen, 1972. *Human Understanding*. Princeton: Princeton University Press.

Turbayne, Colin Murray, 1970. *The Myth of Metaphor*. Columbia, South Carolina: University of South Carolina Press. Revised edition.

Turing, A. M., 1964. Computing machinery and intelligence. In *Minds and Machines*, Alan Ross Anderson, ed. Englewood Cliffs, New Jersey: Prentice-Hall.

Tversky, Amos, 1977. Features of similarity. *Psychological Review* 84:327–352.

Verbrugge, Robert, and Nancy McCarrell, 1977. Metaphoric comprehension. *Cognitive Psychology* 9:494–533.

Warren, N., ed., 1977. *Advances in Cross-Cultural Psychology*, vol. 1. London: Academic Press.

Weinreich, Uriel, 1969. Travels through semantic space. In *Semantic Differential Technique*, James G. Snider and Charles E. Osgood, eds. Chicago: Aldine Atherton.

Weinreich, Uriel, 1972. *Explorations in Semantic Theory*. The Hague: Mouton.

Wheelwright, Philip, 1962. *Metaphor and Reality*. Bloomington, Indiana: Indiana University Press.

White, Hayden, 1978. *Tropics of Discourse: Essays in Cultural Criticism*. Baltimore: Johns Hopkins University Press.

Whorf, Benjamin Lee, 1967. *Language, Thought, and Reality*. Cambridge, Mass.: MIT Press.

Wilson, Deidre, 1975. *Presupposition and Non-Truth Conditional Semantics*. London: Academic Press.

Wilson, E. O., 1978. *On Human Nature*. Cambridge, Mass.: Harvard University Press.

Wordsworth, William, 1950. *Selected Poetry*, Mark Van Doren, ed. New York: Modern Library.

Yates, F. A., 1966. *The Art of Memory*. Chicago: University of Chicago Press.

Yeats, W. B., 1953. *The Collected Poems of W. B. Yeats*. New York: Macmillan.

Zadeh, L. A., 1965. Fuzzy sets. *Information and Control* 8:338–353.

Zadeh, L. A., 1971. Quantitative fuzzy semantics. *Information Sciences* 3:159–176.

Index